FRENCH AND ORIENTAL LOVE IN A HAREM

MARIO UCHARD

1st WORLD
LIBRARY
Literary Society

French and Oriental Love in a Harem

Mario Uchard

© 1st World Library, 2007
PO Box 2211
Fairfield, IA 52556
www.1stworldlibrary.com
First Edition

LCCN: 2007934228

Softcover ISBN: 978-1-4218-9661-8
Hardcover ISBN: 978-1-4218-9761-5
eBook ISBN: 978-1-4218-9561-1

Purchase *"French and Oriental Love in a Harem"*
as a traditional bound book at:
www.1stWorldLibrary.com/purchase.asp?ISBN=978-1-4218-9661-8

1st World Library is a literary, educational organization
dedicated to:

- Creating a free internet library of downloadable ebooks

- Hosting writing competitions and offering book publishing
scholarships.

Interested in more 1st World Library books? contact:
literacy@1stworldlibrary.com
Check us out at: www.1stworldlibrary.com

1ˢᵗ World Library Literary Society

Giving Back to the World

"If you want to work on the core problem, it's early school literacy."

- James Barksdale, former CEO of Netscape

"No skill is more crucial to the future of a child, or to a democratic and prosperous society, than literacy."

- Los Angeles Times

"Literacy... means far more than learning how to read and write... The aim is to transmit... knowledge and promote social participation."

- UNESCO

"Literacy is not a luxury, it is a right and a responsibility. If our world is to meet the challenges of the twenty-first century we must harness the energy and creativity of all our citizens."

- President Bill Clinton

"Parents should be encouraged to read to their children, and teachers should be equipped with all available techniques for teaching literacy, so the varying needs and capacities of individual kids can be taken into account."

- Hugh Mackay

CHAPTER I

CHATEAU DE FEROUZAT, ..., 18...

No indeed, my dear Louis, I am neither dead nor ruined, nor have I turned pirate, trappist, or rural guard, as you might imagine in order to explain my silence these four months since I last appeared at your illustrious studio. No, you witty giber, my fabulous heritage has not taken wings! I am dwelling neither in China on the Blue River, nor in Red Oceania, nor in White Lapland. My yacht, built of teak, still lies in harbour, and is not swaying me over the vasty deep. It is no good your spinning out laborious and far-fetched hyperboles on the subject of my uncle's will: your ironical shafts all miss the mark. My uncle's will surpasses the most astonishing feat of its kind ever accomplished by notary's pen; and your poor imagination could not invent, or come anywhere near inventing, such remarkable adventures as those into which this registered document has led me.

First of all, in order that your feeble intellect may be enabled to rise to the level of the subject, I must give you some description of "the Corsair," as you called him after you met him in Paris last winter; for it is only by comprehending the peculiarities of his life and character that you can ever hope to understand my adventures.

Unfortunately, at this very point, a considerable difficulty arises, for my uncle still remains and always will remain a sort of legendary personage. Born at Marseilles, he was left an orphan at about the age of fourteen, alone in the world with one little sister still in the cradle, whom he brought up, and who subsequently became my mother: hence his tender regard for me. Nevertheless, and notwithstanding the fact that we two constituted the whole family, I only saw him during the intervals on shore of his sea-faring life. Endowed with truly remarkable qualities and with an energy that recognized no obstacles, he was the best fellow in the world, as you must have observed for yourself; but certainly he was also, from what I know of him, a most original character. I don't believe that in the course of his eventful career, he ever did a single act like other men, unless, may be, in the getting of children—yet even these were only his "god-children." He has left fourteen in the Department of Le Gard, scattered over the different estates on which he lived by turns after he had quitted the East; and we may well believe he would not have stopped short at that number, but that four months ago, as he was returning from the South Pole, he happened to die of a sunstroke, at the age of sixty-three. This last touch completes the picture of his life. As to his history, all that is known of it is confined to the following facts:

At the age of twenty-two my uncle turned Turk, from political conviction. This happened under the Bourbons. The character of his services in Turkey during the contests between Mehemet Ali and the Sultan was never very clear, and I fancy he was rather muddled about them himself, for he served both these princes by turns with equal courage and equal devotion. As it happened, he was on the side of Ibrahim at the time that the latter defeated the Turks at the battle of Konieh; but being carried away in that desperate charge which he himself led, and which decided the victory, my unfortunate uncle suffered the disgrace of falling wounded into the hands of the vanquished party. Being a prisoner to Kurchid-Pasha, and his wound having soon

healed, he was expecting to be impaled, when, to his great joy, his punishment was commuted to that of the galleys. There he remained three years without succeeding in effecting his escape, when one fine day he found his services in request just at the right time by the Sultan, who appointed him Pasha, giving him a command in the Syrian wars. What circumstance was it that cut short his political career? How was it that he obtained from the Pope the title of Count of the Holy Empire? Nobody knows.

All that is certain is that Barbassou-Pasha, tired of his honours and having returned two years since to settle down in Provence, started off one morning for Africa, on a ship that he had bought at Toulon. Henceforth he devoted himself to the spice trade.

It was after one of these voyages that he published his celebrated ontological monograph upon the negro races, a work which created some stir and gained for him a most flattering report from the Academy.

These leading events of his Odyssey being known, the more private facts and deeds of the life of Barbassou-Pasha are lost in obscurity. As for his physical characteristics, you will remember the great Marseillais six-foot high, with sinewy frame and muscles of steel; your mind's eye can picture still the formidable, bearded face, the savage and terrible eye, the rough voice, the complete type in short of "the pirate at his ease," as you used to say, when laughing sometimes at his quiet humour. After all, an easy-going soul, and the best of uncles!

As for my own recollections, so far back as they go, the following is all I have ever known of him. Being continually at sea, he had placed me at school quite young. One year, while at his chateau at Ferouzat, he sent for me during the holidays. I was six years old, and saw him for the first time.

He held me up in his arms to examine my face and features, then turning me gently round in the air, he felt my sides, after which—satisfied, no doubt, as to my build—he put me down again with great care, as if afraid of breaking me.

"Kiss your aunt!" he said.

I obeyed him.

My aunt at that time was a very handsome young woman of twenty-two to twenty-four, a brunette with great black, almond-shaped eyes, and fine features on a perfect oval face. She placed me on her knees and covered me with kisses, lavishing on me the most tender expressions, among which she mingled words of a foreign language which sounded like music, so sweet and harmonious was her voice. I conceived a great affection for her. My uncle let me do just as I liked, and allowed no hindrances to be put in my way. Thus it happened that at the end of my holidays I did not want to return to school again, and should certainly have succeeded in getting my way, if it had not been that Barbassou-Pasha's ship was waiting for him at Toulon.

You may imagine with what joy I returned to Ferouzat the next year. My uncle welcomed me with the same delight, and betook himself to the same examination of my physical structure. When his anxieties were satisfied, he said to me—

"Kiss your aunt!"

I kissed my aunt: but, as I kissed her, I was rather surprised to find her very much altered. She had become fair and pink-complexioned. A certain firm and youthful plumpness, which suited her remarkably well, gave her the appearance of a girl of eighteen. Being more bashful than at our former interview, she tendered me her fresh cheeks with a blush. I noticed also that her accent had undergone a modification, and now very much resembled the accent of one of my school-fellows who was Dutch. As I expressed my surprise at these changes, my uncle informed me that they had just returned from Java. This explanation sufficed for me, I did not ask any more questions, and henceforth I accustomed myself every year to the various metamorphoses of my aunt. The metamorphosis which pleased me the least was that which she contracted after a voyage to Bourbon, from which she returned a mulattress, but without ceasing still to be remarkably handsome. My uncle, it should be mentioned, was always very good to her, and I have never known a happier household.

Unfortunately Barbassou-Pasha, being engaged in important affairs, stayed away three years, and when I returned to Ferouzat, he kissed me and received me by himself. When I asked after my aunt, he told me that he was a widower. As this misfortune did not appear to affect him very seriously, I made up my mind to treat it with the same indifference that he did.

Since that time I never saw any woman at the chateau, except once in an isolated part of the park, where I met two shadowy beings, closely and mysteriously veiled. They were taking a walk, accompanied by an old fellow of singular aspect, clothed in a long robe with a *tarbouch* on his head, who greatly excited my curiosity. My uncle told me that this was His Excellency, Mohammed-Azis, one of his friends at Constantinople, whom he had taken in with his family after they had undergone persecution at the hands of the Sultan. He lodged him in another little chateau adjoining Ferouzat, in order that they might be able to live more comfortably in Turkish style: those young persons were two of his daughters.

After that year, I never again stayed in Provence: for my uncle, having settled in China and Japan, was absent five years, and my only relations with him were through his banker at Paris, with whom I enjoyed that solid and unlimited credit which you envied so much, and of which I availed myself with such easy grace and in such a superbly reckless spirit.

You remember that I received a few months ago a letter announcing this sudden misfortune, and requesting my immediate presence at Ferouzat, to remove the seals and open the will: my poor uncle had died in Abyssinia.

Well, the day after my arrival, I had only just got up, when Feraudet, the notary, was announced. He came in, literally armed with documents. I did not want to act like a greedy heir, but rather to put off for a few days all the most material questions; my notary, however, informed me that "there were certain clauses in the will which demanded an immediate examination." My uncle had charged me, he said, with numerous trusts and legacies "for the benefit of his god-children and of other parties living a long distance off." All this was uttered in a mournful tone suited to the occasion, and at the same time with the manner of a person aware that he was the bearer of an extraordinary document, and preparing me for its effect. Finally he opened the will, which was worded as follows:

"*Chateau de Ferouzat*, ... 18..

"I, the undersigned, Claude-Anatole-Gratien Barbassou, Count of Monteclaro, do hereby declare that I elect and designate as my universal legatee and the sole inheritor of my property: of all my real and personal estate, and all that I am entitled to of every description soever, such as ..., &c.: my nephew Jerome Andre de Peyrade, the son of my sister: And I hereby command him to discharge the following legacies:

"To my much-beloved wife and legitimate spouse, Lia Rachel Euphrosine Ben-Levy, milliner, of Constantinople, and dwelling there in the suburb of Pera, First, a sum of four thousand five hundred francs, which I have agreed by contract to pay her; Second, my house at Pera, in which she dwells, with all the appendages and appurtenances thereof; and Third, a sum of twelve thousand francs, to be distributed by her, as it may please her, among the different children whom she has by me.

"Likewise, to my much-beloved wife and legitimate spouse, Sophia Eudoxia, Countess of Monteclaro (whose maiden name is De Cornalis), dwelling at Corfu: First, a sum of five hundred thousand francs, which I have agreed by contract to pay her; Second, the clock and the Dresden china, which stand on my mantle-piece; Third, 'The Virgin,' by Perugino, in my drawing-room at Ferouzat.

"Likewise, to my much-beloved wife and legitimate spouse, Marie Gretchen Van Cloth, dwelling at Amsterdam: First, a sum of twenty thousand francs, which I have agreed by contract to pay her; Second, a sum of sixty thousand francs, to be distributed by her, as it may please her, among the different children whom she has by me; Third, my dinner-service in Delph, known as No. 3; Fourth, a barrel-organ, set with four of Haydn's symphonies.

"Likewise, to my much-beloved wife and legitimate spouse, Marie Louise Antoinette Cora de La Pescade, dwelling at Les Grands Palmiers (Ile Bourbon), my plantation upon which she lives, including the annexes of Le Grand Morne.

"Likewise, to my much-beloved wife and legitimate spouse, Anita Josepha Christina de Postero, dwelling at Cadiz: First, a sum of twelve thousand francs; which I have agreed by contract to pay her; Second, my pardon for her little adventure with my lieutenant Jean Bonaffe."

If some very precise person should seek to insinuate his criticisms upon my uncle's matrimonial principles, my reply would be that Barbassou-Pasha was a Turk and a Mussulman, and that consequently he can only be praised for having so faithfully obeyed the Laws of the Prophet—laws which permitted him to indulge in all this hymeneal luxury without in the least degree outraging the social proprieties—and for having in this matter piously fulfilled a religious duty, which his premature death alone, so far as we can judge, has hindered him from accomplishing with greater fervour. I trust that the God of the Faithful will at least give him credit for his efforts.

Having said so much on behalf of a memory which is dear to me, and having enumerated the chief clauses of the will, I may add in a few words that, after the payment of my uncle's matrimonial donations, and the various legacies to his "god-children," with those to his sailors in addition, there remained for me about thirty-seven million francs.

"But, these children of my uncle's?" said I.

"Oh, sir! everything is in order! The Turkish law not recognising marriages contracted abroad with unbelievers, excepting in the case of certain prescribed formalities which your uncle happens to have neglected to go through, it results that his will expresses his deliberate intentions. Moreover, he had during his lifetime provided for the future of all his people."

I listened with admiration.

"So much for the legal dispositions of the will, sir," said the notary, when he had finished reading it out.

"Now I have a sealed letter to hand to you, which your uncle charged me to give after his death to you alone. I was

instructed in the case of your death preceding his, to destroy it without acquainting myself with its purport. You will understand, therefore, that I know nothing of its contents, which are for you only to read. Have the kindness, please, to sign this receipt, declaring that you find the seals unbroken, and that I have left it in your possession."

He presented a paper, which I read and signed.

"Is that all?" I asked.

"Not quite, sir," he replied, as he took another package out of his pocket. "Here is a document similarly sealed which was addressed to me. I was only to open it in the case of your uncle's will becoming null and void through your death preceding his. This document, he told me, would then give effect to his final wishes. Your presence being duly established, my formal written instructions are to burn this document, now rendered useless and purposeless, before your eyes."

Again he made me attest that the seals were untampered with, and taking up a candle from the writing-table and lighting it, he forthwith committed to the flames this secret document the provisions of which we were not to know. He then departed.

When left alone, and still affected by these lively recollections of my poor uncle, I began to think of the letter which the notary had left with me. I divined some mystery in it, and had a vague presentiment that it would contain a decree of my destiny. This last message from him, coming as it were from the tomb, revived in my heart the grief which had hardly yet been allayed. At last, trembling all the while, I tore open the envelope. These were its contents:—

"My Dear Boy,

"When you read this, I shall have done with this world. Please me by not giving way too much to your grief, and act like a man! You know my ideas about death: I have never allowed myself to be prejudiced into regarding it as an evil, convinced as I have been, that it is nothing but the transition which leads us to a superior state of existence. Adopt this view, and do not cry over me like a child. I have lived my life; now it is your turn. My desire is, that this old friend of yours should be cherished in your memory: you shall join him with you in your happiness, by believing that he takes part in it.

"Now let us have a talk."

"I leave you all my property, desiring to create no business complications for you: my will is drawn up in proper form, and you will enter into possession of your inheritance, which, you may rest assured, is a pretty handsome one. There is, however, one last wish of mine for the fulfilment of which I rely simply upon your affection, feeling sure that between us there is no need of more complicated provisions for ensuring its execution.

"I have a daughter, who has always shared with you my dearest affections. If I have kept this second paternity a secret from you, I have done so because circumstances might occur which would render useless the revelation which I am now approaching. My daughter had a legal father who had the right to reclaim her when sixteen years of age; she is free now, her legal father is dead, she will soon be seventeen, and I entrust her to your charge. Her name is Anna Campbell, she lives at Paris at the Convent of Les Oiseaux, where she is completing her education. Her only relation is an aunt, her mother's sister, Madame Saulnier by name, who lives at No. 20, Rue Barbet de Jony. It will be a sufficient introduction for you to call on this lady and tell her your name. She is aware that I have appointed you moral guardian to my daughter, and that it is you who will take my place. In short, she knows *all my intentions*.

"I underline these words, for they sum up my fondest aspirations. I have brought up Anna with the view of making her your wife, and thus dividing my fortune between you; and I rely upon you to carry out this arrangement. If marriage is for a man but a small matter, it is for a woman the most serious event in life. With you, I am confident that the dear girl will never be unhappy, and that is the thing of most importance. If I never return from this last voyage, you will have plenty of time to enjoy your bachelor's life; but I count upon your friendship to render me this little service by marrying her when the right time arrives. At present she is scarcely full-grown, and I think it will be best for you to wait one or two years. I can assure you her mother had a fine figure. You will find their portraits in one of the velvet frames in the drawer of my desk. (Don't make a mistake: it is the one numbered 9.)

"Now that this matter is settled, it only remains for me to give you one last injunction. If Ferandet has followed my instructions, as I suppose, he will have burnt a paper in your presence. This was a second will, by which my daughter Anna Campbell would have been appointed my universal legatee, had you not been living. So long as all happened in the right order, you surviving me, you will understand I should not have wished to complicate your affairs, by leaving you confronted with a lot of legal formalities and intricacies. Such would be the consequence of a female minor who is a foreigner inheriting jointly with you: this would have plunged you into a veritable mire of technicalities, restrictions, registrations, and goodness knows what. Nevertheless, it is necessary to provide fully for the possibility of an accident arising to you before your marriage with Anna. Our property would go in that case to collaterals ... and God only knows from how many quarters of the world these would not be forthcoming! As I wish my fortune to remain with my children, it is indispensable that you should not forget to make testamentary dispositions in favour of your cousin, so that the whole property may go to her in the event of your death, without any more dispute than there has been in your own case. I leave this matter in your hands. You will find at my bankers all the indications of surnames, Christian names, and descriptions which you will require to enumerate, on the first page of my private ledger, where the account which was opened for her commences, and yours also, forming a separate banking account for you two. Madame Saulnier is accustomed to draw what is required for her: therefore, until your marriage, it is unnecessary for you to occupy yourself with this detail—all you have to do is to confirm her credit.

"Now that we have settled this matter, my dear boy, go ahead! I do not need, I am sure, to remind you to think occasionally of your old uncle: I know you well, and that satisfies me. I thank you for what you have been to me, and bless you from the bottom of my heart!

"Come, don't give way, old fellow: I am in Heaven, my soul is free and rejoicing in the glories of the Infinite. Is there anything in this for you to mourn over? Farewell."

After reading this letter, my dear Louis, need I tell you that I did the contrary to what my poor uncle bade me, and that I gave way to my grief. The tears streamed down my cheeks, my heart was breaking, and I could no longer see this last word, "Farewell," as I pressed the letter to my lips.

Such a mixture of tenderness and elevation of tone, such touching solicitude to console my grief, such boundless confidence in my love and fidelity! I felt crushed with my grief, proud only to think that I was worthy of the generosity with which this noble-hearted man was overwhelming me, prodigal as a father in his kindness. It seemed to me at that moment that I had never loved him enough, and the grief at his loss mingled itself with something like remorse. As if he were able hear me, I swore to him that I would live for the accomplishment of his wishes: from the depths of my soul, indeed, I felt certain that he saw me.

When the flow of my tears had ceased, I did not want to tarry a moment in the accomplishment of his last behests. I ran to his bed chamber, opened his desk, and found the two portraits. One, a valuable miniature, represents a woman of twenty-five, the other is a photograph of Anna Campbell at the age of fifteen. Although not so pretty as her mother, perhaps, she has a charming childlike face; the poor little thing felt uncomfortable, no doubt, when they made her sit, for her expression is rather sulky and unnatural. Still she gives promise of being attractive when she has passed the awkward age. I felt myself suddenly possessed by a sentiment of affection for this unknown cousin, whose guardian I had become and whose husband I am to be. Upon this cold picture I repeated to my uncle the oath to obey his wishes; then, taking up a pen, I wrote a will appointing Anna Campbell the universal legatee of all the property which my uncle left us.

But one part of my inheritance, the most remarkable and the least expected, was at present unknown either to the notary or to myself.

I don't wish to make myself out better than I really am, my dear Louis: I must declare, nevertheless, that in spite of the very natural bewilderment which I felt on finding myself the owner of such a fortune, my first thought, when once I had disposed of the legal matters, was to pay a tribute of mournful regrets to the memory of my poor uncle. I should have considered it base ingratitude, not to say impiety on my part, to have shown myself too eager to enjoy the wealth bequeathed to me by so generous a benefactor. His loss really left a cruel void in my heart. I decided, therefore, at least to live a few months at Ferouzat. I wrote immediately to the aunt of Anna Campbell, to express my resolution to fulfil the wishes of my second father, begging her to dispose of my services in every way as those of a protector and friend ready to respond to every appeal. Four days afterwards, I received from her a most cordial and elegantly-worded letter. She assured me of her confidence in all the good accounts which my uncle had given of me; and she gave me news of my *fiancee*, "who for one who is still only a child, promises already to develop into an accomplished woman."

Having discharged these conventional duties, I shut myself up in my retreat, and set to work.

For me to say that my retirement was not more distracted than I would have desired, might perhaps be called a dangerous assertion; but what could I do? Was it not my duty to acquaint myself with all that my uncle bequeathed to me? And the Lord knows what marvels my chateau of Ferouzat contained! Every day I made some fresh discovery in rooms full of curious furniture and antiquities of all ages and of all countries. Barbassou-Pasha was a born buyer of valuable objects, and the furniture was crammed with rich draperies, hangings, costumes, and objects of art or curios: my steward himself could not enumerate them all.

But the most delightful of all these marvels is certainly Kasre-el-Nouzha, my neighbouring property. Kasre-el-Nouzha was a Turkish fancy of my uncle's. These three Arabic words correspond to the Spanish Buen-Retiro; or, literally translated, they signify "Castle of Pleasures." This was the retreat, separated only by a party-wall from Ferouzat, that was formerly inhabited by the exiled minister who had fled from the persecutions of the Sultan. Picture to yourself, hidden in a great park whose umbrageous foliage

concealed it from view, a delightful palace of the purest Oriental architecture, surrounded by gardens, with flowering shrubs covered with a wealth of blossoms, standing in the midst of green lawns, a sort of Vale of Tempe transplanted, one might imagine, from the East. My uncle Barbassou, conscientious architect that he was, had copied the plan from one of the residences of the King of Kashmir. In the interior of the Kasre you might fancy yourself in the house of some grandee of Stamboul or of Bagdad. Luxuries, ornaments, furniture, and general domestic arrangements, have all been studied with the taste of an artist and the exactitude of an archaeologist. At the same time European comforts are gratefully mingled with Turkish simplicity. The silken tapestries of Persia, the carpets of Smyrna with those harmonious hues which seem to be borrowed from the sun, the capacious divans, the bath-rooms, and the stores, all contribute in short to the completeness of an establishment, suitable to a Pasha residing under the sky of Provence. A little door in the park-wall gives access to this oasis. As you may guess, I passed many an hour there, and I dreamt dreams of "The Thousand and One Nights."

All this time I had never interrupted my labours; for you need not suppose that my nabob's fortune could make me forgetful of my inclinations towards science. In the midst of my numerous follies, as you know very well, and in spite of the distractions of the more or less dissipated life which I have led up to my present happy age of twenty-six, I have always preserved my love of study, which fills up those hours of forced respite that even the pleasures of the world leave to every man who is conscious of a brain. The Polytechnic School, and the search for x, in which my uncle trained me, developed very inquisitive instincts in me. I ended by acquiring a taste for transcendental ideas. This taste is at least worth as much as that for angling. For my part, I confess that I class among the molluscs men who, being their own masters, content themselves with eating, drinking, and sleeping, without performing any intellectual labour. This is why you call me "the *savant*."

I worked away, then, at my book with a veritable enthusiasm, and my "Essay upon the Origin of Sensation" had extended to several long chapters, when the critical event occurred which I have undertaken to relate to you.

I had lived thus all alone for two weeks. One evening, on my return from Arles, where I had been spending a couple of days upon some business, I was informed that His Excellency, Mohammed-Azis, the old friend of my uncle, whom I remembered to have seen on one occasion, had arrived at the chateau the evening before, not having heard of the death of Barbassou-Pasha. I must admit that this news gave me at the time very little pleasure; but in memory of my dear departed uncle, I could not but give his friend the welcome he expected. I was told that His Excellency had gone straight to his quarters at Kasre-el-Nouzha, where he was accustomed to dwell. I hastened to send my respects to him, begging him to let me know if he would receive me. He sent word that he was at my disposition and waiting for me. I therefore set off at once to call upon him.

I found Mohammed-Azis on his door-step. Gravely and sadly he received me with a salute, the respectful manner of which embarrassed me somewhat, coming from a man of his age. He showed me into the drawing-room, in each of the four corners of which bubbled a little fountain of perfumed water, in small basins of alabaster garnished with flowers. He made me sit down on the divan covered with a splendid silk material, and which, very broad and very deep, and furnished with numerous cushions, extends round the entire room. When seated, I commenced uttering a few phrases of condolence, but he replied to me in Turkish.

This mode of conversing had its difficulties, so he, seeing

that I could not understand him, started off into a *Sabir* or Italianised French, pronounced in an accent which I will not attempt to describe.

"Povera Eccellenza Barbassou-Pacha!—finito—morto?"

I replied in Italian, which he spoke indifferently well. We thus managed to get along.

I then related to him the accident which had brought about the death of Barbassou, my uncle and his friend. He listened to me with a greatly distressed air.

"Dunque voi signor padrone?" he replied, uneasily; "voi heritare di tutto?—ordinare?—commandare?"—

"Let me assure you, Your Excellency," I answered, "nothing that concerns you will be changed by my uncle's death. I shall make it a point of honour to fill his place exactly."

He appeared satisfied with this reply, and breathed freely, like a man relieved of a great burden. In another minute he asked me if I would like to make the acquaintance of all his people.

"I should be delighted, Your Excellency, if you would present me to your family."

He walked towards the door and summoned them by clapping his hands.

I was expecting to see the wives or daughters of my host appear according to Mussulman custom, covered up with their triple veils. An exclamation of surprise escaped me when I saw four young persons enter, dressed in beautiful Oriental costumes, their faces unveiled, and all four endowed with such glorious beauty and youthful grace that I was, for the moment, fairly dazzled. I took them for his daughters.

Hesitating and bashful, they stopped a few steps from me. In my bewilderment I could not find a word to say to them, until after their father had said something to them, they came up to me, first one, then another, and with shy graces and indescribable charms, each bowed and saluted me with her hand to her forehead, then took my hand and kissed it.

I must admit that I completely lost my head. I don't know what I stammered out. I believe I assured them that they and their father would find me, in the absence of my uncle, their respectful and devoted friend; but, as they did not understand a word of French, my speech was lost upon them. However that may have been, after a minute or so they were sitting with their legs crossed on the divan, and all I was anxious about was to prolong my visit as much as possible. Mohammed told me their charming names. These were, Kondje-Gul, Hadidje, Nazli, and Zouhra. He, like a proud father, was not backward in praising their beauty, and I joined in chorus with him, and certainly succeeded in flattering him by my enthusiasm regarding them.

Indeed, all four of them were of such striking beauty, and yet so different in type, that you might have thought them grouped together in order to form the most ravishing picture, their large dark eyes, sweet, timid, and languishing like the gazelle's, with that Oriental expression which we do not meet with in these climes; lips which disclosed pearly teeth as they smiled; and complexions which have been preserved by the veil from the sun's rays, and which—according to the ancient simile—appeared really to be made up of lilies and roses. In those rich costumes of silk or of Broussan gauze, with their harmonious colours, revealing the forms of their hips and of their bosoms, they exhibited attitudes and movements of feline lissomness and exotic grace, the voluptuous languor of which can only be realised by those who have seen it in Mussulman women. I imagined myself the hero of an Arabian story, and mad fancies entered my brain.

While I was endeavouring, for appearance's sake, to talk with their father as well as I could, they, growing tamer by degrees, began to whisper together—now and then came a little burst of laughter, in which I seemed to detect some mischief. I playfully responded by holding up my finger to let them know I guessed their thoughts, and again they burst out laughing like sly children—this going on until, after half an hour or so, quite a nice feeling of familiarity was established between us; we talked by signs, and our eyes enabled us almost to dispense with the laborious intervention of Mohammed's interpretations. Moreover, he seemed delighted to see us frolicking in this way.

In order to teach them my name I pronounced several times the word "Andre." They understood and tried in their turn to make me say their names. Hadidje's was the occasion of much laughter, by reason of my difficulty in articulating the guttural breathing. Seeing that I could not manage it, she held me by both hands, her face almost touching mine, and shouted "Hadidje!" I repeated it, "Hadidje!" This was charming and intoxicating. I had to take the same lesson from each of them; but when it came to the turn of Kondje-Gul, it was a delirium of joy. By some chance she let slip a word of Italian. I questioned her in this language, and found she knew it pretty well. You may imagine my delight! Immediately we overwhelmed each other with a torrent of questions. Her sisters watched us with looks of amazement.

At this moment a Greek servant came in, followed by two other women, bringing in the dinner on trays, which they laid upon small low tables of ebony inlaid with mother-of-pearl.

Propriety and good breeding impelled me to take my leave

after this very long visit, and I prepared to do so. Upon this my young friends murmured out a concert of confused words, in which I seemed to detect regret at my departure. Fortunately His Excellency intervened by inviting me to stay to dinner with them.

Need I tell you that I accepted!

I sat down on the carpet, as they did, with my legs crossed, and we commenced a delicious banquet. Champagne was brought in for me, an attention which I appreciated. My place was next to Nazli; on my left was Kondje-Gul, and opposite me, Hadidje and Zouhra. I will not tell you what dishes were served, my thoughts were set elsewhere.

"How old art thou?" asked Kondje-Gul, employing in her Italian, which was tinctured with Roumanian, the Turkish form of address.

"Twenty-six," said I, "and how old art thou?"

"Oh, I shall soon be eighteen." This "thouing" of each other was charming. She then told me the ages of the others. Hadidje was the eldest, she was nineteen: Nazli and Zouhra were between seventeen and eighteen, the age of fresh maturity among the daughters of the East, who ripen earlier than ours. Our gaiety and the prattle of their voices went on without cessation; but as they were drinking nothing but water, I said to Kondje-Gul, thoughtlessly,

"Won't you taste the wine of France?"

At this proposition she gave such a scared little look that the others asked her to explain what I had said. This caused a great excitement, followed by a discussion in which the father took part. I was beginning to fear that I had given offence to them, when His Excellency at last said a few

words which seemed to be decisive. Then Kondje-Gul, blushing all the while, and hesitating with divine graceful-ness, took up my glass and drank—first with a little grimace like a kitten trying strange food, so droll and amusing was it; then, later on, with an air of satisfaction so real that all of them burst out laughing.

By Jove, I must say that at this frank abandonment I felt my heart beat just as if her lips had touched my own in a kiss. Imagine what became of me when Zouhra, Nazli, and Hadidje held out their hands all at the same time to claim my glass. They passed round the glass and drank, and I after them, perturbed by emotions impossible to describe. This unconstraint varied with bashful reserve, these fascinating scruples, which they overcame one after another, fearing no doubt to offend me by refusing things which they thought were French customs; all their little ways in fact stimulated me, ravished me, and yet daunted me at times so much that I dare no longer brave their looks—although the presence of their father was a sufficient guarantee of the innocent character of these familiarities.

When the meal was over, the same Greek servants cleared the tables. Night-time arrived and they lighted the chandeliers. Through the closed shutters there came to us perfumes of myrtle and lilac. Cigarettes were brought: Zouhra took one, lighted it, and after drawing a few mouthfuls, offered it to me. I abandoned myself to their caprices.

Now, Louis, can you picture your friend luxuriously reclining on cushions, and surrounded by these four daughters of Mahomet's Paradise, in their lovely sultana's costumes, frolicking and prattling, and all four of them so beautiful that I don't know which I should have presented with the apple if I had been Paris? I assure you, it required an effort to convince myself that all this was real. After a little while I noticed that Mohammed Azis was no longer present;

but thanks to Kondje-Gul, who had quite become my interpreter, our conversation became brisk and general. Hadidje taught me a Turkish game which is played with flowers, and which I won't try to describe to you, as I hardly understood it.

If I were to tell you all that happened that evening, I should be relating a story of giddy madness and intoxication. I taught them in return the game of "hunt the slipper;" you know it, don't you? We played it as follows: there was a ribbon knotted at both ends, which we held, sitting on the floor in a circle, and on which slips a ring, which one of the players must seize in his hands. This, upon my word, finished me up. What laughter, and what merry cries! Each of them, caught in her turn, chose me of course as her mark. Every moment I found myself seized and held prisoner in their naked, snowy arms. Upon my soul, it was maddening!

It was nearly midnight when His Excellency returned. I had lost all reckoning of the time; now I felt I must really make off. While I was getting ready and saying a few words to Kondje-Gul, Mohammed Azis spoke to Zouhra, Nazli, and Hadidje. I fancied that he was questioning them, and that they replied in the negative. Then he spoke at greater length to Kondje-Gul; he appeared to me to be pressing her to give him an account of my conversation with her, and that the result did not please him. I was annoyed with myself at the thought that, maybe, I had been the cause of her being reprimanded. At last he certainly ordered them to retire, for they came to me, one after the other, and each of them, as on entering, bowed to me in a respectful manner, saluting me with her hand to her forehead, and kissed my hand; after this they went out, leaving me in a frame of mind disordered beyond description.

I was just about to offer some apologies to Mahommed, and make my peace with him before I left (for I feared that he might for the future place obstacles in the way of similar evening performances), when he said to me, with an anxious air, in that dialect of his which I translate, in order to avoid reproducing the scene of the *mamamouchis* in the "Bourgeois Gentilhomme:"

"May I be allowed to hope that your lordship is satisfied?"

"Satisfied, Your Excellency?" I exclaimed, affectionately grasping his hands; "why, I am delighted! You could not give me greater pleasure in this world than by treating me exactly as you treated my uncle."

"The young ladies, then, did not displease your lordship?"

"Your daughters? Why, they are adorable! My only fear is lest I should not find them reciprocate the sentiments which they inspire in me."

"Ah! Then it is not because your lordship is displeased that you will not remain here to-night?" added he, with an anxious look.

"That I will not remain here?" I replied. "What do you mean?"

"Why, Your Excellency has not expressed his will to any of them."

"My will! What will, then, could I express to them?"

"Considering that they belong to your lordship," he continued.

"They belong to me? Who?"

"Why, Kondje-Gul, Zouhra, Hadidje, Nazli."

"They belong to me?" replied I, overcome with stupefaction.

"Certainly," said Mahommed, looking as astonished as I did. "His Excellency, Barbassou-Pasha, your uncle, whose eunuch I had the honour of being, commanded me to purchase four maidens for his harem. Since he is dead, and your lordship takes his place as master—I had supposed—"

"Ah!!!"

I won't attempt to render for you the full force of the exclamation to which I gave vent. You may guess the feelings conveyed in it. In very truth I thought I should go out of my senses this time. The dream of "The Thousand and One Nights" was being realised in my waking hours! This extraordinary and sumptuous palace was a harem, and this harem was mine! These four Scheherazades, whose glorious youthfulness and fascinating charms had scorched me like fire, they were my slaves, and only awaited a sign or token of my desire!

Mohammed, incapable of conceiving my agitation, regarded me with a pitiful, confused look, as if he anticipated some disgrace. At this moment the old Greek woman brought him the keys: there were four. He handed them to me.

"Thank you," I said; "now you may leave me."

He obeyed, saluted me without a word, and went out.

As soon as I found myself alone, not intending to restrain my feelings any more, I began to march about the drawing-room like a madman, and gave free vent to the outburst of a joy which overwhelmed me. I picked up from the carpet a ribbon dropped there by Kondje-Gul, I pressed it to my lips with avidity; next some scattered flowers, with which Hadidje and Zouhra had played.

Louis, I hope you do not expect me to analyse for your benefit all the extraordinary sensations which I experienced at that moment. The events which befel me verged upon the supernatural—the supernatural cannot be described—and I know not any legend, romance, or novel, relating to this world, which has ever treated such an astounding situation as that of which I was the hero. Those severe middle-class parents who give their daughters, for New Year's presents, M. Galland's "Arabian Nights," with illustrations of the amorous adventures of the Caliph of Bagdad, would find such a romance as mine quite too "strong," simply because the scene is not laid in Persia, or at Samarcand. Nevertheless, my story is identical in character, and the most modest young lady might read it without a frown, if only my name were Hassan instead of Andre.

Would you like to know everything that can agitate the mind of a mortal in such a position as mine? Listen, then.

When I had succeeded in reducing to some extent my exaltation of spirit, when I had at last persuaded myself of the reality of this splendid fairyland, I sat down with my elbows on the window-sill—I felt the need of a little fresh air. It was just striking midnight. What were *they* doing? Were they thinking of me, I wondered, as much as I was thinking of them? I began to examine the four keys which Mohammed had left me. Each key had a tiny label, with a letter and a name on it—Nazli, Zouhra, Hadidje, or Kondje-Gul. My eyes were still filled with their beauty. Although far from artless, I felt embarrassed in spite of myself, I might almost say shy. After the fascinations of this evening, I knew that I was in love; I loved with a strange passion suddenly developed; I loved to overflowing these beautiful beings, without being able to separate one from another. So completely were they mingled in my fancy, they might have possessed but one soul between them. By reason of my certitude of equal possession, Kondje-Gul, Hadidje, Nazli, and Zouhra constituted in my imagination a single existence, exhaling its unrivalled perfume of youth, beauty, and love.

All this may appear absurd to you. I daresay you are right, but I am only analysing for you an enchantment which still influences me like a dream. While longing for the virginal delights which awaited me, my tumultuous senses were plunged into certain apprehensions at once anxious and sweet. How am I to explain it to you? Sultan though I have been in my life, never before have I come in for such a delightful windfall of pleasures, my heart having been generally occupied, as you know, with much less worthy objects. All at once I was overwhelmed by the idea that they had doubtless misunderstood the reserve which I had affected in their company. According to their harem traditions, customs, and laws, I was their legitimate master and husband: was it not quite likely, then, that they believed me indifferent or even disdainful of their charms? Troubled at this reflection, I was seized with a dreadful pang of conscience. What could they suppose? Good heavens! Ought I to wait till the next day to dissipate their doubts, and justify myself for such strange coldness—coldness which may have seemed like indifference? I had no sooner conceived this thought than my desire concentrated itself upon one object, to see Kondje-Gul again.

I knew all the domestic arrangements of El Nouzha. In the centre of the edifice is a vast circular hall, to which the daylight is admitted by a cupola of ground glass, supported by pillars of white marble. Lamps hanging between the pillars give out a mysterious light. Once arrived there, I listened. All was silent. I found Kondje-Gul's chamber, and went close up to it. I listened again, with my ear to the door. An indistinct rustling which I heard, apprized me that she was not yet in bed. With key in hand, I still hesitated before opening. At last I made up my mind.

Picture to yourself a sweetly perfumed room, both rich and coquettish in its arrangements, lined with Indian silk hangings of gay colours, and illumined by the soft light of a small chandelier of three branches. In front of a large glass Kondje-Gul was seated, her long hair reaching down to the floor. With her bare arms uplifted, and her head turned backwards, she held in her hand a golden comb. Seeing me, she uttered a little cry, got up with a bound, and blushing all the while, and fixing upon me her great frightened eyes, she rested motionless and almost in a tremble. Her agitation communicated itself to me.

"Did I frighten you?" I commenced, trying to speak with a firm voice; "and will you pardon me for coming in like this?"

She did not answer a word, but lowered her eyes, a smile glanced furtively over her lips, and then, with her hand on her bosom, she bowed to me.

"Kondje-Gul! Dear Kondje-Gul!" I exclaimed, touched to the depths of my soul by this act of submission.

And springing towards her, I took her in my arms to chase away her fears; I kissed her brow, which she offered to me, pressing her face against my bosom, with a lovely bashful look of alarm.

"You have come, then!" she whispered.

"Did you imagine I did not love you?" said I, as truly affected as she was.

At this question she raised her head with an inexpressible languor and smiled again, looking into my eyes, and so close that our lips met.

Louis, is it true that the ideal embraces the infinite, and that the human soul soars into regions so sublime that the blisses of this world below cannot satisfy it?... I did not want to quit the harem without having also seen Hadidje, Zouhra, and Nazli. Poor little dears, no doubt they already fancied themselves disdained! I must dry up their tears.

You will understand by this time the complications in my uncle's will which have prevented me, these four months past, from finding a minute to write to you.

I will relate to you the incidents of this remarkable situation, of this quadruple passion by which I am possessed to such an extent that I am sincere in all my professions. You may tell me, if you like, from the commonplace standpoint of your own limited experiences, that it is all madness. I love, I adore, after the manner of a poet or a pagan—as you like, in fact—but what does it all amount to? My uncle, who was a Mussulman, leaves me his harem; what could I do?

If it should happen that your work leaves you a little leisure, *don't* come to Ferouzat; you understand? That's what we sultans are like! The girls are dying to see Paris; very likely I shall turn up there one of these days.

I need hardly impress upon you, I suppose, the advisability of keeping this letter most carefully from the eyes of your wife.

CHAPTER II

Madam, let me be very candid; I have a warm temperament, certainly—more so, perhaps, than an ordinary Provencal. I will confess to even more than this, if your grace so wills it, and I will not blush for it; but pray condescend to believe that I am also a respecter of conventional proprieties, and that I should feel most keenly the loss of your esteem in this regard. Now, from a few words of satirical wit, concealed like small serpents under the flowery condolences of your malicious letter, I concluded that this miserable fellow Louis, abandoning all considerations of delicacy, and at the risk of ruining my reputation, had played me a most abominable trick, by reading out to you all the nonsense which I wrote to him last week. You need not deny it! He confesses it to-day, unblushingly, in the budget of news which he sends me, adding that you "laughed over it." Good gracious! what can you have thought of me? After such a story, I certainly could never again look you in the face, but that I can clear myself by assuring you at once that all this tale was nothing but a mystification, invented as a return for some of his impertinent chaff regarding my uncle Barbassou's will. Louis fell into the trap like any booby. But for him to have drawn you with him, is enough to make me die of shame.

Madam, I prefer now to make my confession. I am not the hero of a romance of the Harem. I am a good young man, an advocate of morality and propriety, notwithstanding the fact that you have often honoured me with the title of "a regular original." Be so good as to believe, then, that the most I have been guilty of is a too artless simplicity of character. I did not suppose that Louis would show you this eccentric letter, for I had expressly enjoined him to keep it from you. My only crime therefore in all this matter has been that I forgot that a woman of your intelligence would read everything, when she had the mind to do so, and a husband like yours.

In fact, madam, I hardly know why I have taken the trouble to excuse myself with so much deliberation. I perceive that by such apologies I run the risk of aggravating my mistake. What did I write, after all, but a very commonplace specimen of those Arabian stories which girls such as you have read continually in the winter evenings, under the eyes of their delighted mothers? When I consider it, I begin to understand that your laughter, if you did laugh, must have been at the feebleness of my imagination—you compared it with the Palace of gold and the thousand wives of the Caliph Haroun-al-Raschid.—But please remember, once more, that I am a poor Provencal and not a Sultan.

"My tastes are those of a simple bachelor."

Observe moreover that, out of regard for probability, no less than from respect for local colouring, I was obliged to decide upon a somewhat simple harem, and to confine it within the strictly necessary limits. Like a school-boy, falling in love with the heroine he has put into his story, I found myself so charmed with my fancy, that in order to further enjoy my pleasures of illusion, I determined not to overstep the limits of a perfectly realisable adventure.

But since I abandoned myself to this folly, does it not seem to you, reconsidering the matter, that a great deal would have been lost if such a romance had never occurred to me? And above all if it had stopped short at the first page? Is it not astonishing that no author had thought of writing such a thing before? Would not this have been just the work for a moralist and a philosopher, worthy at once of a poet and of a scholar? This poor world of ours, madam, moves in a narrow circle of passions and sensations, so limited that it seems to me as if every soul rather more lofty than the average must continually feel itself imprisoned. What felicity it must be, by a single flight of the imagination, to escape from this prison locked by prejudice! To fly away into the regions of dreamland! Slave of our civilized conventions, what bliss to run away unfettered into the shady paths of the pagan world, peopled with its merry, enchanting nymphs! Or again to wander, like a happy child of Asiatic climes in gardens of sycamores, where young sultanas bathe and disport them-selves in basins of porphyry. The Bois de Boulogne is a charming place, no doubt, madam; but you will admit that it is inferior to the Valley of Roses, and that the painted and bedizened young women you see there will bear no comparison with my houris.

What, then? Does my thirst after the ideal merit any censure? Do not you consider, you who read novels, that it would, on the contrary, be an instructive as well as a curious study to follow up the strange incidents which would necessarily result from such a very natural conjunction of oriental love transferred to the midst of our own world? What contrasts they would provoke, and what strange occurrences! Does not the absence of such a study leave a void in our illustrious literature?

But I divine upon your lips a word which frightens me— "Immoral! Immoral!" you say.

Madam, this word shows me that you are strangely mistaken about my pure intentions. You are a woman of considerable intelligence; let us understand each other like philosophers or moralists. Suppose my name to be Hassan. You would read without the least ruffle on your brow the very simple narrative of my pretended amours, and if they were hindered by any untoward obstacles, you would perhaps accord them a small tribute of tears, such as you have doubtless shed over the misfortunes of poor Namouna. The question of morality therefore, is in this case simply a question of latitude, and the impropriety of my situation would disappear at once if I inhabited the banks of the Bosphorus, or some palace at Bagdad.

Perhaps you take your stand upon the more elevated ground of "sentiment?" Well, this is precisely the pyschological point of view that I am about to discuss, madam. Yes, if it were only in order to inquire whether the human soul freed from all constraint, is capable of infinite expansion, like a liberated gas. To mix positive and materialist science with etherialised sensualism, such is my object. A simple passion, we all know what that is; but to adore four women at a time—while so many honest folk are well content to love one only—this seems to me a praiseworthy aspiration, fit to inspire the soul of a poet who prides himself upon his gallantry, no less than the brain of a philosopher in search of the vital elixir and the sources of sensation. Such a study would, assuredly, be arduous and severe, and would at any rate not be without glory, as you will admit, if it should happen to terminate logically in the triumph of the sublime Christian love over pagan or Mahometan polygamy.

Again, madam, in reprimanding me for my poor little harem, do you mean to preach against King David, or the seven hundred wives of Solomon? Without going back to the biblical legends of these venerable sovereigns, have you not read the classics? In what respect, may I ask, is the poem of Don Juan more moral than my subject? And did good old Lafontaine drop any of his artless probity, when he dipped his pen into the Boccaccian inkpot? The morality of a given book, madam, depends entirely upon the morality of its

author, who respects himself first by respecting his public, and who will not lead the latter into bad company, not wishing to corrupt it with bad sentiments.

It gives me pleasure to draw the picture of those ideal amours which every warm-blooded youth of twenty has at one time or other cherished in his thoughts; to substitute virginal charms and graces for vice and harlotry—and after the manner of those charming heathen poets who have so often filled our dreams with their fancies, to mingle the anacreontic with the idyllic. Open any of your moral stories, madam, and I'll wager my harem you will find that the interest in them is always kept up by adultery, in thought or in deed, which has been erected into a social institution! The same Minotaur has served for us since the time of Menelaus. Adultery, adultery, always adultery! it is as inevitable as it is monotonous!

Do you prefer the novel of the day, on the lives and habits of courtesans? revelations of the boudoir, where all is impure, venal, and degrading? No, madam, I won't proceed any farther, out of respect alike for you and for my pen.

Possibly your taste inclines you to those moralist's studies of "Woman," in which the author warns his readers on the first page that "he does not speak for chaste ears." Madam, it is my boast that I have never written a line which a virtuous woman might not read.... My book will certainly lose thereby in the circulation which it will obtain; but I shall console myself by the thought that if I sometimes cause you to smile, that smile will never be accompanied by a blush. Being the nephew of a Pasha, it struck me as a capital idea to lay the scene of a Turkish romance in Provence, and to found upon it a study in psychology. Every romance must be based upon love. Am I to be blamed, therefore, because oriental customs prescribe for lovers different modes of love? Confess, if you please, that my heroines are more poetic than the young women *a la mode*, into whose company I had as much right as any other author to conduct my hero if I had so chosen. I will excuse myself by saying, like the simpleton De Chamfort, "Is it my fault if I love the women I do love better than those I don't?"

P.S. Above all things, not a word to Louis about the mystification of which I am making him a victim.

You wretch! Here's a fine pickle you've got me into! What, after I confided to you the extraordinary adventures which I have passed through, relying upon your absolute secrecy and discretion, you go straight off and read my letter to your wife, at the risk of bringing upon me by your recklessness the most cruel gibes on the subject of my pasha-ship! Can't you see that if this story gets wind, Paris will be too hot a place for me? I shall become the butt of the Society journals and the halfpenny press, who will treat me as a most eccentric and romantic personage. Never more shall I be able to set foot in club, theatre, or private drawing-room, without being followed by the stares of the inquisitive and the quiet chaff of the ribald! I can picture myself already in the Bois, with all the loafers in my train pointing out "the man with the harem." Have you lost your senses, that you have betrayed me in this abominable fashion?

In all seriousness I now rely upon you to repair this blunder, by accepting, in the eyes of your wife, the part of one mystified, which I have made you assume. I wrote to her that not one word of this story is true, and that it is a romance I have been composing in order to occupy the leisure hours which I am forced to pass in the solitude of Ferouzat, while the business connected with my inheritance is being wound up. In short, as I am positive that the first thing she will do will be to show you her letter, I expect you, if your friendship is good for anything, to pretend to believe it. Upon this condition only will I continue my confidences; and

I suspend them until you have given me your word of honour to observe discretion.

Having received your promise, Louis, I now resume my narrative at the point where I broke off. Now you will see what you might have lost.

Just one word by way of preface.

I am relating to you, my dear friend, a story which is more especially remarkable for the multitude of unaccustomed sensations with which it abounds, and which I experience at every step—for my amourous adventures, as you will agree, bear no resemblance to the ready-made class of amours. It would really have been a great loss for the future of psychology, if the hero of such adventures had not happened to be, as I am, a philosopher capable of bringing to bear upon them powers of correct analysis.

First of all, if you wish really to understand the peculiarities of my situation, you must banish from your mind all that you have ever known of such amours as come within the reach of the poor Lovelaces of our everyday world. Those uncertain, ephemeral connections of lovers and mistresses whose only law is their caprice, and which mere caprice can dissolve; those immoral and dubious ties whose permanence nothing can guarantee, and in which one jostles one's rival of yesterday and of the morrow—in all amours of this sort there is something precarious and humiliating. With our habits and customs no secret, no mystery, is possible; for however loving or beloved a woman may be, her beauty is exposed to every eye. It is like the enjoyment of communal property. In my harem, on the contrary, the charms of Zouhra, Nazli, and Kondje-Gul, concealed from all other eyes, have never excited any passions but mine; my tranquil possession is undisturbed by the anxious jealousies which recollections of a former rival always awaken. Nor is the future less assured than the present, for their lives are my property; they are my slaves, and I their master, in charge of their souls. So much for my preface; now I will proceed.

I will not disparage your powers of memory by reminding you that my interesting narrative was broken off *au premier lendemain*—at the first glimmer of our honeymoon. The complete bliss, the enchantment of such moments, is certainly the most exquisite thing I have experienced. First the timid blushes, then the growing boldness and the fresh impression of first sensations—all this and more, mingled with the contentment of entire possession. One gives oneself up entirely; all barriers are broken down by love—participation in one tender secret has already united the lovers' souls, which seek each other and mingle together in a common existence.

I had returned to the chateau before my people were up; after a bath I slept again, and did not wake before noon. I breakfasted, and then waited till two o'clock before returning to El-Nouzha. Too great a haste would have seemed to indicate a want of delicacy, and I wished to show that I was discreet as well as passionate; this time of day seemed appropriate from both points of view.

To describe to you the condition of my feelings would be about as easy, you may imagine, as to describe a display of fireworks. There are certain perturbations of the heart which defy analysis. The enchantment which held me spell-bound, intoxicated my mind like fumes of haschisch, and I could hardly recognise myself in this fairy-world character; it required an effort on my part to assure myself of my own identity, and that I was not misled by a dream. No, it was myself sure enough! Then I remembered that I was going to see them again. My darlings were waiting for me. No doubt they had already exchanged confidences. What kind of reception should I have? My duties as Sultan were so new to me that I trembled lest I should commit some mistake which would lower me in their eyes; I was walking blindfold in this paradise of Mahomet, of whose laws I was ignorant. Ought I to maintain the dignified bearing of a vizir, or abandon myself to the tender attitudes of a lover? In my perplexities I was almost tempted to send for Mohammed-Azis, to request of him a few lessons in deportment as practised by the Perfect Pasha of the Bosphorus; but perhaps he would disturb my happiness? As to introducing a hierarchy into my harem, I would not hear of such a thing; for to tell the truth, the choice of a favourite would be an impossibility for me. I loved them all four with an equal devotion, and could not even bear the thought of their being reduced to three without feeling the misery of an unsatisfied love.

At last the hour having arrived without my mind being decided, I wisely determined to act as circumstances might dictate, and started off in the direction of my harem. I think I have already told you that a small door of which I alone possess the key, communicates between my park and El-Nouzha. From this door a sort of labyrinth leads to the Kasre by a single narrow alley, which one might take for a disused path. When I reached the last turn in this alley which terminates in the open gardens, I perceived under the verandah Mohammed-Azis, who seemed to be watching me—he ran towards me with an eager and delighted appearance, and *salem aleks* without end.

By his first words I gathered that he knew all.

When I asked after them, he told me that I was expected; then all at once I heard merry voices, followed by the noise of hurrying footsteps mingled with rustlings of silk dresses. Soon I saw coming out under the verandah, struggling together to be the first to reach me, Hadidje, Nazli, Kondje-Gul and Zouhra; they threw themselves into my arms all four at once, laughing like children, hugging me, and holding up their rosy lips, each vying with the other for my first kiss. What laughter, what merry, bird-like warbling of voices! And all this with the natural abandonment of youth and simplicity—I was about to say innocence—so much so that I was quite taken aback. But all of a sudden, at a word from Mohammed, who was looking at us affectionately, and more and more delighted every minute, they stopped quite confused. He had, no doubt, reprimanded them for some breach of decorum, for they, slipping gently aside, held their hands up to their foreheads. You may guess I soon cut short these respectful formalities, by drawing them back into my arms.... Whereupon renewed laughter and merriment ensued, accompanied with little glances of triumph at poor Mohammed, who assumed a scandalised expression, lifting up his hands as if to make Heaven a witness that he was not responsible for this neglect of all Oriental etiquette! After this scene, you will easily understand that I did not trouble my head any more about the difficulties which I had anticipated in my family duties. I had apprehended a very delicate situation, aggravated by growing jealousies; by the susceptibilities of rivals, offended airs, perhaps even the reproaches and tears of betrayed love.

Five minutes later we were running about the gardens. Having only arrived two days before, they had not yet been outside the harem. The sight of their domain pleased them immensely, and their young voices prattled away with a musical volubility fit to gladden the hearts of the very birds. At each step they made some new discovery, some bed of flowers, or some shady path at the bottom of which the sound of a waterfall could be heard, carried off by sparkling brooks running on beds of moss over the whole length of the park until they lost themselves in the lake; over these brooks were placed at intervals little foot-bridges painted in bright colours. All these things gave rise to questions. Naturally Kondje-Gul was always the interpreter; they all listened, opening their eyes wide; then they started off again, plucking

flowers from the bushes, which they placed in their hair, in their bosoms, and round their necks. In order to attract my admiration for these adornments, each of them kept running up to me as if she wanted a kiss.

If you want to know the thoughts and feelings of a mortal under these circumstances, I must confess that it is quite beyond my power to explain them to you. I was bewildered, captivated, and surprised by such novel sensations that without reflection or conscious analysis, I simply abandoned myself to them. If you wish to understand them, my dear fellow, you must first acquire some aesthetic notions which, artist though you are, you do not yet possess; you must familiarise yourself with these entirely exotic charms of the daughters of the East, their youthful simplicity and ease combined with a certain voluptuous *nonchalance*, the undulating movements of their hips acquired by the habit of moving about in Oriental slippers, their lissom and feline graces, and the overwhelming fascination of their languishing eyes. You must see them in these strange picturesque costumes, so artistically revealing their graceful forms, in wide silk trousers, tied round at the ankles, and drawn in at the waist by a rich scarf of golden gauze: you must see them in their jackets embroidered with pearls, and open bodices of Broussan silk transparent as gauze; or in the long robe open in front, the train of which they hold up by fastening it to the waist when they want to walk about freely—all these things in soft well-toned colours, blending wonderfully together. It was a dazzling scene of fresh beauty and strange enchantment, such as I cannot attempt to describe.

Once we arrived at the end of a ravine, where we were obliged to cross the brook by stepping-stones set in its bed. Thereupon they cried out with fright. I prevailed upon Zouhra, who seemed to be the bravest, to cross holding my hand. Hadidje followed her; but when it came to Nazli's turn, the timid creature hung to my neck as if terrified by some great danger; so I took her up in my arms and carried her across to the opposite side. Kondje-Gul, like a coquette that she is, followed her example.

"Oh! carry me too," she cried.

As I was holding her over the brook, one of her slippers fell into the water. You may guess how they laughed; there was Kondje-Gul hopping about on one foot while I was fishing out the little sandal, which I had to dry in order to avoid wetting her soft green-silk stocking.

It was one of the most charming spots in the park: a great carpet of turf shaded by a clump of sycamores. We all sat down....

You have, doubtless, seen plenty of pictures on the subject of "Dreams of Happiness." There is a delightful garden, at the bottom of which stands the temple of Love; the figures, handsome young men and handsome young women, are always found reclining. Well, if you exclude from such a picture details somewhat too academic for Ferouzat, you may see me on the grass, enjoying the fresh air with my houris lying down around me, in the charming abandoned attitudes of young nymphs who have never heard of such a thing as stays, but display in bold relief the well-rounded forms of their beautiful and lissom figures.

I had passed my arm round Zouhra's neck; she, with a fond look, rested her head against me, and Hadidje imitated her on the other side. I began to talk to Kondje-Gul, the sole interpreter of my amours. You may guess how curious I was to learn their thoughts. I questioned her about the events of the morning, and what they had been saying to each other. Directly she replied, I learnt that when they first got up there was, as the result of their mutual confidences, a general astonishment. But Mohammed explained everything, by telling them that "such is the custom in the French harems." This explanation was sufficient for them. You may be sure I did not contradict such a flattering assurance.

"Well then, you like my country," I said to her; "and they are all content that they have come here?"

"Oh, yes!" she exclaimed, "especially since we saw you! Mohammed had led us to believe that you were old. We feared we were about to enter upon a dull and formal existence. So you may imagine how delighted we were when you arrived, and he told us our master was you! At first we could not believe it, but as he had let us appear unveiled, we were constrained to admit that he had not deceived us. And then, when I heard you speak to him—I understood all. Immediately I repeated to them your words, and how that you found us handsome."

"And so," I replied, "I may believe you really love me? And do *they* also?"

She looked at me with an astonished air, as if this question conveyed no meaning to her.

"Why, of course; since you are kind, affectionate, and nice to us!"

The others listened attentively without understanding a word; their handsome eyes wandered from Kondje-Gul to me, and from me to Kondje-Gul, with an indescribable expression of curiosity.

"But *you*," she replied after a moment, "is it really true that you mean always to love us all, one as much as another, as you have done to-day?"

"Certainly," I replied with assurance; "this is the custom in our harems, as Mohammed told you. Does not that please you better?"

"Oh, yes!" she exclaimed, "but we always thought that you Franks never loved more than one woman."

"That's what they keep saying in Turkey, to injure us, and out of jealousy, because we do not ordinarily marry more than one wife, to whom it is our duty to be faithful."

"But—what happens then, when a man has four, as you have?" she inquired.

"We are equally faithful to all the four!" I replied, without wincing.

"Oh, what happiness!" she exclaimed, clapping her hands with joy.

And immediately, with the volubility of a bird, she began to talk to the others, translating to them everything which we had just been saying. They were all in transports of merriment.

Louis, I won't proceed any further. I can guess the stupid reflections which will occur to you on the subject of this very simple situation which you, like one left behind, buried deep in the ruts of your absurd prejudices, take the liberty of judging from afar. Yes, confess it without reserve; you, moving in the limited sphere of your own feeble experiences, are about to pronounce my amours eccentric. On the fallacious ground that it is unnatural to love and be loved by four women at a time, you, like any other miserable sceptic, are shocked by the freedom of simple sentiments which you are unable to appreciate. First, then, let me assure you that in their own minds none of them conceived the slightest irregularity in their position. According to the laws and customs of their country, they believed themselves to be my wives by a tie as perfect and as legitimate in their eyes as that of marriage in ours. They are my *cadines*, a position which creates for them duties and rights defined by the Koran itself.

Next, out of consideration for your poor intellect, let me inform you also that under the blessed skies of Turkey the wife has no such presumptuous ambition as that of possessing a husband all to herself. Reared with a view to the harem, the young girl aims no higher in her ambitious fancy than to become the favourite and outshine her rivals; but never, never in the world, does she conceive the outlandish notion of becoming the sole object of the affections of lover, master, or husband. The ideal of girls like Zouhra, Nazli, Hadidje, and Kondje-Gul, is the life which I am now giving them; they abandon themselves to it, as to the realisation of their hopes. Their notions respecting the destiny of woman do not go beyond this happiness, which they now possess, of pleasing their master and being loved in this way by him. It is no use, therefore, for you to string together a lot of conventional abstractions with a view to drawing from them any deductions applicable to the laws of the Kingdom of Love.

The truth is that Hadidje, Nazli, and Zouhra burst into transports of joy when Kondje-Gul repeated to them my promise to be "faithful to all four of them."

My dear fellow, there is a great deal of the child remaining in these creatures, who seem to have been only created to expand their beauty, as flowers are to exhale their perfume. Cloistered in the life of the harem, their ideas do not reach beyond the horizon of the harem. Their hearts and their minds have only been cultivated by recitals of wonderful legends and of superstitious romances of love; they know nothing else.

You may say, if you like, that they are just pretty little animals without souls—but you would be wrong. Again I repeat, most of our so-called refined and civilised ideas about sentiment, virtue, propriety, and modesty, are conventional ideas, differing according to place, climate, and habits; and this you will see clearly by following my story, which I may with good reason call natural history, for when I take the instincts of my little animals by surprise, they display for a moment bold impulses which bear much more resemblance to genuine innocence of mind than do certain affectations of modesty practised by the young ladies of our educated society.

The slipper being nearly dry, Kondje-Gul put it on her little arched foot, with its famous light green silk stocking, and we recommenced our course through the park. I will say nothing about a row we took in a boat on the lake, with great willows on its banks. The swans and the Mandarin ducks followed us in procession.

Mohammed, like a wise man, had foreseen that I should stay at the Kasre. The dinner this time was served in the French style. He did not sit down with us as he had done the day before; I had no longer need of him, and he returned to the obscure position which he was henceforth to occupy during my visits. I sat down to table, therefore, with my houris; and this meal, in which everything was new to them, became a veritable feast. They nibbled and tasted a bit of everything with exclamations of surprise, with careful investigations, and with little gourmandish airs of inexpressible charm. I should tell you that my cook only won their unanimous approbation at dessert, when they commenced to make a sort of second dinner of sweets and cakes, creams and fruit. The champagne pleased them above all things, and would have ended by turning their little heads, but for my careful attention. Whilst they vied with each other in merriment and gay prattle, I was thinking of that oriental meal of the night

before in which I had seated myself by them in the reserved attitude of a stranger. What a dream fulfilled! What fairy's wand had produced this magical effect? I tell you it was a regular transformation scene. At dessert Hadidje bent her head down to me with a mischievous look, and laughed as she spoke some Turkish word.

"Sana yanarim!" I replied, emphasizing the sentence with a kiss on her hand. I had learnt from Kondje-Gul that it means "I love you," or more literally, "I am burning for you."

You may guess how successful this was, and with what shouts of joy it was received. Of course there followed a little make-believe scene of jealousy on the part of the others.

"Kianet! ah, Kianet!" they repeated, laughing, and threatening me with uplifted fingers. This expression signifies "ungrateful."

When evening arrived I took them into the park to calm the warmth of their emotions down a little. It was a splendid moonlight night, and the long black shadows of the trees stretched over the walk. As we passed these dark places the timid creatures pressed close about me.

Ah! well, you don't expect me, I suppose, to tell you how this day was concluded? Affairs of the harem, my dear fellow!— affairs of the harem!

As to my other news, I hardly need tell you that nobody in this neighbourhood has a suspicion of the secrets of El-Nouzha. In my external life I conform to all the social requirements of my position. I visit my uncle's old friends, Feraudet the notary, and the good old vicar, who calls me the Providence of the place. Once a week I dine with the doctor, Morand; who has a son, George Morand, an officer in the Spahis, on leave for the present at Ferouzat; and an orphan niece, a young lady of nineteen, lively and sympathetic. She is engaged to her cousin the captain, who is a regular *Africain*, a fire-eater you may call him, but a good fellow in the full sense of that word—one of those open natures made for devotion, like a Newfoundland dog, or a poodle. He is both formidable and patient. Such is my friend! We were playmates as children, and he would not brook the slightest insult to me in his presence. He wonders very much at my anchorite's life, and in order to divert me from it, endeavours to draw me into the hidden current of rustic gallantries which he indulges in while awaiting the day of Hymen.

CHAPTER III

In the detailed account which I gave you, my dear Louis, of my honeymoon, I described pretty nearly the history of every day which has passed since I last wrote. "Happy nations have no history," said a wise man; happiness requires no description. First then, you must understand that I am now writing after recovery from the natural excitement into which my strange adventures had plunged me. Three months have passed; I am now enjoying my life like a refined vizir, and no longer like a simple troubadour of Provence, transported of a sudden into the Caliph's harem. I have recovered my analytical composure.

As you may well imagine I set to work, after the second day, to learn Turkish, an easy task after my studies in Sanscrit. Add to this that, with the aid of love, my houris have learnt French, with all the marvellous facility and linguistic instinct of the Asiatic races. You will not be astonished to learn, then, that I can now share with them all the pleasures of conversation; a happy result which will permit me henceforth to furnish a more complete description of their different characters.

Having said this, I will give you in the present letter, with a view of enabling you to understand this narrative more perfectly, the most precise details upon the following subjects:

First—The organisation, laws, and internal regulations of my harem;

Second—Full-length portraits of my odalisques, and a description of their characters;

Third—A careful dissertation upon the advantages of polygamy, and its applicability to the moral regeneration of mankind.

I will first confess, without any presumption, that the ingenious system established for the conduct of my harem is all due to my uncle Barbassou, who, as much as any man in the world, was always particularly careful to maintain what the English term "respectability." In the eyes of the whole neighbourhood, nay, even of my own household, Mohammed-Azis is an exile, a person of high political rank, to whom my uncle had given a hospitable retreat.

Barbassou-Pasha always addressed him respectfully as "Your Excellency," nor did any servant in the chateau speak in different terms of him. He had had the misfortune to lose one of his daughters—so the story goes—for he seems to have had originally five. Whether his daughters are young or old, no one knows. In the interior of the Kasre all the services are performed by Greek women, who do not know a word of French; they never go out of doors. The gardeners have to leave the gardens at nine o'clock in the morning. All these arrangements, as you will perceive, are extremely correct. The story about Mohammed is a very plausible one; his solemn and melancholy expression together with his solitary life, are thoroughly in conformity with the fallen grandeur of a minister in disgrace. He is writing, according to report, a memoir in justification of his conduct. He works at it both day and night, and it is well-known that I very often sit up quite late with him, in order to assist him in this task.

As for me, I do not suppose you imagine that, like the Knight Tannhauser on the Venusberg, I am continually wasting my spirit and my strength over what Heine calls "the sweets and dainties of love;" or that the philtres of Circe have transformed me into a hog like the companions of Ulysses.—Go gently, my dear fellow! I am a representative of the learned cohort, please to remember! I keep a careful diary of my observations, from which I intend to draw up a report for the Academy. Like those bold investigators of pathological science who inoculate themselves with a deadly virus in order to study its effects upon themselves, I, a serious analytical student, am devoting myself to a course of experiments in pure sensualism, to the sole profit of Science. Without restrictions, but in full consciousness of the high mission which I have undertaken; without cheating myself with too small a dose of the intoxicating draught, I act like an honest Epicurean. I take of the voluptuous delights of my harem as large a dose as an intelligent and refined student of nature ought to require, but without imprudently overstraining the springs of sensation. Armed with the dexterity of superior wisdom, I, floating on this Oriental stream of Love, know how to remain faithful to my charge, by avoiding the rocks of satiety and the shipwreck of illusions.

Every day then, about three o'clock, after having devoted the morning to my business affairs or to my "Essays on Psychology," I go to El-Nouzha, and stay there usually until the middle of the night. However, I sometimes go there of a morning, for a bath; I am teaching my houris to swim. I must tell you that in this matter, indispensable for the comfort of the sultanas, Barbassou-Pasha designed a marvel. In the middle of an island in the lake (which is taken from the delightful garden of See-ma-Kouang, the famous Chinese poet), picture to yourself a great marble basin surrounded by a circular arcade, a sort of *atrium* open to the sky. Under a colonnade and in its cool shade, a fine Manilla mat covers the flag-stones. The base of the inner walls is enlivened with frescoes, after Pompeian and Herculanean models. Round the white pillars cling myrtles and climbing roses, reaching up to the terrace ornamented with vases and statues, which stand out in relief against a mass of purple drapery. Here are set capacious divans in leather, hammocks, carpets, and cushions to recline upon. Such is the aspect of this enchanting place. On many a hot morning we have break-fasted there, and it is from there that I write to you to-day, dressed in a Persian robe with wide sleeves, while around me sports my harem; affording me, therefore, an excellent excuse for at once proceeding to sketch the portraits of my *almees*.

In all beings the internal character is so closely allied to the external form, that it appears to be only an equation of the latter. Thus certain features of the face announce peculiarities of nature, inclinations, and instincts even to the vulgar; the physiologist, with his more special knowledge, discovers quite a series of concealed revelations in the innermost recesses of that pretty sphinx which constitutes God's masterpiece, and which we call woman. In the same way grace is always the result of the harmony of lines; from the slightest outline, from the position of a dimple, or the tension of a smile, from a glance, or from the most transient gesture, one can always trace the origin of a feeling, and lay bare the mind. Thus, at this moment, I behold Hadidje leave the water, and saunter quietly in the direction of Nazli and Zouhra, who are reclining on cushions and smoking cigarettes. By the air of indifference that she affects I could wager that she contemplates playing them some trick!

And indeed, when close to the smokers, she suddenly shook her hair. The two others jumped up under the spray of sparkling water, and ran after her, beating her with their fans and fly-flaps.

Kondje-Gul, the heedless beauty, who is rocking herself in

her hammock beside me, scarcely raises her lazy head to follow them with a glance, at the sound of their cries and laughter. Since her name is at the end of my pen, I will begin my series of portraits with her.

Kondje-Gul is a Circassian by race. Her name in Turkish signifies a variety of rose which we are not acquainted with in France; she was brought when quite a child to Constantinople by her mother, attached to the service of a cadine of the Sultan. She is now eighteen. Imagine the Caucasian type in the flower of its beauty, tall, with the figure of a young goddess, an expression of natural indolence which appears to indicate a consciousness of her sovereign beauty, and a fine head crowned with thick chestnut hair falling down to her waist. Her features are clean cut, and of a remarkably pure type. Large brown eyes with heavy eyelids, imparting a languishing expression; lips somewhat sensual, which from her habit of carrying her head erect, she seems always to be holding out for a kiss; a mixture of Greek beauty with a strange sort of grace peculiar to this Tcherkessian race, which still remains a trifle savage. All these characteristics make up an *ensemble* both exotic and marvellous, which I could no more describe to you than I could explain the scent of the lily. Of a loving and tender nature, she exhibits the disposition of a child in whom ardent impulses are united with a profound gentleness of sentiment. She is the jealous one of my household—but, hush! the others know nothing of this.... Certainly she is the most remarkable and the most perfect of my little animals.

Hadidje is a Jewess of Samos, a Jewess of a type singularly rare among the descendants of Israel. She is a blonde of a mingled tint, soft and golden, of which the Veronese blonde will give you no idea. Her beauty is undoubtedly one of those effects of selection and crossing admitted as the foundation of Darwin's system.... England has left her trace there! Picture to yourself one of those "Keepsake" girls escaped from Byron's

"Bride of Abydos" or his "Giaour;" take some such charming creature, fair and fresh-complexioned, white and pink, and plunge her in the atmosphere of the harem, which will orientalise her charms and give her that—whatever it is—which characterises the undulating fascinations of the sultanas.

My dear friend, an incredible event has happened—an event astounding, unheard of, supernatural! Don't try to guess; you will never succeed, *never!* It surpasses the most prodigious and miraculous occurrence ever imagined by human brain.

Yesterday I had broken off my letter, distracted by Hadidje, at the very moment when I was tracing her portrait for you. The day passed away before I again found leisure to finish it. This morning I was breakfasting at the chateau all alone in my study, where I generally have my meals, in order not to interrupt my work. While I was ruminating over the last number of a scientific magazine, my ear was struck by the noise of a carriage rolling over the gravel walk. As I very seldom receive visits, and my friend George, the spahi, always comes on foot, I thought it must be my notary coming to stir me up about some business matters; he had been reproaching me the last fortnight for neglecting them. The carriage stopped in front of the doorsteps. I heard the servants running across the antichamber. Suddenly I heard a cry, followed by confused voices, which sounded as though trembling with fright, and finally fresh sounds of steps, rushing headlong, as in a sudden rout. Wondering what this might mean, I listened, when all of a sudden a stentorian voice shouted out these words:—

"But what's the matter with those blockheads? How much longer are they going to leave me here with my bag?"

Louis, imagine my amazement and stupefaction! I thought I recognised the voice of my dead uncle, which in the brazen notes of a trumpet grew louder and louder, adding in a pompous, commanding tone—

"Francois! if I catch you, you rascal, you'll soon know what for!"

I jump up, run to the window, and see quite distinctly my uncle, Barbassou Pasha himself.

"Hullo! you here, my boy?" says he.

As for me, I leap over the balcony, and fall into his arms; he lifts me up from the ground, as if I were a child, and we embrace each other. You may guess my emotion, my surprise, my transports of joy! The servants watched us from a distance, frightened and not yet daring to approach near.

"Ah, well!" repeated my uncle; "what on earth's the matter with them? Have I grown any horns?"

"I will explain everything," I said; "come in, while they take up your luggage."

"All right!" he replied; "and get some breakfast for me, quick! I'm as hungry as a wolf."

All this was said with the dignity of a man who never allows himself to be surprised at anything, and in that meridional accent, the ring of which is sufficient to betray the origin of the man. My uncle speaks seven languages; at Paris, as you know, he pronounces with the pure accent of a Parisian, but directly he sets foot in Provence, that's all over; he resumes his brogue, or as they call it down here, the *assent*.

He came in, stepping briskly, and holding his head erect; I followed him. Once in my study, and seeing the table laid, he sat down as naturally as if he had just returned from a walk in the park, poured out two large glasses of wine, which he swallowed one after the other with a gulp of deep satisfaction; and then made a cut at a pie, which he attacked in a serious manner, rendering it quite impossible to mistake him for a spectre. I let him alone, still contemplating him with amazement. When I considered him ready to answer my questions, I said—

"Well, uncle, where have you come from?"

"Te! I come from Japan, you know very well," he answered, just as if he were referring to the chief town of the department; "only I have dawdled a bit on the way, which prevented me from writing to you."

"And during the last five months what has happened to you?"

"Pooh! I made an excursion into Abyssinia, in order to see the Negus, who owed me two hundred thousand francs. He has not paid me, the scamp! But how odd you do look! And that great *arleri*, Francois! how he stares at me with his full round eyes, as if I were going to swallow him up. Is there anything so very fierce about me? Hullo, you have altered my livery!" he went on; "they all look like ecclesiastics; have you taken orders, then?"

"Why, uncle, these five months past we have been in mourning for you."

"In mourning for *me*? You must be joking!"

"These five months past we have believed you to be dead, and have received all the documents proving your death!"

"Perhaps these documents informed you that I was buried, then?" he added, without changing countenance.

"Why, yes, certainly!" I said. "We have also the certificate of your interment!"

At this my uncle Barbassou could restrain himself no longer, and was seized with one of those fits of silent laughter which are peculiar to him.

"In this case—you would be my heir?" he said, in the middle of his transport of gaiety, which hardly permitted him to speak.

"I am already, my dear uncle," I replied, "and am in possession of all your property!"

This reply put the finishing touch to his hilarity, and he started off again into such a fit of laughter that I was caught by it, and so was Francois.

But suddenly my uncle stopped, as if some reflection had crossed his mind, and seizing my hand with a sudden impulse he said:

"Ah! but now I think of it, my poor boy, you must have experienced a severe blow of grief!"

This was said with such frank simplicity, and proceeded so evidently from a heart guiltless of any dissimulation, that I swear to you I was stirred to the bottom of my soul; my eyes filled with tears, and I threw myself on to his neck to thank him.

"Well, well!" he said, patting me on the shoulder to calm me, while he held me in his arm; "never mind, old fellow, now that I'm back again!"

When breakfast was finished and the table cleared, we remained together alone.

"Come, uncle, as soon as you have explained to me what has happened to lead to this story of your death, the next thing will be to take early steps for your resuscitation."

"Take steps!" he exclaimed, "and for why?"

"Why, to re-establish your civil status and your rights of citizenship as a live person."

"Oh, they'll find out soon enough, when they see me, that I don't belong to the other world!" said he, quite calmly.

"Now that you are regarded as defunct, you will not be able to do anything, to sign, to contract—"

"So, so! Never mind all that. Barbassou-Gratien-Claude-Anatole doesn't trouble himself about such trifles."

"But your estates?" I said; "your property which I have inherited?"

"Have you paid the registration fees?" he asked me, in a serious tone.

"Certainly I have, uncle."

"Well! Do you want to put me to double expense for the benefit of the government, which will make you pay it all over again at my real death?"

"What is it you mean to do, then?" said I.

"You shall keep them! Now's your turn," he added, in a chaffing tone; "all these forty years I have had the worry of them; it's your turn now, young man! You shall manage them, and make them your business; it will be for you now to pay my expenses and all that!"

"I hope you don't dream of such a thing, my dear uncle!" I exclaimed. "Why even, supposing that I continue to manage your property—"

"Excuse me," he said, "*your* property! It is yours, the fees having been duly paid."

"Well, *our* property, if you like," I replied, with a laugh; "all the same, I repeat you cannot remain smitten with civil death."

"Bah! Bah! Political notions! But first explain to me how I come to be dead—that puzzles me."

I then related to him what I have told you of this strange story; the notary's letter informing me of the cruel news brought by my uncle's lieutenant Rabassu, confirmed by the most authentic documents, and accompanied by a portfolio containing all his papers and letters, securities in his name, and agreements signed by him; proving, in short, an identity which it was impossible to dispute.

"My papers!" he exclaimed. "They were not lost then?"

"I have them all," I replied.

"I begin to understand! It's all the fault of that stupid Lefeburc."

"Who is this Lefebure?" I asked.

"I am going to tell you," replied my uncle; "the whole thing explains itself and becomes clear.—But I wonder, did not Rabassu with the news of my death bring some camels?"

"Not a single camel, uncle."

"That's odd! However, sit down, and I will tell you all about it."

I sat down, and my uncle gave me the following narrative. I write it out for you faithfully, my dear Louis; but what I cannot render for you, is the inimitable tone of tranquillity in which he related it, just as if he were describing a fete at a neighbouring village.

"In returning from Japan," he said, "I must tell you that I put in at Java. Of course I landed there. On the pier-head, I recognised Lefebure, a sea-captain and an old friend of mine; he had given up navigation in order to marry a mulattress there, who keeps a tobacco-shop. I said to him 'Hullo, how are you?' He embraces me and answers that he is very dull. 'Dull?' I reply, 'well, come along with me to Toulon for a few days; my ship is in the harbour here, I will give you a berth in her, and send you home next month by "The Belle-Virginie!" My proposal delights him, but his answer is that it is impossible. 'Impossible? Why?' 'Because I have a wife who would not hear of it!' 'We must see about that,' I say to him. Well, we go to their shop; the wife makes a scene, cries and screams, calling him all sorts of names, and they fight over it. At last, while they are taking a moment's rest, I add that I shall weigh anchor at six o'clock in the evening. 'I will wait for you until five minutes past six,' I say; and then I go off to my business. At six o'clock I weighed anchor, and began to tack about a bit. At 6:10 I was off, when I saw a barque approaching. I gave the order 'Stop her.' It was Lefebure, who was making signs to us to stop. He comes up, gets on board, and off we go."

Fifteen days after that we put in at Ceylon for a few hours. On the twenty-sixth day, as we arrived in sight of Aden, we observed a good deal of movement in the harbour. There was an English man-of-war displaying an admiral's flag, which they were saluting. On shore I learnt that she was carrying a Commission sent out to make some diplomatic representations to the Negus of Abyssinia. And who should I meet but Captain Picklock, one of my old friends whose acquaintance I made at Calcutta, where he was in one of the native regiments. He informed me that he was in command of the escort accompanying the envoys. I said to Lefebure 'By the by, the Negus owes me some money—shall we go and make a trip there?' Lefebure replied, 'By all means let us!' I bought four horses and half-a-dozen camels, which I sent on board with my provisions; and we started with the envoys. We had some amusement on the way. I knew the country very well myself, but when we were half-way, at Adoua, where we halted for half a day, Lefebure picks up with an Arab woman. He wants to stay with her until the next day, and says to me, 'Go on with the captain; I will join you again to-morrow with the convoy of baggage.' I started off accordingly. Next day, no Lefebure. That annoyed me rather, because he had kept the camels. However, I continued my journey, thinking that I should find him again on my return. Finally I arrived at the Negus's capital, just in time to hear that they were on the point of dethroning him. My intention was to apply to the English commissioners to help me in getting my little business settled. I found, however, that my portfolio and papers were with Lefebure, who had the baggage; fortunately, I still had the gold which I carry in my belt. Then I naturally availed myself of this opportunity to go off and wander about the interior, as far as Nubia, where I had some acquaintances. I commissioned Captain Picklock to tell Lefebure to come on and join me at Sennaar, with the camels. So off I go, and arrive in ten days' time at Sennaar, where I find the King of Nubia, who was not very happy about the political situation; he treats me very hospitably, and I buy ivory and ostrich feathers of him.

Three weeks go by, but no Lefebure! So I naturally avail myself of the delay, for pushing on a bit into Darfour; when, lo and behold! just like my luck, on the ninth day, as I am entering the outskirts of El-Obeid in Kordofan, I am met by a predatory tribe of Changallas! They surround me; I try to defend myself, and a great burly rascal jumps at my throat, and trips me up. I feel that I am being strangled by him; I deal him a blow in the stomach with my fist, and he tumbles backwards; only, as his hand still grips my throat, he drags me down with him; the others attack me at the same time, and I am captured! My blow appears to have been the death of the negro—which did not mend matters for me. They thrust me, bound fast like a bundle of wood, into a sort of shed, after robbing me of all my gold.

I was carefully guarded. At the end of eight days I said to myself, 'Barbassou, your ship lies in the harbour of Aden; you have business to attend to, and you won't get out of your present scrape without conciliatory negotiations. You must resign yourself to a sacrifice!' I send for the chief, and offer him as my ransom a cask containing fifty bottles of rum, ten muzzle-loading guns, and two complete uniforms of an English general. This offer tempts him; but as I ask him first of all to have me safe conducted to the King of Nubia, he answers that if once I got there I should send him about his business. They confined me in a pit, where I had only rice and bananas to eat, to which I am not at all partial. As to the women, they are monkeys. However, after four months of negotiations we came to an agreement that I should be conveyed back to Sennaar, where I engaged upon my word of honour to give guarantees.

I set off, still bound fast, with ten men to guard me. After a fortnight we arrive in the town. I enquire for Lefebure.—No Lefebure. I then go to the king's palace—but he had just started off on a week's hunting expedition. However, I find the sheik who was in command of the town, and relate my difficulty to him. He informs me that the treasury is closed. I tell my guards that they can return, and that I will have my ransom sent from Aden, but that does not content them; one of them seizes hold of me by the arm, but I gave him a good hiding. Finally the sheik furnishes me with an escort, and I return to Gondar. The English had gone back, and I started on my voyage across to Aden. When I reached Adoua, where I had left my friend Lefebure, I asked for him. Again no Lefebure! However, I had the luck to find his Arabian sweetheart, whom I questioned about him. Her reply is, that the very day I left him, the stupid fellow went and caught a sunstroke, of which he died the same day. I inquire after my baggage and my camels.—No baggage, no camels! They had all been forwarded to the Governor of Aden.

"When I arrived at Aden, the Governor told me that everything which had been received had been sent on board my ship, including the papers found on my friend, and that a certificate of death had been duly drawn up, which my lieutenant was instructed to convey to the family. I asked no more questions, and wrote at once a little note of condolence to Lefebure's wife. I sent the agreed ransom to my Changallas, and at the same time a letter of complaint to the King of Nubia. Altogether, it was four months since my ship had left Aden. The following day I took the mail boat to Suez—arrived last night at Marseilles—and here I am!"

"Yes, indeed," I said to my uncle, when he had concluded; "that explains it all. They drew up the certificate of decease according to the papers found on your friend Lefebure, and as they were yours—"

"Why, they mistook him for me; and that ass Rabassu went off with the ship to bring the notary the news of my death."

"That's clear," I added.

"But what puzzles me most," replied he, "is to know what has become of my camels!"

As you may well imagine, my dear Louis, this unexpected

resurrection of my uncle plunged me into a state of excitement, which took entire possession of me. I could not see enough of him, or hear enough of him; and all that day I so completely forgot everything which did not concern him, that I did not even think of moving outside the chateau. I followed him from room to room, and kept looking at him, for I felt the need of convincing myself that he was really alive. As to him, quickly recovering from the very transitory astonishment into which the news of his supposed death had thrown him, he had resumed that splendid composure, which you remember in him. He superintended all his little arrangements, and unpacked all his boxes, full of all sorts of articles from Nubia, whistling all the while fragments of *bamboulas* which were still ringing in his ears.

After dinner in the evening, he said to me, stretching out his long legs over the divan, with the air of a man who loves his ease:

"By Jove, it's very snug here! If you like, we will stay down here several weeks."

"As many weeks as you like, uncle," I answered—"months even!"

"Well done!—But," he continued, "won't you be rather dull? —for, unless you have some little distraction—"

"Ah!" I exclaimed, remembering all at once my harem; "I forgot to tell you about this little affair!"

"What affair?" he said. "Have you found your distraction already, then?"

"I should just think I have, uncle!"

"Is she pretty?"

"Why, I have four!"

At this information my uncle did not raise his eyebrows any more than if I had told him that I was occupying my leisure by practising the rustic flute; he only stretched out his arm, took my hand and shook it smartly in the English fashion, saying,

"My compliments, my dear fellow!—I beg your pardon for my indiscretion."

"But, my dear uncle, I have quite a long story to tell you!" I added, not without a certain embarrassment "—and it is your death again that has been the cause of it!"

"How was that? Tell me all about it."

"You know, your Turkish pavilion—Kasre-el-Nouzha?"

"I know, well?"

"Well, four months ago, Mohammed-Azis arrived there."

"Hullo!" he said, "Mohammed?"

"Yes, and you had entrusted him with a—a commission," I continued.

"True," he exclaimed, "I had forgotten that!"

"Well, then, uncle—"

"He had accomplished his commission, I suppose," continued he.

"Yes," I replied. "And as you were dead, and Mohammed's commission formed part of my inheritance from you, I thought that it was my duty—"

"*Bigre!*" said my uncle, "you know how to act the heir very well, you do!"

"Why indeed—" I continued, "remember that I could not suppose—"

"In short you've done it," said he, "and it's all over, so don't let us say anything more about it! And once more, forgive me.—Now that I know all about it, nothing more need be said. Turks never discuss harem matters. Only," he added, "in order to avoid the necessity of returning to the subject, let me now recommend you to keep Mohammed; you understand? He knows the run of the ropes. And in order to make everything safe, as it would not do for me to be seen about there any more, tell him to come and see me."

"Do you wish me to send for him at once?"

"No, no, to-morrow will do. We have plenty of time.— Come, give me a little music, will you? Play me something from Verdi—"

And he began to hum in his bass voice, slightly out of tune, snatches from the air:

"Parigi o cara, noi lasceremo."

We passed a charming evening together, what with conversation, music, and cards. He won three francs of me at piquet, with a ridiculous display of triumph. About twelve o'clock I took him to his bedroom. When he was ready to get into bed, he exclaimed:

"*Te!* I have some securities here which I had forgotten!" And taking a penknife, he proceeded to cut the stitches of his coat lining, from which he drew out some papers.

"See!" he said, as he held them out to me, "here are seven hundred thousand francs' worth of bills on London and Paris. You shall get them cashed."

"Very well, uncle," I replied. "And what do you want me to do with the money?"

"Oh, upon my word, that's your affair, my *pichoun*! You may be sure, now that you have come into your inheritance, I am not going to be troubled with such matters!"

"Well, at least advise me about them."

"But, my good fellow, that means that I am still to have all the bother about them—. After all," he continued, "keep the money if you like—it will do for my pocket money."

Thereupon he went to bed, I wished him good night, and was about to leave the room, when he called me back.

"Come here, Andre! Write, if you please, to the notary and ask him to come here to-morrow."

"Ah!" I replied, "you're coming round to that at last!"

"I am coming round to nothing whatever!" he exclaimed, in a most decided tone. "Only I want to know what has become of my camels! As you may guess, I intended to present them to the Zoological Society. I must have them found! Good night!"

I should certainly annoy you, my dear Louis, if I were to endeavour to impress upon you the full significance of the amazing events through which I have passed during these four months. I don't know of a single mortal who has experienced more original adventures. The dreadful letter from the notary, my installation at Ferouzat, my uncle's will, the harem tumbling down upon me from Turkey, the entering into complete possession of my fortune, and the whole crowned by the return of the deceased. Certainly you will agree with me that these are incidents which one does not meet with in everyday life. Nevertheless, if you want to know my ideas about them, I confess that they seem to me at the present moment to be nothing but the Necessary and the Contingent of philosophers, in their simplest application. I would go so far as to assert that, to a nephew of my uncle, things could not fall so to happen, for it would show a want of training in the most elementary principles of logic, to exhibit surprise at such little adventures, when once Barbassou-Pasha has been introduced on the scene as Prime Cause. The substratum of my uncle so powerfully influences my destiny, that to my mind it would seem quite paradoxical to expect the same things ever to happen to me as to any other man. Cease being astonished, therefore, at any strange peculiarities in my life, even if they be eccentric enough to shock a rigidly constituted mind. Like those erratic planets which deviate occasionally from their course, I move around the remarkable star called Barbassou-Pasha, and he draws me into his own eccentric orbit. In spite of a semblance of romantic complications among the really simple facts which I have related to you, I defy you to discover in them the slightest grain of inconsistency. They can be perfectly well accounted for by the most natural causes and the most ordinary calculations of common sense. Cease your astonishment, therefore, unless you wish to fall into the lowest rank in my estimation.

Having postulated the fact that I am the nephew of my uncle, I will now return to the summarising of my situation. Well, my late uncle had come to life again, but he wanted to keep all the advantages of his status as a dead man, by obliging me to remain in possession of his property. I had just said "good night" to him, while he was dreaming about his camels. Nothing could be less complicated than that. If all that is not in strict conformity with the character of Barbassou (Claude Anatole), I know nothing about him. Nevertheless, it was only natural that the day celebrated by his return should give birth to some other incidents of importance.

I had just left my uncle, and was walking towards the library to write at once to the notary, when Francis informed me that a woman from the Kasre had been waiting an hour to see me. One of the Greek servants came sometimes to the chateau, either with messages or to await my orders. I concluded at once that, not having seen me either during the day or in the evening, my little animals had grown anxious and were sending to inquire after me. I went to my room, where Francis said the woman was. As I entered I saw her standing up, motionless, near the window, wrapped in her great black feridjie; but I had hardly shut the door behind me when, all at once, I heard a cry and sobs. The feridjie fell down, and I recognised Kondje-Gul, who threw herself on to my neck and seized me in her arms with signs of the deepest despair.

"Good gracious!" I said, "is that you? *You* come here?"

Breathless and suffocated with tears, she could not answer me. I guessed, rather than heard, these words:

"I have run away! I have come to die with you!"

"But you are mad, dear, quite mad!" I exclaimed. "Why should you die? What has happened then?"

"Oh, we know all!" she continued. "Barbassou-Pasha has returned. He is a terrible man. He is going to kill you; us also; Mohammed also!"

And raving with fear she clung to me with all her strength,

just as if she were already threatened with death.

"But, my dear child," I said, "this is all madness—who in the world has told you such nonsense?"

"Mohammed. He heard of the Pasha's return—he has hidden himself."

"But my uncle is a very kind man—he adores me, and does not even intend to see you. Nothing will be changed for us by his return."

Seeing me so calm, she was gradually reassured. Still she was too much possessed by her Turkish notions to believe all at once in such a departure from correct oriental usages.

"Well then," she said as she dried her tears, "he will only kill Mohammed?"

"Not even Mohammed!" I exclaimed, with a smile. "Mohammed is a poor coward, and I will give him a bit of my mind to-morrow, so that he shan't worry you with any more nonsense of this kind."

"You don't mean it?" she replied. "Then he will only get a beating?"

I was about to protest, when I perceived by her first words that she suspected I wanted to play upon her credulity. There was thus a danger of reviving her worst fears, for she would not believe any more of my assurances. I contented myself therefore with promising to intercede with Barbassou-Pasha. Once convinced that Mohammed's punishment would extend no further than his hind-quarters, she troubled herself no more about it, but with the characteristic volatility of these little wild creatures, began to chatter and examine all the things in my room, touching and feeling everything with an

insatiable curiosity.

"Come now, you must go home," I said to her, not wishing this little excursion of hers to be discovered.

"Oh, no! Oh, no!" she cried, with childlike delight. "It's your home—do let me look at it!"

"Oh, but you must go and comfort Zouhra, Nazli, and Hadidje!"

"They are asleep," she said. "I want to stay a little time here alone with you! Besides," she added, with a little frightened look still lingering on her face, "suppose Barbassou-Pasha has been deceiving you, suppose he is coming to kill you to-night?"

"But once more I tell you, dear, you are *mad!*"

"Well then, why send me back so soon?"

"Because it is not proper for you to leave the harem," I answered. "Come along, off you go!"

"Oh, just a little longer!—I beg you, dear!" she said, with a kiss.

How could I resist her, my dear Louis? Tell me?

I sat down, watching her moving about and rummaging everywhere. I must tell you that under her feridjie (which she had let down on my entrance into the room), she was dressed in a sort of loose gown of pale blue cashmere, embroidered with lively designs in silk and gold. Her snow-white arms emerged from wide, hanging sleeves. This costume produced a charming picturesque effect in the midst of my room, which, although comfortable, was very prosaic in its style—although to her it seemed wonderful. She touched everything, for she could not be satisfied with seeing only, and her questions never ceased.... At last, after half-an-hour, considering her curiosity to be satisfied, as she was beginning to ransack the books lying on my table, I said once more,

"Come, Kondje-Gul, you must go."

With these words, I picked up her feridjie, and took her back to the harem. A pale light was shining through the windows of the drawing-room. Hadidje, Nazli, and Zouhra were still there. To describe the terror which came over their faces directly I appeared, would be impossible. Hearing steps in the night, they made sure their last moments had arrived. At the sound of the door opening, they cried out loud—the three poor miserable things took refuge in a corner.

When they saw me enter with Kondje-Gul, they were thrown into a great consternation. With a few words I reassured them at once.

As to Mohammed, it was impossible to find him. I will confess, moreover, that I felt very little interest in searching for him—I was far from ill-pleased with the thought that he was paying for the trouble which his stupidity had caused my poor darlings, by a night of fear and trembling.

My lamb having returned to the fold, I eventually retraced my steps to the chateau.

Is it necessary to tell you that the surprising events of the day had caused me emotions which I was scarcely able to understand?

My uncle's resurrection—

Lefebure—

The Changallas—

The camels—

They all kept my brain at work the whole night long.

CHAPTER IV

I apologise, my dear Louis, for having left you a month without a letter from me, as you reproach me somewhat severely. You are not afraid, I should hope, that my friendship for you has cooled. The real cause of my silence is that I have had nothing to tell you. The even tenor of my existence permits only of daily repetitions of the same very simple events. My affections being divided between my harem and my uncle Barbassou, I revel in the tranquillity of the fields and woods, which afford to my mind that quiet freedom which is always more or less disturbed by the excited atmosphere of city life.

Do not imagine, however, that we have been living like monastics, disdaining all worldly distractions: the governor is not the man to lead the existence of a Carthusian monk. He is as much on horseback as on foot. In the daytime we make hunting excursions; he visits his "god-children" and my estates: you may rely upon it, I have got an active steward in *him*! In the evening we receive our friends at the chateau— the vicar, the Morands, father and son, and, twice a week, the notary. We play whist at penny points, and very lively games of piquet—only the latter not so often, as my uncle cheats at it. About eleven o'clock the carriages are got ready to take these people home. I then accompany my uncle to his room, and we talk over business matters, and about my *fiancee*; for, of course, my marriage with his "god-daughter" is an understood thing, and we have not even a notion of discussing the question. Finally, when he gets sleepy, he goes to bed, and I go off to El-Nouzha.

Besides these occupations we have another very serious one, namely, rummaging among the mass of curios which he heaped up together in the lumber-room of the chateau.

"Ah, Andre!" my uncle said to me one day, with the reproachful accent of a faithful steward, "you have a lot of fine things up there which you are very foolish to leave in that lumber-hole. If I were you, I would have them all out!"

"Let us get them all out then at once, uncle," I answered.

Thereupon we set to work sorting them out, and you have no idea of the things we found—valuable paintings, works of art, rare old furniture, and arms of all countries. You will see what a museum they constitute, if you make an excursion down here, as you have promised. Really, for an artist of your genius, this alone would be worth the journey.

We also pay visits at the two neighbouring chateaux of the Montanbecs and the Camboulions; but confine ourselves strictly to the customary conventionalities between neighbours, the female element which we encounter at these places belonging, as my uncle puts it, to the very lowest zoological order of beings.

Once a week we dine at Doctor Morand's. He is a man of great ability, who has only missed making his mark through want of a wider field. He is the one mortal capable of exercising an influence over Captain Barbassou, if the character of the latter did not place him out of reach of all external control. In this home family life reigns in its happiest and most charming simplicity, represented by a goodly quiver-full of children. I have already told you about young Morand, the spahi, and his cousin Genevieve.

Genevieve, with her nineteen summers, is the eldest, by several years, of a prolific brood, the offspring of her mother's second marriage. The doctor, who is a rich man for his district, took them all to live with him after his sister's death. A more delightful and refreshing place cannot be found than this heaven-blest home, the very atmosphere of which breathes the odour of peaceful happiness and honest purity. You should see Genevieve, *la grande*, surrounded by her four *petits*, her brothers and sisters, with their chubby faces, all neat and clean, obedient and cheeky at the same time, and kept in order by her with a youthful discipline, flavoured now and then with a spice of playfulness. Is she really pretty? I confess I cannot decide. The question of beauty in her case is so completely put out of mind by a certain charm of manner, that one forgets to analyse it. She has certainly fine eyes, for they hold you spell-bound by the soul shining through them. George Morand, her *fiance*, adores her, and, headstrong *Africain* though he is, even he feels an influence within her which subjugates his fiery spirit. They could not be a better match for each other, and will live happily together. She will chasten the exuberant ardour of the Provencal warrior.

My uncle professes to detest "the brats;" it is needless, perhaps, to add that, directly he arrives, the whole of them rush to him, climb on his knees, and stay there for the rest of his visit. He is their horse; he makes boats for them, and all the rest of it. The other day you might have seen him grumbling as he sewed a button on Toto's drawers (which he had torn off by turning him head over heels), fearing lest Genevieve should scold him.

I am very cordially welcomed by the whole house, and you may imagine what interminable discussions the doctor and I carry on. Having been formerly a professor in the School of

Medicine at Montpellier, he was led by his researches in physiology to a very pronounced materialism. Now that he has read my spiritualistic articles, he tries hard to break down my arguments. On the third side, my uncle, as a Mahometan, wants to convert him to deism; you may judge from this how much harmony there is between us; you might take us for an Academy!

At El-Nouzha the same life goes on still; but I must take this opportunity of correcting a dangerous mistake you appear to have fallen into, to judge from the tone of your letters. In everything that concerns my harem, you really speak as if you had in mind the fantastic and tantalising experiences of a second blessed Saint Anthony, exposed to the continual provocations of the most voluptuous beauties of the Court of Satan. Indeed, one might say (between you and me and the post), that your Holiness was less scared than inquisitive regarding these terrible scorchings. You old sinner! The real truth is that everything becomes a habit after a while, and that, now the first effervescence of passion is over, this life grows much more simple than you imagine. You must not believe that we lead a riotous existence of continual lusts and orgies. Such notions, my dear fellow, are only the fruit of ignorance and of prejudice.

Let me tell you that my harem is to me at the present time a most tranquil home, and that, but for the fact that I have four wives, everything about it has permanently assumed the every-day aspect of a simple household. Our evenings are spent in conversation round the drawing-room table with music and dancing, conducted in a thoroughly amiable and cheerful spirit, and all set off by the accomplishments of my sultanas. I combine in my conjugal relations the dignified oriental bearing of a vizir with the tender sentimentalities of a Galaor, and in this I have really attained to an exquisite perfection.

In fact, it would be the Country of Love in the Paradise of Mahomet, but for a few clouds which, since my uncle's return, have obscured the bright rays of my honeymoon. I have had some trouble with Hadidje and Nazli, who seem determined to make a trip over to the chateau as Kondje-Gul had done; for, as might have been foreseen, as soon as her alarms had subsided, this silly creature, with the view no doubt of exciting their jealousy, and posing as the favourite, had taken care to relate to them all the wonders of this, to them, forbidden place. Of course I refused at once to permit such an irregularity, contrary as it was to all harem traditions. This refusal was the signal for a scene of tears and jealous passions, which I subdued, but which only gave way to the tender reproaches of slighted affections. Well, I try to jog along as well as I can, as all husbands have to do, but I have a vague presentiment of troubles still in the air.

I have reopened my letter.

I hope you won't be astonished, my dear fellow, but—I have another piece of news relating to Barbassou-Pasha.

The day before yesterday, while my uncle and I were chatting together, as is our custom, before he went to bed, I observed that he yawned in an unusual manner. I had remarked this symptom before, and I drew my own conclusion from it, which was that overtaken once more by his adventurous instincts, he was beginning to find life tedious in the department of Le Gard,—he was longing for something or other, that was certain! And I began ransacking my mind to find some new food upon which he might exercise his all-devouring energy, when he said to me, just before I left him—

"By the bye, Andre, I have written to your aunt that I am returned. She will probably arrive some time between now and the end of the week."

"Ah!" I replied; "well, uncle, that's capital! I shall be delighted to have our family life back again."

"Yes, the house will seem really furnished then," he continued. "Well, good night, my boy!"

"Good night, uncle."

Then I left him.

Now, although this legitimate conjugal desire of my uncle's was quite rational on his part, you may nevertheless imagine that I went to bed rather puzzled. Which of my aunts should I see arrive? My uncle had acquainted me with this design in such an artless manner that it never occurred to me to venture any question on the subject. I began therefore to form conjectures based upon his present frame of mind, as to which of his wives he had probably selected.

I commenced by setting aside my aunt Cora, of the Isle of Bourbon. It was not very likely that the Pasha wanted to add to his past ontological researches upon the coloured races. Excluding also my aunt Christina de Postero, whose adventure with Jean Bonaffe had brought her into disgrace, there remained only my aunt Lia Ben Levy, my aunt Gretchen Van Cloth, and my aunt Eudoxie de Cornalis, so that the question was now considerably narrowed. Still I must confess that it was not much use my setting all my powers of induction to work, taking as my premises the captain's age, his present tastes, his plans, &c. All I succeeded in doing was to lose myself in a maze of affirmations and contradictions from which I could find no way out. The best thing to be done was to wait. So I waited.

I had not long to wait for that matter. Two days after, while I was in my room, I saw a carriage drive up. Its only occupant was a lady, who seemed to me to be very handsome and very elegantly dressed. On the box, by the coachman's side, sat a lady's maid; behind were two men-servants of superior style in their travelling livery. The carriage stopped. At the sound of the wheels on the gravel, my uncle's window opened.

"Hoi! is that you?" he shouted. "How are you, my dear!"

"How are you, captain!" replied the lady. "You see you have not been forgotten, you ungrateful wretch!"

"Thanks for that. Nor am I any more forgetful on my side."

"That's all right," replied the lady; "but why don't you come down and give me a hand? You're very gallant!"

"Well, my dear, I'm coming as fast as I can!" said my uncle.

I must confess I still remained somewhat puzzled at the sight of this fair traveller, whose appearance did not recall to me any of my aunts. Could Barbassou-Pasha have contracted another marriage since the date of his will? Out of delicacy I kept out of the way, in order not to disturb their affectionate greetings, but as my uncle passed my door on his way out, he said to me,

"Andre, aren't you coming?" I followed him. We arrived just as the lady was stepping briskly up the doorsteps.

"Too late, captain!" she said, "I could not stay there, penned up in that carriage."

This reproach did not prevent them from shaking hands very heartily. Then as I came up, my uncle said in his quick way,

"Kiss your aunt Eudoxia!"

At this injunction I forthwith embraced my aunt, and I must

admit that as I kissed her I could not repress a smile, recollecting this sacramental phrase of my uncle's.

"My goodness! is that Andre?" she exclaimed, "Oh! excuse me, sir," she continued rapidly; "this familiar name slipped from my tongue, at remembrance of the bonny boy of old times."

"Pray take it for granted, madam!" I answered.

"Then don't call me madam!"

"What does that matter, *my aunt*; to obey you I shall be delighted to return to old times."

"Very well then, *my nephew*," she added; "see that my servants are looked after, and then let us come in!"

All this was said in that free-and-easy tone which denotes aristocratic breeding, and with so much of the assurance of a woman accustomed to the best society, that I was for a moment almost taken aback by it. My early impressions of her had only left in my mind confused recollections of an amiable and fascinating young woman (so far as I could judge at that age), and now my aunt suddenly appeared in a character which I had not at all anticipated. Assuredly I should never have recognised her, although time had not at all impaired the beauty of her face.

I will therefore draw her portrait afresh. Picture to yourself a woman of about thirty-five, although her real age is forty-two. Her figure exhibits a decided *embonpoint*, but this detracts not in the least from its gracefulness, for she is a tall woman, and has also quite a patrician style about her. Her erect head, and the profound dignity of her expression—everything about her in fact—might be taken to denote a haughty nature, were it not for that extreme simplicity of manner which appears natural to her. Notwithstanding the firmness of her language, the tone in which it is uttered is as soft as velvet, and her light, musical accent suggests the frank and easy bearing of a Russian lady of high rank.

Such is the description of my aunt.

My uncle had offered her his arm. As soon as we entered the drawing-room, she said, while taking off her hat:

"Ah, now you must at once explain to me this story of your death, which I received from a notary. For six months I have been fancying myself a widow!"

"You can see that there's nothing in it," replied my uncle.

"That's nice!" she exclaimed, laughing and holding her hand out to him a second time. "Another of your eccentricities, I suppose!"

"Not in the least, my dear; Andre here can tell you that I positively passed for a dead man, and that he went into mourning for me. He has even entered into the possession of my property as my heir."

"It's an ill wind that blows nobody any good," she answered; "but how was it that they put you in the grave by mistake? I am curious to know."

"I was in Abyssinia."

"Close by, is it?" asked she, interrupting him.

"Yes," continued my uncle. "A friend who was travelling with me, stayed behind at a place on our way, while I went forward, and he managed to die in such a stupid and ill-timed manner that, as my baggage was with him, it was from my

papers that his certificate of death was made out. It was only on my return here, five months later, that I learnt that I had been taken for dead. You see what a simple story it is."

"Well, of course," said my aunt, "such things are quite a common occurrence! That will teach you the result of not taking me with you on your travels. Was it also on account of this trip in Abyssinia that I have not seen you for two years? Oh stop, my dear nephew!" she added in an engaging tone, "a family scene is an instructive event; it forms—. Go on, captain, answer me."

"Two years?" replied my uncle. "Is it really two years?"

"Consult your log-books, if they have not been buried with your friend."

"Ah! forgive me, dear Eudoxia, I have had during all this time most important business."

"Yes," continued my aunt, "we all know what important business you have; I've heard some fine accounts of you. Do you know what Lord Clifden told me at St. Petersburg three months ago, while complimenting me upon my widow's mourning, which, by the way, suited me extremely well? He told me that during your lifetime you had been a bigamist."

"What a likely story!" exclaimed my uncle, boldly.

"He assured me that he had seen you at Madras with a Spanish woman, you old traitor! She was young and pretty, and passed openly by the name of Senora Barbassou. It was surely not worth while making me elope with you, in order that you might treat me in this fashion!"

"Lord Clifden told you a story, my dear, and a very silly story too. I hope you did not believe a word of it?"

"Upon my word, you are such an eccentric character, you know!" she answered, with a laugh.

"And what have you been doing yourself?" continued my uncle, whose coolness had not deserted him for an instant; "where have you been?"

"Oh, if I were to reckon back to the day you left me, I should lose myself!" replied my aunt. "A year ago, at this season, I was on my estate in the Crimea, where I vegetated for five months; then I spent the winter at St. Petersburg, and the spring at my chateau in Corfu, where I had the advantage of a comfortable place in which to mourn over you. Finally I had been two months at Vienna, when I received from my steward eight days ago the letter in which you did me the honour of informing me both of your resurrection and of your desire to see me. I quickly made my farewell calls, started off, and here I am! Now," she added, holding out a plaid to him, "if you will kindly allow me to change these travelling clothes, you will make my happiness complete."

"I am waiting to take you to your room," replied my uncle.

"Nephew," she said to me with a curtsey, "prepare to minister to my caprices; I have plenty of them when I love.—In return let me say to you, Take it for granted."

They left the room, and I felt quite astonished at the way they greeted each other. You can already understand the effect which my aunt must have produced on me, and I was no less surprised at the new traits which I discovered in my uncle's character. A complete revolution had been effected. He became all at once very natty in his dress. His rough straggling beard was trimmed in the Henri IVth style, and his moustaches were twirled up at the ends. He left off swearing; his language and his manners at once assumed the most correct tone, without constraint or embarrassment, and with a modulation so natural, that it seemed really to indicate a very long familiarity with fashionable practice. He had not made a single slip. His frank gallantry had nothing artificial about it; he was another man, and it was quite evident this was the only man that Eudoxie de Cornalis had ever known him to be.

"Well! what do you think of your aunt?" he asked me as he came in after five minutes' absence.

"She is charming, uncle, and as gracious as possible!"

"Did you expect to find her a monkey, then?" he exclaimed.

"Certainly not!" I replied. "But my aunt might have been beauty itself, and still have lacked the character and the intellectual qualities which I observe in her."

"Oh, you can't at all judge of her yet!" continued he, in a careless tone. "You'll see what I mean later on. She's a real woman!"

My aunt did not come down again until luncheon-time. Her appearance created quite an atmosphere of cheerful society in the dining-room, usually occupied only by my uncle and his nephew. My uncle was no doubt conscious of the same impression, for leaning towards me, he said to me in his inimitably cool manner, and in a low voice,

"Don't you see how everything brightens up already?"

My aunt sat down, and as she took off her gloves, cast her eyes over the table, the sideboards, the servants in waiting, and the general arrangements of the dining-room.

"Francois," she said to my uncle's old man-servant, "please send the gardener to me at four o'clock."

"Yes, Madame la Comtesse."

"And then send the steward, whom I do not see here."

"Oh, *I* am the steward!" replied my uncle.

"That's capital! My compliments to you," she continued; "I might have known it."

"All the same, I fancy I perform my duties very well: is not this new furniture to your taste?"

"Not only so, but I find it very handsome, and I appreciate your antiquarian passion for rare and choice objects; only there is a want of life about it. What are those great vases, may I ask, whose enormous mouths stand empty to receive the dust?"

"Those Mandarins!" said my uncle; "they come from the palace of the Emperor of China."

"Oh, the men, the men!" exclaimed my aunt with a laugh: "if they were in Paradise they would forget to contemplate the Eternal! Now, captain, my lord and spouse, pray tell me of what use to you are beds full of flowers, if you never rejoice your eyes with the sight of them?"

The luncheon went off charmingly and merrily. As she chatted with us, my aunt signalled to Francis and gave him her instructions for those innumerable comforts which a woman only can think of. My uncle, as if by enchantment, found everything ready to hand; before he had time to ask for anything to drink, he found his glass filled. We had not been accustomed to this kind of service. When we left the table my aunt said,

"Let us take a turn in the grounds."

She took my arm and we started off. I won't trouble you with a description of this walk, in the course of which my aunt and I succeeded in improving our acquaintance. We soon grew to understand each other thoroughly. With supreme tact, and without apparent design on her part, she had led me on by discreet questions to give her, before a quarter of an hour had passed, a complete catalogue from A. to Z. of all my studies, my tastes, and my pursuits, including of course my youthful escapades, which made her smile more than once.

In this outpouring I excepted, as you may be sure, the revelations of my career as a pasha. My uncle walked close to us, but left us to talk together. One might have thought that he was resuming his marital duties, interrupted only the evening before, without their course having been disturbed by any appreciable incident. All at once, we arrived at the foot-path which leads to the Turkish house.

"Ah! let us go into Kasre-El-Nouzha!" said my aunt.

At this I glanced at my uncle with an air of distress; he, without wincing in the least, said:

"The communicating door is walled up. Kasre-El-Nouzha is let."

"Let!" she exclaimed; "To whom?"

"To an important personage, Mohammed-Azis, a friend of mine from Constantinople. You do not know him."

"You ungrateful wretch!" she continued with a laugh: "that's the way you observe my memory, is it?"

She did not press the subject. You may guess what a relief that was to me.

After we had strolled about the grounds for an hour, my aunt Eudoxia had made a complete conquest of me. But although everything about her excited my curiosity, I had put very few questions to her, not wishing from motives of delicacy to appear entirely ignorant of her history; such ignorance, indeed, would have appeared strange in a nephew. She seemed quite disposed, however, to answer all my questions without any fencing, and to treat me as an intimate friend. What I felt most surprised at was the attitude of my uncle, who had never said any more to me about her than about my aunt Cora of Les Grands Palmiers. There reigned betwixt them the affectionate manners of the happiest possible couple; they discussed the past, and I could see that their union had never been weakened or affected, notwithstanding my uncle's Mahometan proceedings, which she really appears never to have suspected. I discovered that she had accompanied him on board his ship, during several of his voyages, and that two years back he had stayed six months with her at Corfu. As for him, he talked in such a completely innocent manner, betokening such a pure conscience, that I came to the conclusion he was probably on just as good a footing with all his other spouses, and that he would not have been the least bit more embarrassed with my aunt Van Cloth, had she chanced to turn up.

When we returned to the chateau, my aunt asked me to have some letters posted for her. I went to her room to take them from her; she had found time to write half-a-dozen for all parts of the world. While she was sealing them, I had a look at the numerous articles with which she had filled and garnished her boudoir. There were on the table flowers in vases, books and albums; on the mantelpiece, several portraits arranged on little gilt easels, among which was a splendid miniature of a young, handsome man, in Turkish costume embroidered with gold, and having on his head a fez ornamented with an egret of precious stones.

"Do you recognise this gentleman," said my aunt, as I was stooping to look at it more closely.

"What!" I exclaimed; "Can that be my uncle?"

"The very man, dressed up as a great mamamouchi. It is a great curiosity, for you are aware of his Turkish notions on the subject. According to these, one ought not to have one's image made."

"Upon my word, that's quite true," I said; "it is the first portrait I have seen of him."

"I have every reason for believing that it is the only one," she replied with a smile; "this was the most difficult victory I ever won over him."

We then began to discuss my uncle and his eccentricities, combined with his remarkable talents. She related to me some events and features in his life which would not be out of place in the legend of a hero of antiquity; amongst other matters she told me the story of their marriage, which runs briefly as follows:—

My aunt, a daughter of one of the richest and noblest Greek families, lived with her father at a castle in Thessaly, a country which is partly Mahometan. During the feast of Bairam, the Turks commenced a massacre of Christians, which lasted three days. Several families, taking refuge in a church, had fortified themselves there, and with their servants were defending themselves desperately against their assailants. The assassins had already broken open the door of the sanctuary, and were about to cut all their throats, when suddenly a man came galloping up, followed by a few soldiers. He struck right and left with his scimitar in the thick of the crowd outside, and reached the doorway, causing his horse to rear up on the pavement. He slays some, and terrifies all. The Christians are saved!

This cavalier with his scimitar was my uncle, who was then in command of the province. The unhappy wretches who had escaped assassination pressed about him, and surrounded him; the girls and the women threw themselves at his feet. My aunt was one of these unfortunates; she was then fifteen years old, and as beautiful as noonday. You may guess how her imagination was wrought on by the sight of this noble saviour. My uncle on his side was thunderstruck by the contemplation of so much beauty. Having to judge and punish the rebels, he established his head-quarters in the castle of the Cornalis. He sentenced twenty persons to death, and demanded Eudoxia's hand in marriage. This, notwithstanding his gratitude, the father refused to grant to a Turkish general.

The lovers were desperate, and separated, exchanging vows of eternal fidelity. Finally, after three months of correspondence and clandestine meetings, an elopement ensued, followed up quickly by marriage. It was as the sequence of this event that my uncle, induced by love, and moreover disgraced again for having exercised too much justice in favour of the Christians, finally quitted the service of the Sultan. His pardon by the Cornalis followed, and it was at this time that he obtained from the Pope the title of Count of the Holy Empire.

All this will serve to explain to you how it is that my aunt, as an heiress of great wealth, possesses in her own right a very large independent fortune in the Crimea.

We have now been living together for a fortnight, and during this time Ferouzat has been completely transformed. My aunt Eudoxia is certainly very *meublante*, as my uncle calls it, and she has brought into the house quite an attractive element of brightness. She has naturally introduced into our circle a certain amount of etiquette, which does not, however, encroach upon the liberties of country life, or disturb that easy-going elegance which forms one of the charms of existence among well-bred people. The Countess of Monteclaro, as might well have been foreseen, having already been intimately acquainted with Doctor Morand, begins to take a most friendly interest in Mademoiselle Genevieve. As a consequence, Genevieve and the children spend almost all their time at the chateau. In the evenings we have gatherings to which all the young people of the neighbourhood are invited; my aunt, who is an excellent musician, organises concerts, and we generally finish up with a dance.

These worldly recreations afford me a clearer insight into the analytical details of my oriental life, which is now more than ever enveloped in the profoundest mystery. I have invented a story of important botanical studies upon the flora of Provence, in order to justify certain daily excursions which naturally terminate in El-Nouzha. It is well-known, moreover, that I sometimes visit His Excellency Mohammed-Azis, but with the discretion which respect for a great misfortune naturally entails. The exiled minister is no longer even discussed among us; everybody knows that "he shuts himself up like a bear in his den," and there is an end of it.

My aunt is the perfection of a woman. Nothing can be more delightful than our conversations. Her manner partakes both of the indulgence of a mother and of the unrestrained intimacy of a friend. She still remembers the child she used to dance upon her knees; and, although I had for a long while forgotten her very existence, my present affection for her is none the less sincere because it is of such recent growth. I must confess that, after my confined existence at school and college, I am delighted with these pleasures of home life, to which I was until lately quite a stranger.

My aunt, as you may guess, is acquainted with my uncle's

famous plan for the future, and knows Anna Campbell, the Pasha's *god-daughter*. You should hear her chaff him anent this god-fathership, on the strength of which she claims that the captain has returned to the bosom of the Church without knowing it. She tells me that Anna is a charming girl. Thus petted and entertained, I live in other respects very much as I like, and sometimes pass the whole day in the library. I should add that my aunt, who is as sharp as a weasel, makes her own comments upon my frequent absences from the chateau.

"Andre," she asked me the other day with a smile, "is your 'Botany' dark or fair?"

"Fair, my dear aunt," I answered, laughing as she did.

In the midst of all this the Pasha, still emulating one of the Olympian gods, proceeds on his course with that tranquillity of spirit which never forsakes him. Two days ago, who should come down upon us but Rabassu, his lieutenant, the Rabassu whom my uncle has always called his "murderer." He has brought home "La Belle Virginie" from Zanzibar with a cargo of cinnamon; for, as you are aware, we (or rather *I*) still trade in spices. Being now the head of the firm, I have to sell off the last consignments. Rabassu heard of the resurrection of Barbassou-Pasha directly he arrived at Toulon. He hurried off to us quite crestfallen, and when he met the captain literally trembled at the thought of the hurricane he would now have to face. But everything passed off very satisfactorily. My uncle interrupted his first mutterings of apology with a gentle growl, and contented himself with chaffing him for his infantine credulity.

However, this incident has revived the vexed question of the camels. "Where are they?" asks the captain. Having promised to send them to the Zoological Gardens at Marseilles, he feels his honour is at stake; they must be found. I support him in this view; my inherited property is of course incomplete without them. Urgent letters on the subject have just been despatched to his friend Picklock, and to the officer in command at Aden. If necessary, a claim will be lodged against England; she is undoubtedly responsible for them.

In my next letter I will tell you all the news relating to El-Nouzha from the time when I last interrupted this interesting part of my narrative. My houris are making progress, and their education is improving. We are going on swimmingly.

CHAPTER V

The Turks are calumniated, my friend, there's no doubt about it. It is not enough for us to say and to believe, with the vulgar herd, that these turbaned people are wallowing in materialism and are not civilised; we must do more than this, and convict them of their errors. We, fortified with a singular infatuation in our ideas, our habits, and our personal associations, venture to settle by our sovereign decrees the loftiest questions of sentiment. The rules to be observed by the perfect lover in the courtship and treatment of his lady-love, have been settled at tournaments, by the Courts of Love of Isaure, and by the College of the Gay Science. Our pretensions to troubadourism have never been abandoned. The affectations of "L'Astree" have been erected into a code of Love, and we have succeeded in establishing the French cavalier as the paragon of excellence in love matters, and the perfect type of gallantry. The saying "to die for one's lady-love" rises so naturally to our lips that the most insignificant cornet might warble it to his Celimene without causing her to smile.

You will nevertheless admit, I hope, that we ought to discard a few of these absurd expressions. That we know how to make love is not much to boast about, after all. The only important point for us as philosophers is to know whether our ideal is really the higher ideal—whether our treatment of woman is really more worthy both of her and of ourselves

than the pagan treatment which prevails among the Eastern nations? Here at once crops up the elementary dispute between the votaries of polygamy and monogamy. Both these institutions are based upon divine and human laws, both are written down and defined in moral codes, and in sacred books. One takes its origin in the Bible, and remains faithful to its traditions; the other has developed at some period, from the simple conventions of a new social order. We must not conclude that we alone possess the knowledge of absolute truth, merely because our conceit postulates for us the superiority of our time-honoured civilisation. All wisdom proceeds from God alone, and truth is for us only relative to place, time, and habit. Was not Jacob, when he married at the same time Leah and Rachel, the daughters of Laban, nearer than we are now to the primitive sentiment of the laws of nature and of revelation? Do you presume to blame him, insignificant being that you are, because yielding to the supplication of his beloved Rachel he espoused— somewhat superfluously it may be—her handmaid Bala, with the simple object of having a son by her? In presence of this idyl of the patriarchal age, what becomes of all our theories, our ideas, and our prejudices, the fruits after all of a hollow and worthless education?

You will not, I trust, do me the wrong of believing that I, wavering in my faith, intend forthwith to abandon the principles in which I was brought up. But a subject so serious as the one I have been devoting myself to, demands the most frank and honest examination. I will not deliver a judgment; I will merely state the facts. Now it is an established fact that the people who permit by their laws a plurality of wives are, even at the present time, far more numerous than the monogamists. Statistics prove that out of the thousand million inhabitants of this globe, Christianity with all its sects, and Judaism thrown in, does not number more than two hundred and sixty millions according to Balbi, or two hundred and forty millions according to the

London Bible Society.

Since the remainder, consisting of Mahometans, Buddhists, Fire-worshippers, and Idolaters, all practise polygamy more or less, it follows that on this globe of ours, the monogamists constitute one-fourth only of the whole population. Such is the naked, unadorned truth!

Are we wrong? Are they right? It is not my business to decide this point. Philosophers and theologians far more patient than I am, have given it up as a bad job. Voltaire, with his subtle genius, settled the question in his own characteristic fashion, by supposing that an imaginary God had from the beginning decreed an inequality in this matter, regulated by geographical situation, in these words:—

"I shall draw a line from Mount Caucasus to Egypt, and from Egypt to Mount Atlas; all men dwelling to the east of this line shall be permitted to marry several wives, while those to the west of it shall have one only."

And, as a matter of fact, it is so.

But having disposed of this important point, there remains a loftier question for us to elucidate—one consisting entirely of sentiment. The treatment of woman being our only objective, our present business is to decide on which side of the line its character is the most respectful, the most worthy and the most flattering towards her. Certainly our doctrine is purer, our law more divine. Nevertheless, as sincere judges, we ought, perhaps, to examine and see whether we do not transgress against our absolute principles. And I must confess that I cannot now approach this delicate question without some misgiving. In the judgment of every tribunal, the case of polygamy is a hopelessly bad one. That I am ready to admit; but might it not be urged against the other side that in practice the court knows very well that the law is not observed? What judge can be found, however austere, who has never offended against it? To sum the matter up briefly (whispering low our confessions, if you like), what man is there among us—I am not talking of Don Juans, who catalogue their amours, nor of Lovelaces, but of ordinary men of say thirty years old—who can remember how many mistresses he has had? What, is this the monogamy we have been making such a flourish about?

Perhaps you will say that we need not see in these irregularities anything more than a sort of licensed depravity, tolerated for the sake of maintaining a virtuous ideal. But consider the fatal consequences of this hypocrisy. What becomes of our aspirations of the age of twenty, of our dreams and poetic fancies, after we have plunged into these wretched connections, these degrading, promiscuous attachments which form the current of our present habits, and from which we emerge at the age of thirty, sceptics, and with hearts and souls tarnished? What do we reap from these frenzies of unhealthy passion, but contempt for woman, and disbelief in anything virtuous?

For the Turk there is no such thing as illegitimate love, and woman is the object of absolute respect. Never having more than one master, she cannot fall in his esteem. Having been bought as a slave, she becomes a wife directly she sets foot in the harem; her rights are sacred, and she cannot any more be abandoned. The laws protect her; she has a recognised position, a title; her children are legitimate, and if by chance—

I suspend this philosophical digression, in order to inform you of a momentous occurrence. El-Nouzha has just been the scene of a sanguinary drama. A rebellion has broken out among my sultanas.

My harem is on strike.

You will ask me how this storm came to break upon me just as I was settling down into the most innocent and tranquil frame of mind? It can only be explained by a retrospective survey of certain domestic circumstances, which the changes that have been going on at Ferouzat had caused me to overlook.

You will not have forgotten the terrible commotion caused in my harem by the news of my uncle's resurrection. My poor houris, dreading some fatal drama of the usual Turkish character, had indeed passed through a cruel time of distress and anguish. When their alarms were dissipated, a revival of animation soon manifested itself in their spirits; but, as ill-luck would have it, and as I have told you, one little detail of this day's proceedings, unimportant as it appeared at the time, was destined to disturb their harmony, so perfect hitherto, and to arouse their jealousies. Kondje-Gul had been to the chateau, and a silly ambition to attempt the same freak had got into the heads of Nazli and Zouhra. I at once expressed a decided opposition to this childish scheme; but, of course, from the moment it met with opposition, it developed into a fixed purpose.

Within the limited circle of ideas in which they move, their imaginations had been excited—curiosity, the attractions of forbidden fruit. The long and the short of it was that, at the sight of their genuine disappointment—a disappointment aggravated by continual and jealous suspicions of a preference on my part for Kondje-Gul—I had almost made up my mind to yield for one occasion, when my aunt arrived, which at once put an end to any thought of such good-natured but weak concessions.

I imagined myself to be armed now with an overwhelming reason for refusing their request, but it turned out quite otherwise. When they heard that my uncle's wife was at the chateau, they asked to be allowed to make her acquaintance.

They said that they were really bound as *cadines*, according to Turkish custom, to pay their respects to my uncle's wife, "whom her position as legitimate spouse places hierarchically above us." I got over this difficulty by telling them that my aunt, being a Christian, was forbidden by her creed to have any intercourse with Mussulmans.

What especially distinguishes the Turkish woman, my dear Louis, from the woman whose character has been fashioned by our own remarkable civilisation, is the instinctive, inborn respect which she always preserves and observes towards man. Man is the master and the lord, she is his servant, and she would never dream of setting herself up as his equal. The Koran on this point has hardly at all modified the biblical traditions. Unfortunately for me, I must confess that in my household I have disregarded the law of Islam. Inspired by a higher ideal, you will understand, without my mentioning it, that my first object has been to abolish slavery from my harem, by inculcating into the minds of my houris principles more in conformity with the Christianity which I profess. I wished, like a modern Prometheus, to kindle the divine spark in these young and beautiful barbarians, whose minds are still wrapped up in their oriental superstitions. I wished to elevate their souls, to cultivate their minds, and in short, to make them my free companions and no longer my helots.

I may assert with pride that I have been partially successful in my task. Three months of this treatment had hardly elapsed before all traces of servile subordination had disappeared. With this faculty for metamorphosis existing in them, which all women possess, but which is for ever denied to us men, and thanks above all to the revelations of our customs and habits contained in novels of my selection, which Kondje-Gul read to them during my hours of absence, and to which they listened with admiration (for they were eager to know all about this world of ours, which was as yet unknown to them), I soon obtained a charming combination.

Their strange exotic mixture of oriental graces, blending happily with efforts to imitate the refinements of our civilisation, their artless tokens of ignorance, their coquettish and feline instincts, their voluptuous bearing in process of attempted transformation into bashful reserve, all these phenomena afforded me the most delightful subject for study ever entered on by a philosopher.

Nevertheless, I must admit that the education of their intellects did not keep pace with the cultivation of their ideas, but rendered them still liable to commit a number of solecisms. I had an interest, moreover, in keeping them in a certain degree of ignorance of the actual laws of our own world. Imbued with their native ideas, their credulity accepted without hesitation, everything which I chose to tell them about "the customs of the harems of France," and they conformed to them without making any pretence to further knowledge of them. None the less, there began to grow up in their minds ideas of independence and self-will, the natural consequences of the elevation effected in their sentiments. The notion of a truer and more tender love was used by them henceforth as a weapon against my absolute authority. Only too happy to be treated as a lover rather than a master, I did not feel any loss in this respect: love is kept alive by these numberless little stratagems of a woman, who loves and desires—yet desires not—and so forth. And then, you must remember, I had four wives.

They on their part, having no aims, no ambitions, but to please me, the sole object of their common love, each tried to effect my conquest in order to obtain the advantage over her rivals—an emulation of which I experienced all the charms. Notwithstanding the fact that I distributed my affections with a rare impartiality, I could not always prevent the occurrence of jealous quarrels among them. Afterwards ensued regrets tender reproaches, and clouds of sadness melting into tears. Peace was restored amid foolish outbursts of mirth. But you

cannot realise what a task it has been for me to preserve the harmony of a well-regulated household among creatures with their impulsive imaginations, which have ripened under the heat of their native oriental sun. They have mixed up their superstitions with those higher principles of which I have endeavoured to inculcate a notion into their minds, and which they often interpret in quite a different sense. All this has been the occasion for the display of charming eccentricities. My little animals have grown into women, and along with the development of a more intelligent love, I have seen manifestations of a coquettish mutinous spirit, upon the slightest evidence of partiality on my part, which they have thought to detect in me.

I must tell you that Kondje-Gul, who is really a very intelligent girl, had begun to study with great ardour, and it naturally followed that she benefited more from her lessons than the others, who treated them rather as an amusement. In three months she learnt French tolerably well—she it was who translated the novels to them. Hence arose a superiority on her side, which must in any case have produced a good deal of envy among the others. On the top of this came her famous excursion to the chateau, concerning which the silly creature gave them marvellous accounts, in order to pose as favourite. I should add that Kondje-Gul, being of an extremely jealous nature, often gave way to violent fits of passion. Hadidje, for some reason or other, more especially excited her suspicions. Hadidje has an excitable temperament. Between them, consequently, a considerable coolness arose: this, however, created nothing worse than a few clouds on my fine sky. For the passive domesticities of the harem, I had substituted love; for its obedience, the free expansions and impulses of the heart.

I must add, however, that while rising to purer conceptions of truth, my houris retained too much of their native instincts not to get their heads turned somewhat by the novelty of their situation. Having equal rights, they claimed the same rank in my esteem. From this it resulted that Hadidje, Nazli, and Zouhra at last took umbrage at the success of Kondje-Gul, who was wrong in trying to outstrip them. "Kondje-Gul," they proclaimed, "wishes to act the *savante*. Kondje-Gul gives herself the airs of a legitimate Sultana." I must confess that the said little coquette was only too careful to impress them with her successes, of which she was rather proud. One evening she sat down to the piano, and, with a careless air, played part of a waltz, which she had learnt on the sly in order to surprise me. You may guess what the effect was. This triumph put the finishing touch to their provocation, and the evening was spent in sulky murmurs.

Finally, one day when I arrived at the harem I found Kondje-Gul shut up in her own room, bathed in tears. The storm which had been impending so long had burst over her proud head—Hadidje, Zouhra, and Nazli had beaten her.

Once more I appeased their discords, by recourse to a new declaration of principles. The reconciliation was celebrated by a general display of cordiality; but a faction had been formed within the ranks. At the very time that I least expected it, Nazli, Hadidje, and Zouhra returned to their idea of a secret visit to the chateau. This project, which so far had only been carried on by detached skirmishes, was still cherished by them, and was now pursued by a compact body of troops, combining their siege-manoeuvres with a rare concentration of boldness and courage. Their weapons were tender caresses and those innumerable cajoleries of women, which nearly always compel us to surrender in desperation to their most unreasonable whims. My oriental *menage* was still walking on a flowery path, but a snare was hidden under the dead leaves.... A few weeks later, when I was completely entangled in the subtle meshes of their cunning, the whole line changed their tactics. They said no more about Ferouzat, but I soon saw exhibitions on every side of frivolous caprices, sudden fits of sulkiness, unexpected refusals, and so forth.

My odalisques had become civilised.

I was too good a tactician to allow myself to be outflanked by this artful little game, the concerted object of which I pretended not to perceive. Whenever they fancied they had obtained a success over me, I immediately transferred my attentions to Kondje-Gul, and the attacking party disbanded, surrendering unconditionally.

Unfortunately Kondje-Gul, relying upon my weakness for her, tried to carry off a decisive victory by a sudden charge. The other evening, having accompanied me up to the secret door, she rushed through it with a laugh, and made off for the chateau, right through the grounds of Ferouzat. I ran after her and soon caught her, encumbered as she was by her oriental slippers and her long train. I took her back to the harem, where the others seemed to be awaiting, in a great state of excitement, the result of this most audacious attempt. Then I learnt that "she had boasted she would obtain this fresh triumph over them." This was a flagrant offence. After such an act of rebellion it was necessary to make an example: I spoke severely, and there was a tremendous scene. Kondje-Gul had too much pride to humiliate herself before her rivals, who were rejoicing over her defeat. Distracted with vexation and carried away by her foolish impulses, she made the breach between us complete. For three days she remained haughty and arrogant, accepting her disgrace, but too proud to make any advances for a reconciliation. Needless to say, Nazli, Hadidje, and Zouhra were more affectionate and attentive to me than ever.

Such was the condition of affairs when the critical incident took place which I undertook to describe to you.

The other evening, I was in the harem, and Nazli and Zouhra were playing Turkish airs on the zither, while Hadidje, seated at my feet, with her head resting upon her hands, which were crossed on my knees, was singing in a low murmur the words of each tune.

Kondje-Gul stayed near the verandah, looking cool and dignified, and smoking a cigarette in the defiant, and at the same time resigned attitude of a hardened rebel; but the furtive glances which she cast at Hadidje gave the lie to her affected calmness. For two evenings past we had not exchanged a word with each other. She had dressed herself that day with remarkable care, as if to impress me with the splendours of the paradise I had lost: her glorious hair streamed down in long tresses, somewhat disorderly, from under her pearl-embroidered cap. Notwithstanding a great gauze veil with which she pretended to enshroud herself in order to conceal her charms from my profane eyes, her bodice was so slightly fastened that it dropped down just low enough to expose to view the charming little pits under her arms and the snowy-whiteness of her breasts. Like a wrathful Venus, the expression on her face was both mutinous and resolute. She had put *kohl* under her eyes (a thing which I forbid), and had blackened and lengthened her eyebrows so that they met together, in Turkish fashion. In this get-up the little sinner looked ravishing!

Now you can picture to yourself the scene, and guess my state of mind. The weird tones of the zither, with their penetrating and singularly melancholy vibrations, the strange yet graceful costumes, the scent of those flowers with which the daughters of the East always adorn themselves, the all-pervading voluptuous atmosphere the enchantment of which I cannot explain to you; finally, the fair rebel gloomy and jealous, in the corner of the picture! All this, without my being any longer surprised by it, kept me in a sort of happy contentment, like that of a well satisfied vizir, which defies all analysis, but which you will understand.

All at once the music ceased.

"Andre," said Hadidje to me, "won't you come into the garden for a little while?"

"Come along!" I replied, and rose up to go.

She took my arm. Zouhra and Nazli followed us. As I went out by the verandah, I passed close to Kondje-Gul; she drew back with a superb air of dignity, as if she feared lest her dress should be ruffled by me. Then darting a look of withering scorn at Hadidje, she wrapped herself up in her veil and leant against the balustrade, watching us go off. It was a delicious autumn evening, the air was soft and the sky clear and starry. Under our feet the dry leaves crackled. Hadidje wanted to have a row in the boat, so we went towards the lake. As we rowed along we caught glimpses of Kondje-Gul from time to time, through the openings between the trees; her motionless figure stood out like a solitary shadow in front of the illuminated window of the drawing-room.

"That's capital!" said Hadidje, who was rowing with Nazli; "How dismal she looks! But then why does she try to get privileges over us? Let us stay here."

"Oh!" answered Zouhra in an indifferent tone, as she lay back on the cushions, "Not the whole evening, I hope, for it's rather cold."

"Why didn't you bring your *feridjie* then," said Nazli; "you poor sensitive creature?"

"I will go and fetch it if you like," I said to Zouhra.

"Oh, no!" she answered quickly; "if you leave us we shall

be afraid."

"Very well then, *I'll* go," said Hadidje, who wanted to carry out her plan. "Let us row to the bank."

We pulled up to the point nearest to the chateau, and Hadidje, not without some nervousness after all, left us and ran off.

"Keep your eye on me all the time, won't you?" she said to me as she picked up her long skirt.

Soon we saw her reach the verandah without any adventure. She ascended the steps and passed in front of Kondje-Gul. It seemed to us that Kondje-Gul spoke very passionately to her, and that she answered her in the same tones. At last they both had gone in, when all at once we heard piercing shrieks. Apprehending some skirmishing between my two jealous houris, I rushed off, followed at a distance by Zouhra and Nazli, who were frightened at the thought of being left alone. As I entered the harem I found Hadidje and Kondje-Gul, with their hair dishevelled and their clothes torn, struggling together. Kondje-Gul was armed with a little golden dagger, which she wore in her hair, and was striking Hadidje with it. When she saw me she fled and ran to her room to shut herself in.

We hastened to the assistance of poor Hadidje. She had been wounded on the shoulder, and blood was flowing. Happily the weapon, too harmless to wound seriously, had not penetrated the flesh; but, breaking with the blow, it had scratched her rather severely. I soon felt reassured, and quieted her cries, but not without some trouble.

Mohammed and the servants had run up to the rescue; I sent them all back, and after calming Nazli and Zouhra, I staunched the wound with some water. In a few minutes,

Hadidje, who had fancied herself murdered, regained her tranquillity of mind, and only complained just enough to keep alive our interest in her grievance.

Then I questioned her, and she told us that as soon as she had entered the drawing-room, Kondje-Gul followed her, and giving vent there and then to an outburst of passion, accused her of being the cause of her disgrace, reproaching her with hypocritical devices for getting over me. Hadidje, according to her version of the affair, had only replied with extreme moderation, when Kondje-Gul, exasperated all of a sudden, rushed at her with her dagger.

I knew Hadidje's character too well to place an implicit belief in the whole of this account; still it was important to put an end to such escapades. The happiness of my household, which had hitherto been so peaceful, was endangered if I failed to act like a just but strict husband. After this outrage committed by Kondje-Gul, my houris, in their indignation, insisted upon a signal vengeance, and demanded forthwith that I should deliver her up to the *cadi*. The *cadi!* that was coming it strong. I had some difficulty, however, in overcoming their persistency; at last they agreed to a less tragic form of punishment, which went no further than the expulsion of this unworthy companion from the harem.

Such escapades might, I feared, get wind outside, and cause a scandal. However much allowance I might make for the tempers of my houris in these demands for a somewhat summary punishment, I could not conceal from myself that, taking everything into consideration, it was really necessary for me to punish the offence severely, into whatever difficulties this adventure might lead me. I promised to give satisfaction to their legitimate indignation. Then, leaving Hadidje to the care of Zouhra and Nazli, I proclaimed that I was going at once to subject the culprit to an examination, after which I should pronounce sentence upon her.

CHAPTER VI

Kondje-Gul was shut up in her room; I found her sitting on her bed, which was disarranged, and the pillows of which seemed to have been rumpled up in a fit of rage and despair; she appeared like one stupified, with her gloomy looks, and hands clasping her knees. Her face and her neck bore the marks of Hadidje's nails. The *kohl* from under her eyes had been smeared on her cheeks, which were smudged all over; she looked just like a little savage, with however the gracefulness of a child.

She did not stir when I came in; I walked right up to her, and in the solemn tone of a judge, said—

"Wretched girl, do you know what you have done?"

She remained silent and motionless, fixing her eyes on the carpet.

"After such an act, will you not answer?" I continued.

"Why do you love her?" she said at last, in a wild voice.

"Say, why should I love *you*?" I replied, "when your bad temper and your jealousy lead you to disobedience, to crime—when you stir up quarrels and discords among us?"

At these reproaches Kondje-Gul all at once drew herself up erect before me, and exclaimed passionately—

"Then you do not love me any longer?"

My questions had not reached their mark.

"This is not the time for me to answer you," I said. "I am now asking you to account for the act which you have just committed."

"Very well! If you love me no more, I want you to confess it, and I will die! What have I done to you, that you should prefer Hadidje to me? Perhaps she is handsomer than I am, is she? If you think me ugly," she added, in a tone of concentrated despair, "tell me straight, and I will go and cast myself into the lake, and you shall see me no more!"

"But no! I did not say that," I replied, trying to cut short this diversion.

"Then what are you reproaching me for? Hadidje loves you better than I do, perhaps?"

"Neither Hadidje's sentiments nor mine have anything to do with the question. I am asking you about your violence, and the wound you have given her with the dagger!"

"Why did she tell me that you love her better than me?" she answered.

"She told you that?"

"Yes; and pretends that you swore to it. For my part, I do not want to be loved like a slave. I have learnt from your books that women in your country die when they are no longer loved. So if you have ceased to love me, I wish to die! You have told me that I have a heart, a soul, and an intellect, as they have, and that a woman's love makes her the equal of her master. Do you mean to tell me, ungrateful man, that I do not love you? Have I ever been jealous of Zouhra, or of Nazli? Why should this Hadidje be everything in your eyes? If you do not want me any more," she added, in a transport of grief, "say so, then; crop my hair, shave off my eyebrows, and place me among the servants!"

As she said these words, she threw herself down at my feet, which she hugged in a delirium of passion. Her tears coursed down her cheeks, and upon my hands, which she covered with kisses. In her intense emotion her voice betokened such bitter distress, that in spite of my determination to punish her, I felt softened towards her. In presence of these transports of a passion, which admitted no other motive but that of her jealous rage, I saw that it was in vain for me to attempt to awaken her conscience to the sense of her guilty conduct. She could neither hear nor feel anything but the echo of her own grief. I loved her no longer, and I loved Hadidje! These words returned to her lips over and over again, amid sobs so heart-rending that, overcome by pity, and forgetting my resolution, I could not help uttering a word of protestation. I had hardly spoken, when she exclaimed—

"Is that true? Do you really love me? Will you swear it?"

I then understood the imprudence I had committed, but it was too late. Kondje-Gul, passing at once from affliction to joy, had clasped me in her arms. I wanted to remain stern; but how could I contend by any arguments with such outbursts of mad jealousy? She would not listen to me: she implored me with all the frenzied entreaties and reproaches of which an unreasoning nature is capable. At one moment I believed that I had at last brought her mind to realise the actual situation between us, and the justice of my complaints against her conduct.

"Well, yes!" she said, "I have been very foolish. I ought to have thrown myself at your feet three days ago! Ah, if you only knew how wretched your coldness made me! Listen: when you came in just now, thinking that I had lost your love for ever, I was considering how I could kill myself. But you have forgiven me, have you not?—No, no! don't speak to me about *them*!" she continued, sharply, seeing that I was about to answer. "You know very well that I am no longer like them; you have formed my heart for a different love to that of the harem. I no longer love you just as they do. No! As for you, you shall love me just as you please—as your servant, if such is your will. Imprison me, if you like, as a punishment; all I want is to see you, and to love you. Yes, I was wrong in striking that Hadidje. You know very well that I am still a savage, for you have often told me so. Well, then, teach me your own ideas, your religion. Tell me what you wish me to be?" she added finally, in tones so soft and tender that I was quite overcome by her.

I was astounded by this language, by this impassioned eloquence which I had never suspected in her, and which I now heard from her lips for the first time. The butterfly of love had spread out its wings. Psyche was born for love! No longer for that passive and vague love which was but the awakening of the senses and of pleasure, but for that love of the heart which is life itself, with its sorrows, its joys, and its ecstacies. I contemplated it full of surprise, experiencing the fascination of some new enchantment.

Louis, how can I describe it? Within an hour after I had entered Kondje-Gul's room; our quarrel, her jealousies, her offence, and the punishment I had resolved upon, were all forgotten!

Nevertheless, appreciating more completely now the defeat to which I had submitted, I could not fail to perceive the embarrassment which such strange conduct would cause me.

It would, at any rate, be remarkably awkward for my wives to learn that the violent scene which had passed, and poor Hadidje's dagger-wound, had actually become the occasion for a reconciliation with Kondje-Gul. How could I show my face before the victim to whom it was my duty to grant justice? It was really impossible for me to show such contempt for *fas* and *nefas* as I should do were I to reward her assault upon Hadidje in such an extraordinary fashion as by pardoning her. What in the world would Zouhra and Nazli say? It would be all over with my authority and my reputation.

At any cost, therefore, it was necessary for me to conceal my very imprudent weakness until their passions had calmed down, or until some conciliatory advances on the part of Kondje-Gul to Hadidje had led to the forgiveness of this deplorable folly. But directly I attempted to appeal to her reason, Kondje-Gul, full of pride at having won me back, and even making use of my desertion as a weapon in her hands, would not hear of humiliating herself before a rival. In vain I represented to her that my own dignity, "the proprieties," and justice were at stake; she held fast to her victory, and would not forego any of its advantages.

Finally, however, she comprehended the gravity of the situation.

"Well, do you know what we'll do?" she said; "it will be so nice! They will all believe that you have given me a tremendous scolding. And so you have, for you *were* cruel when first you came in!"

"I suppose you did not deserve it then?" I answered.

"Hold your tongue, sir!" she said, putting her finger up to her mouth, and pouting like a little child. "You're going to begin again! Let me tell you my plan, which will settle all our difficulties."

"Let me hear your plan."

"Very well; you shall tell them that you have been inexorable, and that you have treated me as an odious creature. For my part, I shall look still more angry with you. Before them, we will scowl at each other, and make them believe that all is quite at an end between us, and that you have decided to send me away and have me sold."

"What a capital idea!" I said to her.

"Yes, do let us. It will be so delightful, so clandestine! And then I shall feel that you love me better than them!"

"Because we shall deceive them, I suppose."

"Yes, yes!" she exclaimed, with a laugh; "because we shall deceive them! Besides," she added in a tone of conviction, "you must know very well yourself that there is no other rational course for us. In the first place I swear I will never beg the pardon of this miserable Hadidje—never!"

For the present it was clearly necessary to agree to this compromise, which at least provided for the exigencies of decorum. When I left Kondje-Gul I returned to the chateau from motives of prudence, in order to avoid rousing the suspicions of my wives.

Nevertheless I must admit it was not without some apprehensions that I returned the next day to the harem. But I was soon reassured when I saw the amiable satisfaction which prevailed among my houris. The absence of Kondje-Gul, who remained in stoic seclusion, left no doubt in their minds that she was in complete disgrace and would certainly be sent away. I even gathered that the silly creature had shown Nazli some blue marks which she had made on her own skin, and told her that I had beaten her! Hadidje, rather proud of her wound, continued to give herself interesting airs as the principal heroine of this terrible tragedy. As it was in reality merely a scratch, which hurt her very little, her only object in complaining was to emphasize her caprices. After the stormy days we had just gone through, this morning passed like an idyl. Their spirits were all harmonious; and I left them firmly convinced that from the way I performed my great act of justice they had no longer anything to fear at the hands of a rival.

Satisfied at this termination of the incident, which had caused me no small anxiety, I was returning to the chateau, when lo and behold! as I was passing the bushes, who should appear but Kondje-Gul, who ran up and threw herself into my arms.

"How's this?" I said to her; "you here!"

"Yes, dear; I wanted to see you and kiss you," she exclaimed, bounding with joy like a child; "and to hear you tell me that you love me still!"

"You mad creature, suppose anyone were to see you!"

"All right!" she replied; "I jumped down from my window, for they think I am a prisoner there. I slipped under the verandah, so as not to be noticed by Mohammed, and came here to wait for you. Now, don't scold me. Now that I have seen you I am going back, for fear I should rouse the suspicion of your *wives*. Tell me if I'm not clever!"

Then, just as she was running away again, she added in a little tone of importance,

"And mind *you're* careful too!"

Eight days have passed since the dramatic events, of which I have related to you the singular termination. Here I am involved in a regular conspiracy of deceit; I have a secret intrigue with one of my wives. Kondje-Gul plays her part of estrangement in a most curious fashion, with an affectation of melancholy, combined with haughtiness, and the silly creature is delighted with her efforts. After two or three days of seclusion, she reappeared, talked cynically of her approaching departure, and rejoiced over it. We treat each other like spouses definitely divorced from each other, who are nevertheless paying each other, as well-bred people should do, a final tribute of strict politeness after the irreparable breach. Hadidje, Nazli, and Zouhra, confident in a dominion which appears to them henceforth assured, admire my great qualities as a dispenser of justice.

My dear Louis, do you wish me to confess to you the most remarkable consequence of this business? Yes, of course you do. I promised that this psychological study should be conducted with sincerity, and that nothing should be shirked. Well then, in the course of my analytical observations, this mystery with Kondje-Gul, these tastings of forbidden fruit, form certainly the most exquisite experience I have met with. You may tell me, if you like, that I am a *pandour*, and that my taste has been perverted by a life of unbridled Epicureanism; you may tell me that the charms of duplicity, of falsehood, and of this connivance in the guise of a childish deception, are exercising a morbid fascination over my demoralized heart. You may be right. I would only ask you to express yourself somewhat less bluntly. At any rate, you will not, I presume, expect me to account for the frailties of our mortal nature. I guess what you are thinking—out with it!

Notwithstanding my fine array of principles and the strict vows I made to myself to distribute my affections equally between my *cadines*, it certainly looks very much as if I have selected a favourite. Have I fallen to this extent? I don't know. What is the good, moreover, of arguing about it? Is it true that undisturbed possession is the rock upon which love splits, and that constraint, on the contrary, acts as a spur to it? Instead of arguing aimlessly about such inconsistencies in human nature, it seems to me much simpler to recognise in them, as Kondje-Gul does, a decree of Fate. Can you blame me for sacrificing futile theories to the higher motives by which I am guided?

The fact is that this necessity for dissimulation, these deceptions, and these clandestine interviews, have produced between Kondje-Gul and me a sort of spring-tide of delightful expansion of the affections. You should see us in the daytime, both of us as stiff as starch in the presence of the others. You should see the manoeuvres we perform in order to exchange a sly smile or a shake of the hands out of sight. You should see also what pretty little airs of disdain she puts on for her rivals, who are slumbering in their paradise of illusion! If we are alone by chance, she says,

"Quick! *your wives* are not here," and throws herself into my arms.

Those words coming from her lips, will reveal to you quite a new order of sentiments, a strange form of love, which could only spring from the education of the harem. Although civilised already at heart, Kondje-Gul being still backward in her ideas and traditional associations, does not trouble herself about my other wives. She could not conceive of my being reduced to such a singular state of destitution as that of a poor or a miserly man, who abstains from the luxury of a few odalisques. In her eyes, Hadidje, Zouhra, and Nazli, form part of my establishment, and of my daily routine; while *she* possesses me in secret. For her sake, I am unfaithful to them, I enter her chamber at night by the window, which I climb up to when all are asleep.

All this, you will tell me, is folly on my part. Ah, my dear fellow, our pleasure in life is only made up of such trifles, which our imagination generally provides for us. In those secret interviews I discovered in Kondje-Gul, who was certainly endowed with a frank and straightforward mind, a number of graces which I had never been able to detect before during our intercourse in the harem. Nothing could be stranger or more fascinating than the love of this poor slave-sweetheart, still so humble and timid, and dazzled as it were by the brilliancy of her dream. Her oriental ideas and the superstitions of her childhood, mingled with the vague notions which she has acquired of our world and of a truer ideal, form within her heart and in her mind a most original collection of contrasts. One is reminded of a bird suddenly surprised at feeling her wings, but not yet venturing to launch out into the open. Add to all these attractions the impulses of a passion, exalted perhaps by solitude or by satisfaction at her victory over her rivals, and, even if you blame my conduct, you will at least understand the seductions which precipitated my fall.

At Ferouzat we have great news: the camels have been discovered! A letter from Captain Picklock informed us of this. My uncle is quite jubilant; and we have planned a trip to Marseilles to meet them. Another piece of news is that my aunt has undertaken with Doctor Morand, without appearing to have a hand in it, a great philanthropic work. I must tell you that a few years ago the doctor discovered here a hot spring of ferruginous water, the effects of which upon the few patients whom he was able to induce to visit this hole, have been simply marvellous. What is wanted now is to establish there some sort of hospital for convalescents. My aunt at once decided that she, my uncle, and I should find the funds for it. A hundred thousand francs are more than sufficient for the modest foundation which we contemplate. But from motives of delicacy, and in order to avoid any appearance of ostentation, we arranged with the mayor and the vicar to open a subscription, in order that the enterprise might appear to be supported by public charity, and that all personal liberality should be concealed by associating the whole district with it. The consequence was that Ferouzat has had a visit from the Prefect of the Department, accompanied by several members of the General Council, and that, in addition to this, my aunt has organised a committee of the leading inhabitants of the neighbourhood. Of course I am her secretary, and I leave you to guess whether her activity overworks me. I assure you my aunt has in her the making of a statesman.

My dear friend, an incident of noteworthy importance, and of quite exceptional gravity, has just thrown me into the greatest perturbation of mind.

The other morning my aunt started upon a round of calls on behalf of her great enterprise.

"Andre," she said to me, "come with me like a good nephew; I need your help."

So off we started in the carriage, down the great drive of the chateau; I thinking that we were going to the doctor's, or else to the Camboulions. When we arrived at the gate, Bernard asked from his box for his orders.

"To El-Nouzha," said my aunt.

"What!" I exclaimed, "to Mohammed-Azis?"

"Yes," she replied; "His Excellency's name will look very nice on our list. It will be a sort of pledge of our excellent foreign relations."

"Have you forgotten? A Mahometan!"

"Certainly: an infidel's charity is quite as good in its effects

as a Christian's."

"But he lives a very retired life. Such a visit will take him very much by surprise."

"You are intimate with him; you introduce me. Nothing could be more correct; that's why I brought you with me."

In truth nothing could be more correct; I was caught in her trap, and could say nothing more, for fear of exciting suspicion in her alert and penetrating mind. I had no doubt in my own mind that my aunt's real object was to satisfy a curiosity which she had cherished for a long time past. How could I oppose this tenacious purpose of hers? By what plausible pretext could I divert her from taking a step so natural, and so cleverly justified? I was caught, and my only hopes rested in Mohammed's behaviour, and in his gibberish dialect, which would at least render conversation so difficult, that it would be easy for me to intervene. We rolled on in the carriage; my aunt was delighted. I succeeded pretty well in concealing my apprehensions. After all, the chief danger seemed to be over directly my aunt stopped at the official entrance of El-Nouzha. The "selamlik," inhabited by Mohammed, where we were received, is according to the Turkish custom, entirely separated from the harem, the gardens of which are walled off from it, and hidden from sight.

In a quarter of an hour we arrived in front of His Excellency's abode. The gate was shut, as it always is. The footman got down and rang, but no one answered the bell. For a moment I had hopes; but at the third ring of the bell (which my aunt ordered), one of Mohammed's servants, a Cerberus stationed on this side of the house, showed himself at the grating of the inner door.

"His Excellency Mohammed-Azis is at home, is he not?" shouted my aunt. "Tell him that Monsieur Andre de Peyrade has called to see him."

Recognising me in the carriage, Cerberus hesitated. He was actually going to open the gate to let the carriage pass through. I sharply commanded him to do as my aunt told him. To give Mohammed warning, was at once to put him on his guard.

"There is no need for taking the carriage in," said my aunt; "we will cross the lawn on foot. The lawn is there still, I suppose?"

"Yes, aunt."

"Well, then, give me your hand to get out, and now forward! If His Excellency will not receive us, I shall at least have had a glimpse of a corner of the park. What a funny idea it was of the Captain to let him this place!"

She led me on without any more ado, and we entered.

"Oh! the sycamores have grown splendidly," she said.

At that moment we noticed Mohammed coming down the steps, and walking towards us.

"Ah, His Excellency has not forsaken his old ideas!" said my aunt; "he still wears the costume of the true believers. As he is coming, let us hurry on, to be polite."

The danger was impending, nothing could now save me from it. I summoned up all my self-control. When I was a few steps off His Excellency, I slipped away quickly and ran up to him.

"Be careful," I said to him in a whisper; "it is my aunt. Keep your counsel, and don't let her suspect anything."

Then I went through the formal introduction, delivering it in the famous *sabir* which I told you of. Mohammed in the same idiom was fashioning a compliment as profound as it was difficult to understand, when my aunt all at once answered him in the purest Turkish.—I felt myself quite lost.

A minute afterwards we were ensconced in the drawing-room of the "selamlik." My aunt described the object of her visit. I must tell you that this rascal Mohammed played his part with the most affable gravity imaginable, albeit somewhat timidly, as if he felt whizzing through the air a shadowy reminder of the stick with which, no doubt, my uncle had trained him. I kept my eye on him all the time, and his eye wandered from me to my aunt with a distressed expression. Great drops of perspiration started from his face. Finally, at a sign from me, he generously promised his subscription, and on the whole got through the ordeal very well.

My anxieties being now removed, I was beginning to breathe more fully, when my aunt, just as the interview was coming to a close, expressed to him, in the most gracefully delicate manner possible, her desire to pay a visit to his daughters, whose acquaintance she would be delighted to make.

I was stupefied. To have refused the *entree* of the harem to a lady of my aunt's rank would have been an offence to her; she was too well acquainted with Mussulman customs for it to be possible to put her off with any pretext. Mohammed, still maintaining his dignified attitude, replied without any hesitation, by a gesture of delighted acquiescence, and without the least embarrassment got up, saying that he was about to inform them of their good fortune. I felt rather reassured. From the manner in which the old fellow had acted "His Excellency," it was clear that this was not the first time he had been called upon to "save the situation."

"You would like to follow me, I daresay," said my aunt with a laugh, as soon as he had left us.

"Why, of course," I replied, in a careless enough tone. "Still, if his daughters take after him, you will admit that it may be better to content myself with my illusions."

"You dear innocent boy! Why, with a Turk, you never know what to expect!"

Mohammed came back to tell my aunt that her visit had been announced, and then, preceding her with a dignified bow he opened for her the gates communicating with the harem. I remained behind. What would happen? Although the remarkable self possession of my eunuch had set me more at my ease, it was a critical moment. It was evident that there would be great excitement among my houris. They would feel at home gossiping with my aunt, as she spoke Turkish, and they would very likely let out everything. If one of them mentioned my name only, my aunt would guess it all.

I waited in a state of suspense such as you can imagine. Finally, after half-an-hour of cruel anxieties, the sound of the closed door in the neighbouring room informed me that I was about to know my fate. My aunt came in, and I did not dare look her in the face. Fortunately I gathered from her first words that I had nothing more to fear; she complimented Mohammed upon his good fortune as the father of such charming daughters, promising often to return to spend a few hours with them, and then at last we said "Good-bye" to His Excellency.

On our return, my aunt persisted in her eulogiums upon the young Turkish women, chaffing me about my long solitary period of waiting for her, separated only by a few walls from those pretty birds shut up in their golden cage. During the whole of luncheon she regaled my uncle with her description of these wonderful beauties. He kept looking at me from the corner of his eye with a furious expression.

As soon as I could escape, I ran off to El-Nouzha to question Mohammed about what had happened in the harem. He related the whole scene to me in detail. Nazli, Hadidje, and Zouhra were alone when he went to prepare them for my aunt's visit. As Koudje-Gul was reading in her room, she had not been informed of it. At the news of such a great event my houris screamed with joy. Trained as he had been by my uncle never to forget his part as the father, he had taken care to remind them that, in accordance with French usage, they must not allow it to be in the least suspected that they knew me. They promised to do as he wished them, swearing faithfully to keep all his commands. My aunt was then introduced. When they saw her, my houris rose up rather frightened, but she soon set them at ease with a kind word, and then conversation began. Needless to say, the countess's toilet formed the chief topic of discourse.

I will not try to depict for you the state of excitement in which I found my sultanas, nor the accounts which they had to give me themselves of this great event. Their sanguine imaginations were already occupied by the absolute necessity, as they deemed it, of returning my aunt's call. Her kindness had very naturally charmed them to the point of believing that no obstacle could arise to hinder the continuance of friendly relations so well inaugurated. They went on chattering all the evening about the incidents of this lucky and delightful event, taking particular pleasure in repeating before Koudje-Gul who had been absent (and whom they confidently hoped to exclude from their new relations), all the kind things which the pasha's wife had said to them. It was certainly a splendid revenge upon their rival for that evening escapade which she had boasted so much about.

Poor Kondje-Gul, disappointed as she was already at having

had no share in this unexpected treat, listened without a word, her sad eyes questioning me all the time. I reassured her with a nod, letting the silly creatures prattle away in their glee, and amuse themselves with sanguine projects of such a revolutionary character that it would have been impossible to discuss them.

I began to consider for myself the best way to cut short these unforeseen complications. Although I was out of danger for the present, the veil which concealed the secrets of El-Nouzha was only supported by a thread. My aunt was not the woman to remain long deceived, and with her quick mind, the slightest imprudent word, the slightest clue, would suffice to arouse her suspicions. I did not even feel sure but what my aunt, impelled by her curiosity, might be only too eager to exchange visits with His Excellency's daughters, and the very thought of this was enough to make me tremble.

The result of my cogitations was a resolve to take decisive measures for putting a stop to such extremely delicate and critical complications as I apprehended. It might, indeed, have been possible for me, while carefully mystifying every one, to have continued unabashed my oriental pursuits and avocations under the secure shelter of the walls of El-Nouzha. They represented, after all, nothing worse than one of those intrigues in the neighbourhood with which my aunt had herself credited me, but after this visit to the Kasre which had brought her into contact with my houris, the most ordinary respect for the proprieties required me to prevent such conjunctures from recurring. Moreover, our time at Ferouzat was drawing to a close, for we were to spend the winter in Paris. I therefore determined to anticipate our departure, and to remove my harem immediately. Once lost in the crowd and din of Paris, my secret would be safe.

The removal is now settled. A talk with my uncle simplified matters. As you may imagine, I had to explain to him the risks

entailed by such an occurrence as my aunt's visit, which might lead her mind to revert to some incidents in the Captain's past life which had so far remained unintelligible. Barbassou Pasha did not trouble himself very seriously about it, but he approved of my decision, and, contenting himself with a few growls at me by the way, affectionately proceeded to give me the assistance of his experience. It seems that he has—or rather I have—a house at Paris, which was furnished expressly for the use of His Excellency Mohammed Azis during my uncle's visits there. Orders have already been sent to have it ready. Then plausible reasons for my departure have been invented; some pretended business of importance, which we have been discussing several days past before my aunt, and which "might necessitate my presence in Paris." Truly my uncle's composure is wonderful!

As to my houris of El-Nouzha, I need hardly tell you that the coming journey has been the subject of a most extraordinary enthusiasm on their part. The idea of seeing Paris has quite turned their heads, and caused them to forget their proposed visits to Ferouzat. In order to put all conjectures off the scent, Mohammed is going to start to-morrow ostensibly for Marseilles, as if he were returning to Turkey. The cool November weather having set in, nothing could be more natural than this return to his native land. The end of his journey, however, will be the Faubourg St. Germain, to which he will direct his course by a circuitous route, and where I shall rejoin him on my arrival at Paris next week.

CHAPTER VII

The deed is done! We managed everything without the slightest hitch. I write to you from Paris, from our house in the Rue de Varennes; it seems like years since I was last there, so many things have happened during the six months since I left it. All my surroundings belong to a life so different from my present one, that it requires an exertion of thought to identify myself and realise my position here.

My harem is established in the Rue de Monsieur—in the former "Parc aux Cerfs" of my uncle—a splendid mansion, the gardens of which reach to the Boulevard des Invalides. My uncle has absolutely the genius of an ancient Epicurean transferred by accident into our own century. To look at the street, with its cold and deserted aspect, one might imagine oneself in a corner of aristocratic Versailles. My mystery is safely hidden away there. Mohammed while at Paris is no longer an exiled Minister, but simply a rich Turk who has acquired a taste for European civilisation. His name is Omer-Rashid-Effendi, a name under which he has already passed here twice.

My houris are astonished with all they see, and their pleasure is indescribable. Of course my first care was to Europeanise their toilettes. In pursuance of my orders (for, as you may be sure, I do not appear in such matters) a fashionable dressmaker was sent for by Mohammed. What a business it was! The difficulty was to avoid making them, with their oriental styles and deportments, look stiff and awkward when confined for the first time in the garb of our civilised torture-house.

By a happy compromise between fashion and fancy, the clever *artiste* has contrived for them costumes which are marvels of good taste and simplicity. Nothing could be more successful than this metamorphosis; their *coiffures* complete the picture, and I can hardly recognise my almees under the bewitching little hats worn by our Parisian women. I assure you it is a transfiguration replete with surprises and unexpected charms. Attired like our women of fashion, their striking and original beauty, which was my admiration at El-Nouzha, impresses me in quite a novel manner, which I seem to understand better as I compare them by the side of our own women. Like young foreign ladies of distinction habited in the costumes of our civilisation, they seem to shed around them wherever they go a sort of exotic fragrance.

Everything, of course, had to be changed now that they are in Paris; they could no longer follow the routine of their former existence within the four walls of the harem. They were now at liberty to go out walking, and take little trips; but here at once appeared a most serious difficulty for them to overcome. How could they show themselves in the streets, the Champs Elysees, or the Bois, without their veils just like infidels? That was a serious question! It was impossible for them to make up their minds to such a shameful breach of Mussulman law; and, if I must admit it, I myself experienced a strange sort of revulsion at the thought of it. Yes, to this have I come! Nevertheless, on the other hand, it was quite out of the question for them to shew themselves out of doors enshrouded in their triple veils, attracting wherever they went the remarks of the idle crowd.

At last, after a great many hesitations, Zouhra, who is the

bravest of them all, ventured to go out with me, buried in the recesses of a brougham, and protected by a very thick kind of mantilla, which after all was hardly any less impenetrable than a *yashmak*. Then they grew bolder, and impelled by curiosity, their coquetry getting the better of their bashful timidity, they took a drive one day in a landau to the Bois with Mohammed. I mounted on horseback and met them, without appearing to know them. Everything went off as well as could be.

The carriage which I had purchased is severely simple in style, as is suitable for a foreigner of distinction. In his European disguise Mohammed maintains that expression of serene dignity which so excellently suits his part of a father escorting his three daughters. There is, in short, nothing about the latter to excite attention. If a dark pair of eyes is sometimes distinguishable through the embroidered veils, the fashion, at any rate, permits the features to be sufficiently disguised to conceal the beauty of my sultanas from over-bold glances.

Of course poor Kondje-Gul, still living away from the others, does not take part in these frolics; but we thus gain some hours of liberty. On the second day, while my *wives* were driving in the Bois, we took our opportunity of going out, like true lovers, arm in arm; it was most delightful!

We went on foot to the Boulevards. You may guess what raptures Kondje-Gul was in each step we took. It was the first time she had been out with me alone, the first time she had felt herself free and released from the imprisonment of the harem. Many an inquisitive fellow, seeing us pass, and struck with her dignified manner, stopped of a sudden, and tried to distinguish her features through the veil. We quietly laughed at his disappointment.

When we arrived at the Rue de la Paix, we went into some of

the well-known jewellers' shops. At the sight of so many marvels, you may guess how she was dazzled. She felt as if in a dream. We spoke in Turkish; and the puzzled shop-keepers gazed in astonishment upon this strange display of Asiatic charms, which they had evidently met with for the first time. All this amused us; and it is unnecessary to add that I quitted these haunts of temptation with a considerably lighter purse than when I entered them.

We have already had several of these little sprees, and nothing can be more fascinating than Kondje-Gul's childish delight; everything is new to her. Transported, as if by magic, from her monotonous existence at El-Nouzha into the midst of these splendours, this free life, and this animated world, she feels like one walking in a dream; the whole atmosphere intoxicates her.

We form plans innumerable. In the first place we have decided that her position in regard to my wives shall be definitely fixed, and that she shall live henceforth separated from them in another part of the house, where she shall have private attendants. We shall thus be able to see each other without any constraint, and she will no longer be subjected to the sneers of my silly houris, who have been treating her apparent disgrace too brutally since our arrival at Paris. My proud Kondje-Gul, in the consciousness of her ascendency over me, would be sure to make a scene with them some day.

Besides, as I have already told you, she furnishes me every day with a more and more engrossing subject of study. I should like you to understand what sweet and seductive labour this progressive initiation is; I am watching the development of a mind which I am myself forming. There is no subject in regard to her, not even her receptive intelligence, which fails to afford me innumerable surprises. Sometimes I discover original views and opinions of hers upon matters connected with our European civilisation, at the correctness of which I am absolutely amazed. Her progress is surprising, and she wishes to learn everything, knowing how much is required in order to become "civilised," as she calls it.

My uncle and my aunt are in Paris.

A month without any news, you say. And you talk sarcastically about my leisure, and rally me upon the subject of that famous system, which I used to boast was a simplification of life. If I might judge from your twaddle, you imagine me to be saddled with the very cares and worries from which I justly boasted that I was exempt. You picture me running backwards and forwards, and incessantly occupied with my four wives, so that I have not even time to write to you.

Absurd fancy: this is my real situation.

As soon as my four wives were settled down in their new home, they permitted me much more freedom than did the least burdensome of my former amours. No anxieties now, no jealousies, no fears for the future. They are not like some of those feminine taskmasters who take entire possession of you, forcing you to follow the adored object to the theatre, or take it to the ball, in order to have the pleasure of watching it flirting bare-shouldered with some intimate friend, who will perhaps be its next lover. No, in my *role* of sultan my amours are modestly hidden from profane eyes in the recesses of my harem, and there I am always welcome whenever I choose to come. I keep the key in my pocket. At any hour of the day or night I can go there in my quality of owner without having to leave my club, my friends, my work, or my amusements a moment earlier than I desire.

Such, then, is the "anxious existence" which you attribute to me. Find me a husband who can act in the same way.

Still, as might have been foreseen, great changes have taken place in the internal arrangements of my household, where it became necessary that the Turkish elements should be partially replaced by others more adapted to the exigencies of western civilization.

A memorable event has occurred.

Hadidje, Nazli, and Zouhra went the other day to the opera. It is needless to say that I was there. I must admit that their nervousness was so extreme at making this bold experiment that, watching them from my own stall as they came in, I thought for a moment that they were going to run away again.

Already in their walks they were getting into training, and in regard to their veils exhibited a certain amount of coquetry; but now it became necessary to disregard the law of Mahomet entirely. They had never seen the inside of a theatre before, so you can imagine that when they found themselves in the box, with their unveiled faces exposed to the gaze of a multitude of infidel eyes, all the bold resolutions which they had made for this decisive effort were put to the rout. Strange as such Mohammedan bashfulness may seem to us, they felt, as they afterwards told me, that appearing there unveiled, was "just like exhibiting themselves naked."

However, as soon as this first impression was overcome, thanks chiefly to the exhortations of Mohammed, who was almost at his wits' ends to manage them, they succeeded in putting on sufficient assurance to dissemble their very sincere dread, so that at a distance it looked merely like excessive shyness. The lifting of the curtain for the first act of "Don Juan" fortunately changed the current of their emotions. During the *entr'acte* their box became the object of attraction to the subscribers and the frequenters of first night's performances. Their indolent, oriental type of beauty, notwithstanding the partial disguise effected by their present costumes, could not fail to produce a sensation.

Who, it was asked, was this old gentleman with his three daughters of such surprising beauty? In the Jockey Club's box, where I went to hear the gossip, everyone was talking about them, as of some important political event; Mohammed was an American millionaire, according to some, a Russian prince, or a Rajah just arrived from India, according to others. When I smiled in a significant manner (as I began to do, on purpose), they immediately surmised that I fancied I knew more about the matter than the rest of them, thereupon they surrounded me, and pressed me with questions.

I had already come to the conclusion that it would be better to calm their minds, and thus avoid all inconvenient enquiries. I therefore gave them an account, which after all was not far from the truth, namely, that Omer-Rashid-Effendi was a rich Turk, "whose acquaintance I had the honour of making at Damascus, and who had come to stay at Paris with his family." I thus insured myself against any suspicion of mystery arising in connection with my visits to the house in the Rue de Monsieur, in the event of these coming to light by any chance.

Our relations, you will see, were thus defined once for all. This new life is nothing but a succession of delights to my almees; and I have really now attained the ideal in the way of harems, through the absence of that monotony which is the inevitable result of the system of rigid seclusion. Under the influence of our civilized surroundings, the ideas of my houris are undergoing a gradual transformation. They have French lady's maids, and their study of our refinements of fashion has opened out quite a new world of coquettish charms to them. My "little animals" have grown into women: this single word will convey to you the whole delicious significance of this story of mine, the secret of which you alone in the whole world possess.

As we had decided, Kondje-Gul has been separated from her over-jealous companions. Hadidje, Zouhra, and Nazli have taken this measure to be a confirmation of her disgrace, and knowing that she lives in a sequestered corner of the house, they fancy their triumph more assumed than ever. I can place implicit confidence in the discretion of my servants—who wait on us like mutes in a seraglio: consequently Kondje-Gul and I are as free as possible. When I want to go out with her, I pay a short visit to my wives, and after a quarter of an hour's talk, leave them and go off in my carriage, in the recesses of which my darling reclines. Now you see what a simple device it is and how ingenious; still it involves a certain amount of constraint for me, and an isolation hard to endure for Kondje-Gul. She reads and devours everything that I bring her in the way of books; but the days are long, and Mohammed, with his time taken up by the others, cannot accompany her out of doors. I therefore conceived the idea of taking her away from the harem altogether, and thus relieving her of the contemptuous insults which my other silly women still find opportunities of inflicting upon her. The difficulty was to procure a chaperon for her, some kind of suitable and reliable duenna whom I could leave with her in a separate establishment; this duenna has been found.

The other day Kondje-Gul and I were talking together about a little house which I had discovered in the upper part of the Champs Elysees, and of an English governess, who seemed to me to possess the right qualifications for a pretended mother:

"If you like," said Kondje-Gul, "I can tell you a much simpler arrangement."

"Well?" I replied.

"Instead of this governess whom I don't know, I would much rather have my mother. I should be so happy at seeing her again!"

"Your mother?" I exclaimed with surprise; "do you know where she is then?"

"Oh, yes! for I often write to her."

She then told me all her past history, which I had never before thought of asking her, believing that she had been left alone in the world. It afforded me a complete revelation of those Turkish customs which seem so strange to us. Kondje-Gul's mother, as I have told you, was a Circassian, who came to Constantinople to enter the service of a cadine of the Sultan. Kondje-Gul being a very pretty child, her mother had, in her ambitious fancy, anticipated from her beauty a brilliant career for her. In order to realise this expectation, she left her at twelve years old with a family who were instructed to bring her up better than she could have done herself, until Kondje-Gul was old enough to be sought after as a cadine or a wife.

This hope on the part of her mother was accomplished, as you know, for the girl was purchased for a good round sum by Mohammed. Thus poor Kondje-Gul fulfilled her destiny. Then she related to me how her mother, several years ago, had found a better situation for herself with a French consul at Smyrna, and had learnt French there.

Kondje-Gul's idea was a happy one, and I was inclined to entertain it. I consented to her writing to Smyrna, and some days later she received an answer to the effect that in about a couple of months her mother would be able to join her providing the requisite means were sent her for this purpose. I have a house in view where they can live together. It is a little house belonging to Count de Teral, who is on his way back to Lisbon: one might really fancy he had got it ready on purpose for me.

What have you to say to this, you profound moralist?

CHAPTER VIII

Again you complain of my silence, in a letter written with the object of overwhelming me with abuse; and you mix up sarcasms (through which your childish curiosity is very transparent) with philosophical remarks which reveal the snobbishness of your nature. In fact, from the tone of your letters, one might imagine I was threatened by strange complications, and that you were hoping every morning to read the account of some catastrophe. For once in a way your longing for an important event will not be disappointed, for I have a weighty piece of news for you. As it belongs to the most strictly moral order of events, you may listen without any anxiety.

As you are aware, my aunt and uncle came to Paris a fortnight ago, and will stay here all the winter. The house in the Rue de Varennes has resumed its gay honours; we give receptions, dinners, and everything else that you are familiar with, but embellished this time by the presence of the charming Countess of Monteclaro, who supplies that lively element of family life which we rather missed formerly. My aunt has discovered here a young cousin of hers, Count Daniel Kiusko, a capital fellow, whom I have quite made friends with.

Having given you these details, I will now proceed with my story.

The other morning, after breakfast, as I was about to return to my room (for whatever you may believe, I am working hard just now), my uncle stopped me, and without any further preliminaries began:

"By the way, Andre, I expect Madame Saulnier and my god-daughter Anna Campbell, your betrothed, to dinner this, evening. I should not mind letting you make her acquaintance. If you happen to be curious to see her, don't make any engagements at the club, and come home punctually."

"Really!" exclaimed my aunt with a laugh, and without giving me time to answer: "from the way you put it, one might think you were talking of some doll that you intended to offer Andre for his birthday!"

"What the deuce do you mean by that, my dear?" asked the captain in his imperturbable way.

"I mean," said my aunt, "that this little acquaintance which you wish they should make with each other before you marry them, seems to me a very necessary preliminary."

"Pooh! They've still a good year before them! Besides, this little matter has nothing to do with romance." Then turning to me he continued; "Well, if that suits you for to-day, I have given you notice."

"Capital!" added my aunt. "Well, Andre! How does it suit you?"

"Why, aunt," I said, laughing in my turn at their little dispute; "I think my uncle may rely equally with you upon the pleasure it will give me."

"All right, that's settled!" continued my aunt in an inimitable tone of hilarity; "at seven o'clock punctually, my dear nephew, you will come and fall in love."

My uncle took no more notice of this last ironical shaft than of the rest, but occupied himself with selecting a cigar, remarking that what he had were too dry. My aunt availed herself of the opportunity of continuing her conversation with me.

"Between you and me," she said, "I may tell you that you are not much to be pitied, for she is a charming girl, and you would really lose a good deal by not making her acquaintance."

"I was only waiting for my uncle to decide the question."

"You must at any rate be grateful to him for letting you meet *by chance* before your wedding-day," she continued.

"Oh, dear! one might think I wanted to marry them at a minute's notice!" said my uncle at these words. "Just like a woman's exaggerations! Perhaps you would have liked me to have introduced her to him before my last voyage, when she was a lass of fourteen, thin, awkward, and gawkish, as you all are at that age."

"Thanks; why don't you say monkeys while you are about it?" replied my aunt with a curtsey.

But my uncle intended to make a speech of it, and continued:

"Who would have left in his mind the disagreeable recollection of a small, flat, angular creature, with arms like flutes, and hands and feet as long as that!"

"Poor little creature! I shudder at the thought of it! However, in your ineffable wisdom, you have fattened her up with mystery."

"Ta, ta, ta!" continued my uncle; "I have made a fine, healthy, solid young woman of her, who promises to make just the right sort of wife for Andre! And I maintain, in spite of your ideas on the subject, that I have done well to bring them up at a distance from each other, in order to preserve the freshness of their feelings, and avoid the necessity of that awkward and painful transformation of the affections which is so difficult for a couple who have grown up together and eaten their bread and butter together as brats in the nursery. To-day they will find each other just as they ought to before they become husband and wife. All the rest of the business must be left to them. If they like each other very much they will make a love-match, if not, a *mariage de raison*, which is just as good."

My uncle having concluded thus, it only remained for me to signify my compliance with his wishes. As you may well understand, I awaited with impatience the hour for this first interview, and I was in the drawing-room that evening some time before my *fiancee's* arrival. My aunt was in the heaven of delight, just like every woman looking forward to a romantic incident, and she did not fail to remark my eagerness. As to the captain, like a being superior to such sentimental trifles, he was quietly reading his paper. He was just commencing a political discussion when the servant opened the folding doors and announced:

"Madame Saulnier and Mademoiselle Campbell."

To tell the truth, I must admit that I felt somewhat nervous. A lady of about forty years old came in, accompanied by a young person in a regulation convent dress. I stood up, while my uncle went forward to meet his *god-daughter*, and kissed her affectionately on the forehead. Then he led me to her by the hand, in a dignified and ceremonious manner, and said without more ado:

"Anna, this is Andre! Andre, this is Anna! Kiss each other!"

This form of introduction, with its laconic precision, had at least the advantage that it left no uncertainty between us, and at once indicated to us our proper course of procedure. Too well trained to my uncle's habits, I did not hesitate a moment, but kissed my betrothed; after which I said, "How do you do?" which, of course, gave me a nice opportunity of looking at her.

Anna Campbell is at the present time just seventeen. She is neither short nor tall, thin nor stout—although the great blue ribbon which she wears over her neck, with a cross suspended from it, already sets off the plump outlines of her bosom. She is neither fair nor dark; her chin is round, her face oval, her nose, mouth, and forehead are all medium-sized, and she has rather pretty blue eyes. Generally speaking, she is more pleasant-looking than handsome, and her features on the whole suggest a very gentle disposition united with good health. My uncle took care to impress upon me that she will continue to develop, since her feet and hands are still large for her age, and promise a handsome completion of her growth.

In short, my lot is far from a disagreeable one—quite the contrary. As my uncle expresses it, "All the symptoms are good."

Our dinner was a very lively one. Anna Campbell, although rather subdued in my presence, did not show any embarrassment. Nothing seemed to be new to her; her manners and deportment, and everything about her, revealed the familiar assurance of a child of the family who had come to take a holiday there, and felt herself as much at home as I did. I perceived that she knew the house as well as if she had been brought up in it, and I learnt that during the time when I was at college she and Madame Saulnier had really lived there for three years.

The result of all this was that Anna Campbell exhibited a pleasant sort of familiarity with my aunt and uncle which I did not at all expect to see. Brought up away from each other, and without any previous acquaintance, we were now meeting for the first time at this common centre of our affections, which, unknown to us, had united us since our childhood. This was both original and sweet to think of.

Once, when my uncle asked for the pickles, Anna said:

"They are near Andre."

When the meal was over we left the dining-room. Following a Russian fashion which my aunt had introduced among us, when we entered the drawing-room, I pressed her hand to my lips, while she kissed me on the forehead. Anna did the same; then, without even appearing to think what she was doing, she quietly held up her two cheeks for me to kiss, and afterwards offered them to her godfather. She then ran to the piano, and sat down to it, while we were taking our coffee.

"Well, what do you think of her?" my uncle asked me.

"She is very nice," I replied.

"Yes, isn't she? Just the thing for you, my boy," he observed, as he stirred his cup, with the tranquillity of a pure conscience. "Go and talk with her," he continued; "you will find she is not stupid."

I went to sit down by Anna.

"Come, play the bass!" she said, moving aside to make room for me, as if we had often played in duet together before.

When the piece was finished, we talked about her convent, her friends, and the Mother Superior, Sainte Lucie, whom she was much attached to; and she spoke about everything in a confident tone of familiarity, which showed me that she had often talked of me, and had been used to think of me as an absent brother. The understanding is that, on account of her youth, our betrothal is to remain a family secret, which will only be made public when the right time arrives.

The evening concluded without any other special incident. At ten o'clock Anna went home to her convent. As she was putting her things on, she held out her hand to me, and said:

"Good-bye, Andre!"

"Good-bye, Anna!" I replied; and then my uncle took me away with him to the club, where he sat down to his party at whist.

While I am on the subject of my uncle, I must tell you about an adventure which he has just had. He is *dead*, as you are aware, for I have inherited his property. This privilege he will not give up, *because the registration fees have been paid*. The result of this peculiar situation is that he is under certain legal incapacities, which, without troubling him more seriously, do nevertheless cause him some annoyance. Three months ago at Ferouzat, he had to renew his gun-license, which he had taken out seven years before; but as his decease had been formally entered at the prefecture, they would not accept this document, bearing the signature of a defunct person. As you may imagine, he did very well without it, and began to shoot as if nothing had happened!

The other morning, however, it chanced, as my uncle was passing our banker's, that he wanted to draw twenty thousand francs for his pocket-money. The cashier, who had known him years ago, was very much surprised to see him in the

flesh, but represented to him that it was now quite impossible for him to open an account in his name, as he was legally dead and buried. My uncle, like a law-abiding man, admitted the justice of this observation, and I had to intervene in order to arrange the matter for him. He took no further notice of it; only as he never does anything by halves, he had his visiting cards printed with "The late Barbassou" on them; and this was the way he signed himself at our banker's, by which means he pretended that he conformed with all requirements.

"You see how simple the whole thing is," he said to me.

My amours with Kondje-Gul have certainly taken a very remarkable turn. The other day I took her to Versailles for an educational and historical excursion; she is continuing her course of civilization, you know. After visiting the palace and the museum, we went into the park. She was in the best of spirits, still excited with the fresh air and freedom which she was enjoying like an escaped prisoner from the harem, and was asking me questions about everything with that charming simplicity of hers which delights me so much, when we arrived in front of Diana's Bath, where we found a group of three young women most brilliantly dressed, two of whom, as I saw at the first glance, were old acquaintances of mine, very well known in the gay world. Young Lord B— accompanied them, and they all recognised me; but Lord B—, with the well-bred tact of a man of the world, seeing the company I was in, only nodded slightly to me. With like discretion, as is usual on such occasions, the women made no movement of recognition; yet they could not help—being struck no doubt with the remarkable beauty of my companion—evincing such evident curiosity, that Kondje-Gul observed it. I, of course, passed without appearing to notice them. Kondje-Gul and I then took a turn up the walk, while I expounded the mythology of the bath to her, and then we went out.

"Who are those ladies?" she asked me as soon as we were at a good distance from them; "they know you, I could see."

"Oh, yes," I replied in an indifferent tone, "I have met them several times."

"And the young man who was with them also looked at you as if he was one of your friends; why did not you speak to him?"

"For discretion's sake, because you were with me, and he was walking with *them*."

"Ah! I understand," she said; "no doubt they are the women of his harem?"

"Just so," I answered quite coolly, "and, as I have often told you, according to our customs, the harem is always—"

I was trying to think of the right word, when she burst out laughing quite loud.

"What are you laughing at, you silly thing?" I asked.

"I am laughing at all those stories about your harems which you still make up for me just as you used to do for that idiot Hadidje. I listen to them all, because,—whatever does it matter to me now that I love you! I prefer the happiness of remaining your slave to that of these women, who have no doubt been your mistresses, and whom you don't even condescend to notice when you meet them."

"What?" I exclaimed in astonishment; "have you got to know so much already, you little humbug, and have concealed it from me?"

"After all you have given me to read to form my mind

according to your ideas, surely it was natural that I should some day discover the truth! I only waited for an opportunity of confirming my new knowledge," she continued with a smile. "There are still a lot of things in your country which I cannot understand. But you will teach me them now, won't you?" she added in a coaxing tone.

"Oh, you young flirt! It seems to me you know everything already!"

"Why, yes, I feel I know that, for all you may say, I am still no more than a curious toy in your eyes—a strange creature, like some rare bird that you are rather fond of, perhaps, for her pretty plumage."

"Ah! you're right upon the last point at any rate!" I replied with a laugh.

"Yes, sir!" she continued in a satisfied tone of pride, "I know that I am handsome!—Now don't laugh at me," she added with a charming reproachful look; "what I have to say is quite serious, for it comes from my heart. I was born for a different life, for different sentiments to yours, and I know that I possess none of those qualities which they say make the women of your country so attractive. Their ideas and associations are very different to mine, which you call the superstitions of a young barbarian, and which I want to forget in order to learn to understand you and to have no rivals."

"Are you quite sure that you would not lose by the change?"

"Thank you," said Kondje-Gul; "that's what I call a compliment."

"The fact is," I replied, "the very thing I like about you is that you do not in any way resemble the women whom we have just met."

"Oh!" she said, with an indescribable gesture of pride, "it's not *those* women I envy! But I see others whom I would like to resemble—in their manners and tone, of course. If you're a nice fellow, do you know what you will do for me?"

"What?"

"It's a dream, a scheme which I have been continually thinking over. You won't laugh at me, will you?"

"No. Let's hear your grand scheme."

"Well, then, if you would like to make me very happy, place me for a few months in one of those convents where your young ladies are educated. You would come and see me every day, so that I should not be too dull away from you."

"That's the queerest idea I have ever heard from you; fancy a Mahommedan girl at a convent!" I said, with a laugh.

I took a great deal of trouble in explaining to her what a foolish project this was; but the result of my attempts at demonstrating the serious obstacles which such ambitious aspirations would encounter, was that in the end I myself entered into her views. The experiment might indeed prove a most instructive one. With Kondje-Gul's character, there was an extremely interesting psychological experiment before me. I had found her to be endowed with marvellous natural qualities. With her ardour and enthusiasm, what would be the effect upon her simple imagination of a sudden transition from the ideas of the harem to the subtle refinements of our own society?

Certainly, I was obliged to admit that such a trial was not without its dangers; but then, was not Kondje-Gul already aware that the marital yoke which my houris still believed in was only imaginary? And was it not better, such being the case, for me to complete this work of regeneration, the fruits of which I should in the end reap for myself?

So I submitted to Kondje-Gul's wishes, and as soon as we returned to Paris this important matter was settled.

The next day I began to look for the means of carrying it into execution, a search which was attended, however, with a good many difficulties.

CHAPTER IX

My uncle is going to send for another of my aunts to come to Paris.

Well! what of that?—My uncle is a Mussulman, you know; and, being a man of principle, his duties are more onerous than yours, that's all!

My services were required to take a little house at Passy, where she is to live. I wonder whether it is my aunt Gretchen, my aunt Euphrosine, or my aunt Cora? He has not given me the slightest hint on this point.

While awaiting this addition to our family, Barbassou-Pasha pursues his eccentric career in a manner that beats description. This visit to Paris has brought out more than ever the quaint independence of his character. One is reminded of a man who stands on a bridge watching the river flow by, but now and then takes a header into it to cool himself. The other day at the club, he lost sixty-three thousand francs to me at baccarat, just for a little distraction. The evening after, he was entertaining at our house his late Lieutenant Rabassu, whom he always speaks of as "the cause of his death," and who has come here upon some business. He won eleven francs from him at piquet, playing for a franc the hundred points. For the moment I felt quite alarmed for the poor victim! But my mind was soon set at ease; for

Rabassu, who is used to his captain's play, knows how to cheat as cleverly as his master. Their losses soon balanced each other.

Putting aside little dissipations of this kind, I should add that "the late Barbassou" is really very steady-going for a man of his temperament. He takes everything which comes in the routine of our fashionable life so naturally, that nobody would imagine he had spent several years at the hulks in Turkey.

My aunt Eudoxia, of whom he stands in wholesome awe, and who keeps him in check, forces him to cultivate the vanities of this world. He escorts her to balls and fetes with all that ceremony with which you are familiar; and quitting the lofty regions of his own philosophical existence, without however permitting anything to disturb his self-possession, he goes forth into the gay and hurried throngs of Paris with as little concern as he would into any village street. In short, he is in exquisite form, and—but for the legal disabilities which deprive him of his rights of citizenship—you would find him still exactly what he was when you knew him five years ago.

However, the other day he received a little shock in connection with a very simple incident, which might have been perfectly anticipated.

We were in my aunt's box at the Opera. The pasha, seated by her side, was listening to a singer who was rather more buxom than elegant; and he appeared to be calculating what her nett weight would be, after making deduction for her queen's crown and robes of state. After a minute or so, he seemed to have solved this equation and lost all further interest in the problem, for he began to examine the audience. All of a sudden he shouted out, quite forgetting himself, in his Provencal brogue:

"*Te!* What's that I see?"

"Hush!" said my aunt, nudging him with her elbow, without turning round.

"But, *bagasse!* it's Mohammed!" he added, in a lower tone.

It was indeed Mohammed, who attracted some attention as he walked with my houris into their famous box.

"Well, you're right," replied my aunt. "I recognise his charming daughters."

You may be sure my uncle put up his glasses. When all my people were settled down in their box, he surveyed them carefully, interrupting his examination occasionally in order to take a furtive scowl at me. But my aunt's presence kept him quiet. His composure was perfect for that matter, except that he seemed extremely puzzled. There were only three of them—that evidently was not the right number for him. As for me, prudence dictated that I should get out of the way as quickly as possible, leaving him to make what observations he pleased.

As I was slipping away quietly to the back of the box, I heard my aunt saying:

"Are you going to speak to him?"

"No; we have had a quarrel!" he growled, looking again for me at his side.

But slam went the door, and I was out in the passage, whence I escaped to the back of the scenes and to the green-room. There he joined me during the *entr'acte*. But, as you are aware, "Turks do not discuss harem matters." All I could see clearly was that he was in a fury with me.

To turn, however, to other things, my perseverance on behalf of Kondje-Gul is at last rewarded with complete success.

After I had spent a whole week in looking about, I found, in the Beaujou district, an institution for young ladies presided over by a Madame Montier, a kind woman of polished manners. She had suffered a reverse of fortune, which seems to have prepared her for the express purpose of civilizing my Kondje-Gul. There are never more than three or four boarders in the house: at the present moment two American girls, daughters of a commodore who is on a mission to the King of Siam, are finishing their education there. Nothing could suit my purpose better.

When the time arrived, however, for putting my plan into execution, I must confess that I could not help feeling considerable embarrassment. I could certainly have introduced Kondje-Gul as a young foreign lady, prematurely widowed, who was anxious to qualify herself for French society; but I soon found that this would create an unnecessary complication. Decidedly the better course would be for Mahommed to introduce her either as his ward or his daughter. Under any circumstances it was desirable that I should explain to her the necessity of extreme prudence.

At last, one evening, when I thought she was about to revert to this great object of her ambition, I started the subject myself.

"I am going to announce an important piece of news," I said to her; "I have found a convent for you where you can stay pending your mother's arrival."

"Really!" she exclaimed, kissing me. "Oh, my dear Andre, how kind you are!"

"Yes; but I must warn you. This realisation of your dream is only possible at the cost of sacrifices, which will perhaps be hard for you to make."

"What sacrifices? Tell me, quick!"

"First, assiduous work, and next, the sacrifice of your liberty; for during the whole time you remain at this establishment, you won't be able to leave the place."

"What does that matter?" she exclaimed, "provided I can see you every day!"

"But that's exactly what will be impossible."

"Why?" she asked, in her simplicity.

"Because, according to our customs, bachelors are never admitted into young ladies' schools," I replied, with a laugh.

"But as I belong to you," she continued, with an astonished look, "they will not be surprised at your coming; are not you my master?"

"This reason, my dear, although a convincing one for you, would constitute the greatest obstacle; for they must not be allowed on any account to suspect that you are my wife. Mohammed alone will introduce you either as his daughter or as a young lady under his charge, and, for conventional reasons, which you will understand later on, this period of study will be a period of separation for us."

I then let her know the whole truth about certain of our social conventionalities, concerning which she was still in ignorance. When she learned that our laws declared her free, and the equal of any Frenchwoman, and that I had no longer any rights over her, she looked inexpressibly pained.

"Good heavens!" she exclaimed, throwing herself into my arms, "what do you mean? Am I free, and my own mistress, and not yours for ever?"

"You are mine, because I love you," I said to her very quickly, seeing her agitation; "and so long as you do not *want* to leave me—"

"Leave you! But what would become of me, then, without you?"

And her eyes filled with tears.

"What a foolish girl you are!" I replied, quite touched at her evident pain; "you are exaggerating the significance of my words: your liberty will make no difference in our relations."

"Why did you tell me this cruel truth, then? I was so happy in the belief that I was your slave, and in obeying and loving you at the same time."

"Still it was necessary for me to tell you, as you wish to learn our ideas and customs. Your ignorance was a source of danger, for even your questions might lead to the betrayal of relations which must remain a mystery for the rest of the world, and, above all, in the 'pension,' where you are about to live with companions."

I had some difficulty in consoling her for this terrible discovery that our laws do not recognise slavery. Nevertheless, her desire for further instruction remained very keen.

Finally, two days afterwards, Mademoiselle Kondje-Gul entered Madame Montier's institution, having been presented by her guardian, the worthy Omer-Rashid-Effendi, who made all the necessary arrangements with the majestic dignity which he displays on every occasion.

Although I have kept myself carefully in the background in all this matter, I watch its progress just the same, and superintend everything. Every evening Kondje-Gul writes to her guardian, and I get her letters at once: I can assure you they constitute quite an interesting romance. For a whole week Kondje-Gul, who had been rather overawed at first and astonished at all her new surroundings, seemed to live like one dazed. She would not trust herself to speak, fearing to appear uncultivated; but she observed, and the results of her observations were most curious. After that I perceived that she was gradually trying her wings; for when she had been initiated a few days into her new life, she soon abandoned her reserve, and has by this time passed the first step in her emancipation. Her simplicity of character, and her quaint Oriental manners, have secured her some very cordial friendships; and nothing can be more charming than the accounts she gives me of her devotion for her friends, Maud and Suzannah Montague, who are the realisation of perfection in her eyes.

Of course Kondje-Gul's educational programme, as fixed by me, is confined within very modest limits. It consists of music, history, and a slight and general acquaintance with literature. But above all she is expected to acquire that indispensable familiarity with our ideas, and those feminine graces and refinements which can only be learnt by contact with women and girls brought up in good society. A few months at Madame Montier's will be sufficient for this purpose, and the cultivation of her mind can be completed later on by private lessons.

My harem in the Faubourg St. Germain retains its Oriental aspect; it is a corner of the world described in the "Arabian Nights," where I indulge from time to time, in the midst of Paris, in the distractions of a vizier of Samarcand or Bagdad. There, when the shutters are closed, in my *gynaeceum* (or women's apartment), illuminated by lamps which shed a soft

lustre upon us, while the bluish-grey smoke from my narguile perfumes the atmosphere, my houris lull me to sleep to the music of their taraboucks.

With all this I am not quite so satisfied, as I would have liked to describe myself, with certain incidents which have occurred in connection with my harem. Certainly, they are all the natural consequences of our life in Paris; for I don't suppose you imagine that I had not foreseen the psychological effect which entirely new ideas would unavoidably produce upon the profoundly ignorant minds of my houris. Besides, a progressive and judicious emancipation from their previous restraints formed part of my programme for them. But the introduction into the harem of certain high-class lady's-maids, indispensable for initiating my little animals into the subtle mysteries of Parisian toilets, has of necessity led to their making a number of discoveries, which have contributed in a remarkable degree to their civilization:—hardly, however, in those elements which I could have most desired. They have all of them got to know a great deal more than was necessary for them about those famous "customs of our harems in France," the principles of which I had endeavoured to teach them. Thus I even noticed the other day that I set Zouhra and Nazli laughing when I reminded them of some point of etiquette. Although they are still imbued with the good principles of their native education, it is evident they are being corrupted by the poison of Liberalism. This I am convinced of by certain airs of assurance which they have put on, by their coquetries, and by novel and unexpected caprices which they now display.

The "Rights of Woman" have clearly been divulged to them. They talk of walking out by themselves, of visiting the popular theatres and music-halls, and even Mabille, the illuminations of which struck their fancy very much the other night, as we were passing the Avenue Montaigne in the carriage, on our way back from the Bois. One little instance will illustrate the situation for you. Mohammed's rank and titles have ceased to impress them with any respect; and the day before yesterday Zouhra actually had the impudence to say "Chut!" to him.

This expression will clearly indicate to you an astonishing progress in the refinements of our language; but it will also, no doubt, afford you a text upon which to declaim in that cruelly sarcastic style which your Philistine genius revels in. I will, therefore, anticipate you by replying:

In the first place, that Mohammed does not understand French—a fact which considerably diminishes the gravity of Zouhra's disrespect;

In the second, that I never doubted but what their stay in Paris would open my houris' minds to new ideas;

And in the third, that neither did I doubt but what they would acquire, in consequence, more precise notions upon the extent of their rights.

Woman, like any other animal susceptible of education, possesses the most subtle faculties of imitation. Now if, her weak nature being overcome by those impulses towards mischief and malice with which she is peculiarly endowed, she is tempted to commit trivial derelictions of conduct— derelictions which, after all, are but faults of discernment—is there any reason why we should make such a fuss about it?

In the midst of the supremely refined existence which my sultanas lead, I seem to discover in these innocent little vagaries a frank simplicity of character, more nearly related to purity of conscience than are the accomplished manners of our most polished coquettes.

While on this subject I must reply to the sarcasms contained in your last letter.

Let me tell you first of all that I have never laid claim to the character of a superior being inaccessible to human vanities, as you are trying to make out. I am quite willing to admit with you that I, like any other man, am possessed by "the stupid satisfaction which every man experiences in watching the success of the woman he loves." It is quite possible that the effect produced by my odalisques upon the idle crowd (or as you term it *la haute badauderie*) of Paris, has suddenly invested them with new charms in my eyes. You say that the mystery with which they are enshrouded, and the silly conjectures which I hear people make about them as they pass by, have excited me and turned my head like that of a simpleton.

Well, I suppose you will hardly expect me to account for the human weakness which leads us to measure our own happiness by the degree of envy which it excites in others? Besides, what is the good of sifting my passion or testing my love in a crucible in order to estimate its value?

In the midst of my pagan indulgences, you ask me if I really love, in the usual sense of that word. This very reasonable question was at any rate worth asking, however simple it may seem. It is concerned with the great problem in psychology which I undertook to solve, namely, as to which predominates in love, the heart or the senses, and whether true love is possible when one loves four women at the same time?

It is clear that in the restricted limits of our ideas, and under the yoke of our customs and prejudices, we can only conceive of passion as concentrated upon a single object. Too far removed from our primitive origin and from the patriarchal age, and moulded by the influences of more refined customs, our minds have been stimulated to the contemplation of a certain recognized ideal. Still, as moralists and philosophers, we must admit that among Orientals there is, doubtless, another conception and another ideal of love, the character of which we cannot grasp. It is only by divesting ourselves of our moral clogs, or the restraints of our social conventionalities, that we can attain to the understanding of this lofty psychological problem. Indeed, no one has ever been able to say what love consists in. "Attraction of two hearts," say some, and "mutual exchange of fancies;" but these are nothing but words depending upon the particular instance in which they are employed.

The truth is that we are full of inconsistencies in all our definitions. From a purely sentimental point of view, we start by laying down, as an absolute axiom, that the human heart can only embrace one object of love, and that man can only fall truly in love once in his life. Yet if we abstract from love the distinct element which our senses contribute to it, it is seen to consist of nothing but a form of affection—an expansion of the soul analogous to friendship and to paternal or filial love, sentiments equally powerful, but which we recognize the duty of distributing between several objects.

Whence arises this strange contradiction?

Do not declare that it is a paradox, for our ideas on the subject proceed entirely from our education and from the influence of custom upon our minds. If we had been bred on the banks of the Ganges, of the Nile, or of the Hellespont, our school of aesthetics would have been different. The most romantic Turkish or Persian poet could not understand the vain subtleties of our emotions. Since his laws permit him several wives, it is his duty to love them all, and his heart rises to the occasion. Do you mean to tell me that his is a different love to ours? Upon what grounds? What do you know about it? Cannot you understand the charms of the obligation he is under to protect them all, in this equal distribution of his affections? It comes to this, in fact, that our ideas on the point are simply and always a question of latitude and of climate. We love like poor helpless creatures of circumstances.

It is these very psychological considerations which form the basis of the social argument which I intend to demonstrate in the important work which I am preparing for the Academy of Science, and which I introduce as follows:—

"Revered Mother,

"Among the learned and celebrated members of whom your illustrious Society so justly boasts, the most competent have already determined to their satisfaction the general principles which should regulate the study of biology. It would be the height of presumption on my part to set up my unworthy opinion against theirs, were it not for the fact that I can adduce, as a justification for doing so, certain data in my own possession which very few, probably, of these highly-respected authorities could have procured under such favourable conditions as I have been enabled to do. As the nephew of a Pasha I have, &c."

As you perceive, this modest preface is well calculated to soothe the delicate susceptibilities of the Institute.

The civilization of my Kondje-Gul has become quite the most delightful subject of study for me. It presents a complete romance in itself, and the denial which I have imposed upon myself adds a certain charm to it. I must tell you that her stay with Madame Montier has gradually produced a number of unforeseen complications. Commodore Montague has returned; one of the consequences of which is that the intimacy between the Misses Maud and Suzannah Montague and the ward of worthy Omer-Rashid-Effendi, which has seemed to him a most desirable one, has been so much encouraged that they have become inseparable, and Kondje-Gul has of course been invited by her young friends to entertainments given by their father—invitations which she has been unable to decline for fear, thereby, of arousing suspicions.

Discretion on my part, you will thus perceive, has become more than ever necessary, so long as Kondje-Gul remains with Madame Montier. Our amorous relations are absolutely reduced to epistolary effusions, and to clandestine meetings, to bring about which we have recourse to all the stratagems employed by separated lovers. There is a certain piquancy in these adventures which affords us much delight—so true is it that the deprivation of a pleasure enhances its value. In the morning Kondje-Gul takes riding-lessons in the Bois with Maud and Suzannah, who are accompanied by their father. I sometimes take a canter that way, in order to watch their party ride by. She looks charming in her riding-habit, and the Montague girls are really very pretty, especially Maud, who has a pert little playful expression which is very fascinating.

I forgot to tell you that Kondje-Gul's mother, Murrah-Hanum, has arrived. She is a woman of forty-five, tall, with a distinguished bearing, and rather handsome still. Yet although she has been Europeanized by her residence at the French consul's at Smyrna, and speaks our language almost with fluency, she retains in her manners all the peculiarities of the Circassian and the Asiatic; she has an easy-going and indolent temperament, and in her large dark eyes you can read the stern resignation of the fatalist races. When she appeared before me, she lavished upon me, in Oriental fashion, the most ardent expressions of devotion. I assured her of my desire to secure to her a share in all the advantages which I wished to confer upon Kondje-Gul. She expressed her gratitude with calmness and dignity, and swore to observe towards me the submissive obedience which she owed to her daughter's husband. In short, you can picture the interview for yourself; it was characterized by all the florid effusiveness of Mahommedan greetings.

CHAPTER X

I don't suppose you will be astonished at a curious encounter which has just taken place.

I must tell you that in my uncle's character while in Paris, Barbassou-Pasha, General in the Turkish cavalry, predominates over Captain Barbassou the sailor. He takes a ride every morning, and I of course accompany him. These are our occasions both for intimate talks and for discussing serious questions; and I beg you to understand that my uncle's notions upon the latter are by no means ordinary ones. He adorns such questions with quite original views—views which are certainly not the property of any other mortal known or likely to be known in this world below. He starts a subject for me, and I give him the cue as well as I can. I know of nothing more instructive than to follow his lines of argument—he has a separate one for each subject—upon different departments of private and political life, judged from his own standpoint. As a legislator I fancy he would commit radical mistakes; but as a philosopher, I doubt very much if a match could be found for him, for I don't think that his methods can be compared with those of any existing school of thought.

The other morning we went to the forest of Mendon; my uncle, as a lover of the picturesque, considers that the Bois de Boulogne, with its lake, looks as if it had been taken out of a box of German toys. We arrived at Villebon, a sort of farm situated in the middle of the forest, with a few fields attached to it. There is a restaurant there, which is much frequented on Sundays during the summer.

My uncle, enchanted with the place, wanted to stop and take his glass of madeira there. So, leaving our horses in charge of a stable-boy, we went into one of the rooms. At a table at the further end, quite a stylish-looking woman, who looked as if she were out with somebody on the spree, was sitting by herself, finishing a liqueur-ice, with her hat off and lying by her side. Her figure, as viewed from the back, was exquisite, with graceful and well-set shoulders, an elegantly poised neck with a lovely little dimple on the nape, crowned by a luxuriant chignon, from which emerged a profusion of rebellious tresses—.

"Waiter! Madeira, please!" shouted my uncle in his formidable bass voice.

At this unexpected explosion, the strange lady jumped up from her chair and looked suddenly round. But directly she saw the captain, she screamed out and fainted away all at once.

I must do my uncle the justice of admitting that when he noticed the remarkable effect he had produced, he exhibited a slight gesture of surprise; which, however, soon passed off. Without calling any help, in four strides he reached the lady's side, and supported her against the table, raising up her pretty head which had fallen back, and slapping her hands. Then, having satisfied himself that she had completely lost consciousness, he began without any more ado to unfasten her dress, tore open her collar, and, with admirable dexterity, unhooked the upper part of her stays—thereby revealing to our gaze two charming globes, imprisoned in lace.

This spectacle, I avow, might have made any other man pause in his zealous operations,—not so my uncle, however; he did not think twice about it, but with his usual unconcerned air proceeded to open out the fair one's stays, then took up the water-bottle, and emptied it with one dash into the hollow between her rounded charms.

A convulsive start, and another scream, indicated immediately the successful effect of this triumphant measure.

"There!" he said to me, "you see that's all that was needed."

Just at this moment the gentleman who belonged to the lady came in. It is hardly necessary to add that when he saw my uncle occupied upon a business so distinctly his own, the new-comer evinced some temper.

"*Bon Dieu!*" he shouted out as he rushed forward, "What's the meaning of this? What's the meaning of this?"

"Nothing serious!" answered the pasha. "Your lady has simply been in a swoon, nothing more; it's all over now!"

"But what have you been about, sir? What do you mean by throwing water like that, right upon people's bosoms—?"

"It was all to do you a service," replied this saviour, quite composedly.

The lady, for her part, looked as if she was going off in another fit, but my uncle, judging no doubt that he had fulfilled his part of the duties, and without troubling himself any further about the mingled alarms and stares of the people of the house who came up, made one of his ceremonious bows to the whole company, and took me away with him, saying,

"Come, let us drink our madeira."

So we went out.

Being accustomed to Barbassou-Pasha's ways, I was certainly not surprised at such a trifle as this. The waiter having served us, ten minutes had elapsed, and while we were discussing the irreparable loss of the Xerez and Douro vines, all of a sudden the door opened. It was the lady's cavalier, and he came in raging like a storm.

"*Bagasse!*" he exclaimed with a furious look, and his hair bristling up like a porcupine. "But you won't get off quite so easily as that, sir! Who ever heard of such a thing? Undressing a defenceless woman like that, and quite a stranger too!! Not to mention that you have spoilt her dress, which looks as if she had been under the pump!"

His words rolled on like a torrent, in the purest Provencal accent. This made my uncle smile, as if at some pleasant reminiscence; and putting on his most engaging expression, he asked the new-comer in a gentle tone of voice:

"What are you to this lady?"

"She is my sister-in-law, sir!" he replied in a fury, his voice swelling louder and louder: "She is my brother's wife, sir; and he's no fool, no more am I, sir!—Twenty-one years of service, eleven campaigns, and sub-lieutenant of the Customs at Toulon, sir!—So you shall just let me know how it was my sister-in-law fainted through your fault; and what you meant by taking the liberty of exposing her in a way that no decent man would be guilty of, not even with the consent of her family, nor if she were in mortal danger of her life, sir!"

"And where do you live?" continued my uncle, sipping his madeira, and still fixing upon the fair one's brother-in-law the same charming gaze.

"Hotel des Bouches-du-Rhone, Rue Pagevin. I am escorting my sister-in-law, and I am responsible for her to her husband."

"My compliments to you, sir! She is a charming young person."

This magnificent composure of my uncle's so completely disconcerted the lieutenant of the Customs that he stopped short. But he had been carried on too far by his hot meridional temper not to launch out again very soon. He followed up with a perfect flood of abuse, interlarded with the most approved insults, with violent epithets and noisy oaths. My uncle listened to him quietly, stroking his chin, and contemplating him as if watching the performance of some surprising feat. The Toulonnais said that he considered this fainting fit of his sister-in-law's, and the very unceremonious proceedings which had followed it, equally suspicious and irregular.

"My brother's honour has been outraged," and so on, he observed.

But at last the good fellow was obliged to pause in order to take breath. Barbassou-Pasha took advantage of the opening.

"Pray what is *your* name?" he asked, still smiling affably.

"My name, my good man," loftily replied the man of Toulon, "is Firmin Bonaffe, lieutenant in the Customs, seen twenty-one years of service and eleven campaigns. And if that is not enough for you—"

"Why, dear me! then this charming young person has married your brother, has she?"

"A week ago, sir, at Cadiz, where she lives! It was because he had to go back over the sea to Brazil that he confided her to my charge. And you must not imagine that I can let your outrageous behaviour to her pass without further notice, sir!"

"You are a man of spirit, sir, that I can see!" replied my uncle. He was gradually falling into his native *assent*, charmed, no doubt, by the soothing example of his adversary. "I can understand your feelings," he continued; "and for my part, my good fellow, I confess I should not have the slightest objection to taking a sabre and slicing off a piece of your person." (He uttered this latter word, *individu*, in French, with the Marseillais pronunciation, *inndividu*.) "Indeed," he continued quite placidly, "I should have no objection to throwing you through the window here, just as you are."

This, following upon his imperturbable coolness throughout, had, I can aver, a most aggravating effect. Being a little man and a braggart, Firmin Bonaffe felt the insult all the more hotly.

"Throw me through the window? *Me!*" he exclaimed, drawing himself up as if he wanted to touch the sky. "Try then! Just try!"

"By-and-by," said my uncle, pacifying him with a good-humoured gesture; "but for the present let us have a talk, my good fellow! Certainly I sympathise with your annoyance; for you must have perceived that I know this lady, and that she knows me. There has even been a little *liaison* between us—"

"*Bagasse!* You confess to it, then?"

"I confess to it!" responded the captain, in a conciliatory manner. "But, my dear fellow, a brother's horns, as the

saying goes, need not trouble one so much as one's own. You will of course agree with me on that point."

"I agree with you there!" replied the Toulonnais, quite gravely, as if struck by a specious argument. "But it does not follow from that—"

"Stop a moment!" interrupted my uncle, who wished to pursue his argument. "*I*, whom you see here, have also had the honour of being made a cuckold, as they say in Moliere. You are acquainted with Moliere, I dare say?"

"I am; go on!" said the lieutenant, who had made up his mind to restrain himself while my uncle was developing his explanations.

"Very well! as you have read him, you ought to know that a misadventure like that is not such a great matter after all. A second or two and it is all over, just like having a tooth out. Besides, remember this, the tooth cannot be replaced, while in the case of a woman, one can find plenty to take her place."

"That's true!" returned Firmin Bonaffe, who opened his eyes wide, as if he wished to follow this chain of reasoning, which evidently astonished him by its perspicuity.

The issue began to be cleared.

"Then we have arrived at the same opinion," continued Barbassou Pasha. "All that remains is to come to an understanding."

"By no means! by no means! I repeat, my brother confided his wife to my charge. You have insulted her in public, and in the name of decency—"

"Oh, no!" interrupted my uncle; "you are exaggerating! In the first place, my nephew and I were the only persons present; therefore there was no very great harm done. Then you brought the people up by your shouting; consequently it is I who have cause to complain."

"*Te!* Are you trying to make a fool of me?" exclaimed the Toulonnais, bursting out upon us like a bomb with another explosion. "Do you suppose, then, that I am going down on my knees to thank you for having undressed Jean Bonaffe's wife?"

"Jean Bonaffe's wife? No, no, my good fellow!" briefly replied my uncle.

"Why 'No'?"

"Why, in the first place, because she is actually my own wife!"

"Yours?"

"As I have the pleasure of informing you. And consequently it is I who would be entitled not to be at all pleased by your intervention in the little domestic occurrence which took place just now."

The Toulonnais, for the moment, was struck dumb with astonishment.

"Then, *bagasse!* who are you?" he asked.

"*The late* Barbassou, retired general, seen fifty years of service, and thirty-nine campaigns, and the husband of your sister-in-law, who is now a bigamist—rather an awkward mistake for a lady."

My uncle might have gone on speaking for the rest of the day, and had it all his own way. The unfortunate lieutenant stared at him, crushed and dumbfounded by this astounding revelation. All at once, and without waiting to hear any more, he turned on his heels, and beat a precipitate retreat by the door.

The late Barbassou indulged in a smile at this very intelligible discomfiture of his adversary. He had finished his madeira, and we went out to get our horses again.

Directly he had mounted into the saddle, he said to me, reverting to the subject of our interrupted conversation:

"Do you know, I think it's all up with the Madeira vines; but as to those of the Douro, with careful grafting, we might still pull them through!"

"I hope so, uncle!" I replied.

And, as a matter of fact, I think he is right. Perhaps we shall soon know.

Come, I must tell you about a new occurrence which is already influencing my romance in the most unexpected manner.

I don't suppose you have forgotten our Captain Picklock and the famous story of the camels which were recovered through his good offices. Well, the captain, having returned from Aden with the fever, and being at Paris on his way home, accepted the hospitality of Baron de Villeneuve, late consul at Pondicherry, whom you know. Two days ago we were invited to a farewell dinner, given in his honour. It was quite a love-feast: half a dozen friends, all of whom had been several times round the world, and had met each other in various latitudes. The ladies consisted of the amiable

Baroness de Villeneuve, Mrs. Picklock, and my aunt. You may imagine what a number of old recollections they discussed during dinner. After the coffee we went into the drawing-room, where a card-table was being set out for whist, when my uncle said:

"By the bye, what has become of our good friend Montague?"

"Oh, Montague," answered the baron; "he is in Paris. He has been prevented from dining with us by an invitation to his ambassador's; but he will look in this evening, and you will see him."

"Ah, that's capital!" exclaimed my uncle; "I shall be delighted to see him again."

When I heard this name mentioned, I pricked up my ears. Still there was nothing to indicate that the Montague spoken of was the commodore. I listened with curiosity.

"Will he stay in Paris any length of time?" my uncle continued.

"The whole winter," replied the baroness. "He has come to pick up his daughters, whom he had left in my charge two years ago, before he went off to the North Pole."

"Ah, yes! little Maud and Suzannah," observed my uncle.

"Yes, captain; only your *little* Maud and Suzannah are now grown-up young ladies," added the baroness with a laugh.

It was impossible for me to entertain any more doubts; and I confess my mind was far from easy when I heard this. At the thought of meeting the commodore, my first idea was to get away at once, before he arrived. Although I was confident of the perfect security of my secret, and although it was the merest chance that had brought about the intimacy which I could not have foreseen between Kondje-Gul and his daughters, I could not conceal from myself the embarrassment which I should feel in his presence. As bad luck would have it, I was already seated at the card-table. I lost my tricks as fast as I could in order to shorten the game, swearing inwardly at the captain and my uncle, who were both of them playing with a provoking deliberation, and lecturing me upon my careless play. At last, having succeeded in losing my three rubbers, I got up from the table, alleging a sudden attack of head-ache, when at this very moment, in the next drawing-room where the baroness was sitting, the servant announced,

"Commodore Montague!"

Just imagine my stupefaction, Louis, when I saw the commodore come in, followed by his two daughters and Kondje-Gul, whom he introduced to the baroness and to my aunt as a schoolfellow of his daughters, Maud and Suzannah!

You may guess what a state of confusion I was thrown into by this spectacle. Whatever would happen? My chances of retreat being now completely cut off, I withdrew myself to the midst of a group who were talking together in a corner of the room. Kondje-Gul was listening timidly to the baroness's compliments, and I heard the latter say:

"I am much indebted, mademoiselle, to our friend the commodore who has done us the favour of bringing you with him; Maud and Suzannah had already spoken to me so often about you, that I had a great desire to make your acquaintance."

The striking beauty of the young foreigner had created quite a sensation, and feeling that all their eyes were fixed on her, she did not venture to look about her. Still it was necessary to anticipate the dangerous consequences of the least imprudence on the part of either of us, by putting her on her guard before the baroness had the opportunity of introducing me to the commodore and his daughters.—By rather a clever manoeuvre, therefore, I managed to slip behind my aunt while she was talking to the American young ladies.

When Kondje-Gul saw me, she could not help giving a start of surprise, but I had time to put my finger to my lips, and signify to her that she must not show that she knew me. Our encounters in the Bois, during our morning rides, had fortunately trained her already for this necessary piece of dissimulation: and she had sufficient self-control not to betray our secret. My aunt turned round at that very moment, and seeing me standing by her chair, said to me:

"Oh, Andre, come and let me introduce you to this young lady!"

Kondje-Gul blushed when I bowed to her, and returned my bow very prettily. I was introduced in the same way to the commodore and his daughters. There was a vacant chair close to them on which the baroness made me sit down, and I soon found myself engaged in a general conversation with them; I may add that the liveliness of the Montague girls rendered our conversation much easier than I had expected. Having been brought up in the American way, they possessed that youthful independence of spirit which is stifled in our own girls by a more strict and formal education, on the false ground of the requirements of modesty. Kondje-Gul, although rather reserved at first, expanded gradually, and I was astonished at the change which had been effected in her whole bearing. Certainly one could still guess that she was a foreigner, but she had acquired quite a new ease in her deportment and in her language. Being reassured by her behaviour against the risks

of this encounter, which I had at first so much dreaded, I freely accepted the peculiar position in which I was placed. There was a positive charm about this mystery, the pleasure of which I can hardly explain to you.

Although this was quite a small and friendly party, there were now enough young people to get up a "hop," so the baroness instructed me to lead off with Miss Suzannah, which I did very willingly, asking her for a polka.

"What do you think of my friend Kondje-Gul?" she said to me, when we sat down after a few turns.

"She is remarkably pretty," I replied.

"I suppose you'll ask her for a dance with you?" she continued, with a smile.

"I shall certainly not fail in this duty to a friend of yours and Miss Maud's!"

"Miss Maud and I thank you very much for the attention," she said, with a ceremonious bow; "only," she added, smiling maliciously at me, "I must prepare you for a disappointment, which you will, no doubt, feel very much afflicted by—our friend does not dance!"

"What, never?"

"We have given several little parties at my father's rooms, and have never been able to persuade her to."

"Ah! that's no doubt because she only knows her oriental dances."

"You're quite wrong there! She has taken lessons just as we have, and waltzes splendidly; but she won't even dance with the professor; it's always Maud or I who act as her partners. She has some principles on this subject which appear to be rooted in her, and which we have not yet succeeded in overcoming."

"If you would help me this evening," I said, "perhaps we can succeed between us."

"What, is it to be a conspiracy?"

"Quite a friendly one, for you must admit that it is for her own interest."

"I won't deny it," she replied, with a laugh; "but how are we to force her?"

Then I noticed poor Kondje-Gul, who was watching us, and seemed to envy us.

"Listen!" I said, as if a sudden idea had struck me. "I know of a likely way."

"Well?"

"Let us take my aunt into our confidence; I see them over there talking Turkish together. My aunt will perhaps be able to exercise sufficient influence over your friend to convince her that she may conform to our usages without committing any offence."

"Yes, that's the way to manage it!" exclaimed Miss Suzannah, in delight. "Our conspiracy is making progress; but how shall we get at your aunt?"

"Does Mademoiselle Kondje-Gul understand English?" I asked her.

"No, not a word."

"Then it's a very simple matter," I added. "After this polka I'll take you back to your seat; you then communicate our scheme to my aunt in English, and ask for her assistance; I come up, as if by chance, and try my luck with her for the next waltz."

We did as we said. I watched from the distance this important conference, all the details of which I guessed. While Miss Suzannah was addressing my aunt in English, I saw her laugh in a sly manner, casting a glance at me. She at once understood our request; then turned her attention again to Kondje-Gul, and continued, quite undisturbed, the subject which she had last commenced talking about with her. I had so perfectly anticipated all the phases of this scene, that I seemed to hear what she said. By Kondje-Gul's face I could tell the moment my aunt approached her on our subject, and the negative gesture with which she replied was so decisive—I was nearly saying so full of horror—that, fearing lest she should cut off her retreat completely, I deemed it advisable to intervene as quickly as possible.

I advanced, therefore, without any more ado, joined their group, and addressing myself to the handsome young foreigner, I said to her:

"I should not like you to think me indifferent to the pleasure of dancing with you, mademoiselle; I meant to have asked you for the first waltz; but, alas! Miss Suzannah tells me that you do not dance!"

"You have come to the rescue, Andre," chimed in my aunt. "I was just endeavouring to convert the young lady to our customs by telling her that she would be taken for a little savage."

At this expression, which she had so often heard me utter, Kondje-Gul smiled and cast a furtive glance at me. Miss Suzannah supported my aunt, and the victory was already won. They were beginning to play a waltz, so Maud took her hand and forced it into mine; I clasped her by the waist and led her off. During the first few turns Kondje-Gul trembled with excitement; I felt her heart beating violently against my bosom, and I confess I was nearly losing my own self-possession. Once we found ourselves some way removed from the rest, and, with her head resting on my shoulder, she whispered in my ear:

"Do you still love me, dear? Are you satisfied with me?"

"Yes, but take care!" I answered hurriedly: "you are too beautiful, and all their eyes are fixed upon us."

"If they only knew!"—she added, with a laugh.

I stopped a moment, to let her take breath. Each time any couple came near us, we appeared to be engaged in one of those ball-room conversations the only characteristic of which is their frivolity, and as soon as they were out of hearing, we talked together in a low voice.

"You naughty fellow," she said, "I have not seen you in the Bois for three days!"

"It was from motives of prudence," I replied. "And now prepare yourself for a surprise. Your new house is ready and you can go there the day after to-morrow."

"Do you really mean it?" exclaimed she, "Oh! what happiness! Then you find me sufficiently Europeanized?"

"You coquette! you are adorable!—What a nice fan you have, mademoiselle!" added I, changing my manner as Maud came close to us.

"Do you think so," she answered, "Is it Chinese or Japanese?"

Maud having passed we resumed our conversation, overjoyed at the idea of constantly seeing each other again. The waltz was just ending and I was obliged to conduct Kondje-Gul back to my aunt.

"Listen!" she remarked, "whenever I put my fan up to my lips, that will mean 'I love you'—You must come back soon to invite me for another dance, won't you?"

"My dear girl, I can't."

"Why?"

"Because it is not usual, and would be remarked," I replied.

"But I don't want to dance with anyone else!" she said, almost with a terrified look.

I had not for once thought of this very natural consequence of our little adventure, and I must confess that the idea of anyone else asking her after me took me quite by surprise— like some improbability which no mortal could conceive.

"What shall I do?" she said.

It was necessary at all costs to repair the effects of our imprudence. I invented for her a sudden indisposition, a dizziness which obliged her to leave off waltzing, and I conducted her back to my aunt. This pretext would be sufficient to justify her in declining to dance for the rest of the evening.

I know very well, my dear fellow, that you will cry out against me when I tell you of this strange feeling which pierced me suddenly like a thorn in the heart, at the notion of seeing Kondje-Gul dance with another man. But how could I help it?

I simply relate to you a psychological fact and nothing more.

You may tell me, if you like, that this is a ridiculous exaggeration, and that I am giving myself the morose airs of a jealous sultan. The truth is that in my harem life, I have contracted prudish alarms and real susceptibilities which are excited by things which would not have affected me formerly. Contact with the outside world will, no doubt, restore me to the calm frame of mind enjoyed by every good husband. Perhaps some day I may even be able to feel pride as I watch my wife with naked arms and shoulders whirling round the room in the amorous embrace of a hussar. At present my temper is less complaisant: my love is a master's love, and the notion that any man could venture to press my Kondje-Gul's little finger would be enough to throw me into a fit of rage. That's what we Orientals are like, you know!

However that be, I led Kondje-Gul back to my aunt's side, and she did not dance any more.

From a corner of the drawing-room I saw some half-a-dozen of my friends march up to get introduced to her, anxiously longing to obtain the same favour as I had, and I laughed at their discomfiture.

Meanwhile the commodore, who, by the way, is a highly educated and thoroughly good-natured man, had marked me out, and was so kind in his attentions to me, that I felt constrained, in spite of my scruples, to accept his advances. His relations with my uncle, moreover, might have made the cold reserve which I had so far maintained appear singular.

Finally, towards the middle of the entertainment, when he was going away with his daughters and Kondje-Gul, whom he had to see home to Madame Montier's, I had, without meaning it, so completely won his good opinion, that I found myself invited to accompany my aunt who was dining with him the next day but one.

Although it was only a fatality that had led to this extraordinary complication, I must own that, when I began to think over it and to contemplate the possible consequences, I felt a considerable anxiety. Hitherto, by a compromise with conscience, which Kondje-Gul's childlike simplicity rendered almost excusable, I had been enabled to deceive myself about the consequences of this school-friendship with two American girls who were strangers to me. This, I thought, would never be more than a chance companionship, and when her time with them was over, the Misses Maud and Suzannah would remain ignorant of her real position, which they had no occasion for suspecting. But I could not fail to perceive that our relations with the commodore must aggravate our difficulties to a remarkable extent.

Our society affords shelter, certainly, to many a hidden romance: we have both honest loves and shady intrigues confused and interlaced in its mazes so that they escape all notice. Yet, certain as I felt that nothing could occur to betray our extraordinary secret, I was troubled all the same at the part which I should have to play in this family with which my uncle was on such intimate terms.

Placed face to face with the inexorable logic of facts, I could not long deceive myself as to the course which the most elementary sense of delicacy prescribed to me. I could see clearly during this last evening party, that Kondje-Gul had no further need of Madame Montier's lessons to complete her social education. Count Terals house being now ready to receive her, I need only settle her there with her mother in order to commence at once the happy life of which we had so often dreamed. Then it would be easy to withdraw gradually from the society of the Montague girls, and thus banish all future risks.

Having decided upon this course, I wrote the same evening to Kondje-Gul to ask her to prepare for her return.

CHAPTER XI

You know, my dear Louis, that whenever I have formed any plan, whether a reckless one or even a wise one, I go straight at it with the stubbornness of a mule. This, perhaps, explains many of my follies. According to my view (as a believer in free-will), man is himself a will or independent power served by his organs; he is a kind of manifestation of the spirit of nature created to control matter. Any man who abdicates his rights, or gives way before obstacles, abandons his mission and returns to the rank of the beasts. His is a lost power, which has evaporated into space. Such is my opinion.

This highly philosophical prelude was necessary, as you will see, in order to fix my principles before proceeding any further; and, above all, in order to defend myself beforehand against any rash accusation of fickleness in my plans. Science has mysterious paths, along which we feel our way, without seeing clearly our destination. The consequence of which is that, just when we fancy that we have reached the end, new and immense horizons open out before us.

But I am getting tired of my metaphor.

It all amounts to this—that having the honour of being my uncle's nephew, nothing happens to me in the same way as to other mortals, and that consequently all the careful arrangements that I made in regard to Kondje-Gul have eventuated in a manner completely opposed to my express intentions. But although my objective has been considerably enlarged, it remains substantially the same, as I think you will remark.

Kondje-Gul and her mother are now settled down in Count Teral's house; and it is hardly necessary for me to describe to you the joy which she felt at the termination of her educational seclusion. The first few days after her return were days of frenzied delight, and we spent them almost entirely together. Her metamorphosis was now so complete, that I felt as if I were witnessing one of the fabulous Indian *avatars*, and that another soul had taken up its dwelling in this divinely beautiful body of hers. I could not tire of watching her as she walked, and listening to her as she spoke. In her Oriental costume, which she occasionally resumes, in order to please me, the American girl's ways, which she has picked up from Suzannah and Maud, produce a most remarkable effect. And with all this was mingled that exquisitely blended aroma of youth, beauty, and dignity, which permeated her and surrounded her like the sweet perfume of some strange Oriental blossom!

We have settled our plan of life. Knowing the whole truth, as she does now, about our social habits, she understands the necessity of veiling our happiness under the most profound mystery. Confiding in the sanctity of a tie which her religion legitimizes, she is aware that we must conceal it from the eyes of the world, like any secret marriage. Besides, what advantage would there be in lifting the veil of mystery, and taking the poetry out of this romantic union—thus reducing it to the vulgar level of an ordinary intrigue? If I were to treat my Kondje like a common mistress, would not that be degrading her?

When I tried to console her for the dulness which this constraint must cause her, she exclaimed, with vehemence—

"Be so good as not to calumniate my woman's heart! What do I care for your country, and its laws, so long as you love me? I don't care to know either your society, or its customs, or its conventionalities. I belong to you, and I love you; that is all I see, all I feel. I am neither your wife, nor your mistress. From the depths of my soul I feel that I am more than either. I am your slave, and I wish to preserve my bonds. Command me, do what you like with me; and when you love me no longer, kill me, that's all!"

"Yes, dear!" I replied, laughing at her rhapsodies, "I will sew you up in a sack, and go and throw you in the Bosphorus some evening!"

She received this remark with a peal of childish laughter.

"Goodness me!" she said, in her confusion; "why, I was quite forgetting that I am civilised!"

Count Teral's house has been quite a find for us; it seems just as if it had been built expressly for Kondje-Gul and her mother. On the ground-floor, approached by a short flight of eight steps, is a drawing-room, which opens into a sort of hall, resembling an artist's studio. The latter serves as picture-gallery, library, and concert-room. Above the wainscoting the eye is relieved by silk hangings, of a large grey-striped pattern on white ground, in contrast with which is the rich garnet of a velvet-covered suite of furniture. There are some curious old cabinets in carved ebony, set out with statuettes, vases, flowers, and nick-nacks. The general effect is lively, enchanting, and luxurious; in fact, just what the home of a young lady of patrician birth, who confines herself to a small circle of friends, should be. On the first floor are the private apartments, and on the second the servants' rooms. The establishment is maintained on the elegant, yet simple scale, which seems proper for members of good society; they keep three horses, and a neat brougham:

nothing more. Their luxuries, in short, are all in the well-considered style suitable for a rich foreign lady and her daughter, who mix in Parisian society with the reserve and delicate taste of two women anxious to avoid attracting too much attention.

Kondje-Gul's private life is contrived, as well as everything else, to preserve her against solitude or dulness. She is completing her "civilisation" with industrious zeal. Every morning, from eight o'clock to twelve, is devoted to work; governesses from Madame Montier's come to continue her course of lessons; then from one to two she practises on the piano. Her curious mind, with its mixture of ardent imagination and youthful intelligence, is really producing a wonderful intellectual structure upon its original foundation of native belief and superstitions. I am often quite surprised by hearing her display, on the subject of our social contradictions, an amount of observation and a grasp of view which would do credit to a philosopher.

After two o'clock she dresses, and takes a walk or a ride, or makes calls with her friends, the Montague girls; for in spite of all my excellent intentions, their intimacy has only increased since they were all emancipated from the restraints of school life. Kondje-Gul being now under her mother's protection, the most regular position she could have in the world, it would have been difficult indeed to find a pretext for breaking it off. Moreover, I had come to the conclusion that, owing to my having been introduced to the commodore's family by my uncle, there could be no danger in these encounters with Kondje-Gul at their house. It was by Maud and Suzannah that I had been presented to their fair foreign companion, and who would suspect it was not at Madame de Villeneuve's party that I had first spoken to her? Consequently, if any unforeseen circumstance should some day betray our secret, I could at least rest assured that Commodore Montague would never think of accusing me of

anything more than a romantic adventure, resulting by a natural train of circumstances from that introduction.

Nothing, as you perceive, could be more correct from the worldly point of view. I am well aware that as a rigid moralist you would not neglect the opportunity, if I gave it you, of lecturing me upon the rashness of my course. Well, for my part, I maintain that our respect for the proprieties consists chiefly in our respect for ourselves. Chance, which led us into the society of the foreign colony, together with Kondje-Gul's charming manner, have naturally created for her a number of pleasant acquaintances, which I should never perhaps have aimed at obtaining for her. All that was needed to secure her this advantage was that we should both pay to the world this tribute of mystery to which it is entitled. Our society is so mixed that I do not think you would have been scandalised if you had met Kondje-Gul at the ball at the British Embassy, where she went the other night with her mother, and Commodore Montague. The admiration which she excited as she passed must certainly have disarmed your objections.

Being always about with the Montague girls, Kondje-Gul soon got invited with them to the balls to which the commodore took his daughters. Having been admitted to two or three aristocratic drawing-rooms, such as that of Princess B—and Marchioness d'A—, she obtained the entry to all the others. With your knowledge of the infatuations of our fashionable world, you can imagine the extravagant style of admiring gossip with which such a beautiful rising star is greeted wherever she goes. I should add that the young sinner understands it all very well, and is very much flattered by it.

The mystery which surrounds her increases the peculiarity of our situation. Being always chaperoned by her mother, whose foreign type of features creates an imposing impression,

Kondje-Gul is taken for one of those young ladies who are models of filial respect. The style of their house and of their dress, and that refined elegance which stamps them as ladies of distinction, designate them no less indisputably the possessors of a large fortune and of high rank. All this, you will perceive, formed a crowning justification for the success which Kondje-Gul's remarkable beauty had of itself sufficed to achieve for her. Then of course the fashionable reporters of the official receptions fulfilled their duty by heralding the advent of this brilliant star. They only made the mistake— one of those mistakes so common with journalists—of describing her as a Georgian.

Confident in the security of our mystery, Kondje-Gul and I find nothing more delightful than the manoeuvres by which we deceive them all. We have invented a code of signs, the meaning of which we keep to ourselves, and which leads to some very amusing by-play between us.

Thus the other evening, at Madame de T—'s, she was sitting by Maud and Suzannah, surrounded by a number of admirers, when the young Duke de Marandal, one of the most ardent of my acknowledged rivals, was lavishing upon her his most seductive attentions. Kondje was listening to him with a charming smile on her face. Now that evening, I must tell you, she had resolved upon a bit of fun; and knowing that in France unmarried girls are not supposed to wear jewellery, she had fastened on her wrist a heavy gold bracelet as a token of her servitude. So while the young duke was talking, she looked at me, playing carelessly the while with what she calls her "slave's ring." You may guess how we laughed together over it.

CHAPTER XII

I have to inform you, my dear fellow, that my uncle, who has always been admired so far for his virtuous conduct, and whom I should certainly have been ready to quote as a paragon of husbands, seems just now on the way to forfeiting his character.

Here is what I have to relate:

Two days ago I went to the Theatre des Varietes to see for the second time the play which is just now the rage. Not having obtained a good place, I left my stall at the end of the first act with the intention of not returning, when, as I passed a rather closely-curtained stage-box, I was quite surprised by seeing Barbassou-Pasha, who had pretended to be going out that evening to an important dinner with some business friends. He was accompanied by a lady whose features were obscured by the darkness.

Being a discreet and respectful nephew, I was about to turn my eyes the other way, when he beckoned me with an imperative gesture to join him in his box. I immediately obeyed this peremptory summons, and, going round by the passage, got the box-opener to usher me in.

"Come in, and sit down," said my uncle, pointing out to me a chair behind him.

Once more I obeyed him, bowing politely to the lady, whose features I could not clearly distinguish. I was hardly seated when I recognised the fair heroine of the fainting fit last week.

Exquisitely attired in a perfectly ravishing costume, Madame Jean Bonaffe replied to my compliments by a charming smile, and a pretty glance from her fine Spanish eyes, which showed me clearly that she was troubled by no remnants of that sudden indisposition which the too unexpected encounter with my uncle had produced.

Our conversation turned upon the play. As she spoke French rather badly (although she understood it very well), she asked my uncle from time to time to tell her the words she was in need of. This he did, pronouncing them with grammatical deliberation, and then leaving us to talk alone, while he surveyed the audience like one superior to such frivolities as feminine smalltalk.

My companion was very gay, and was crunching bonbons all the time.

I, as you may be sure, was gallant and attentive, and I followed her example with the bonbons.

My former aunt, Christina de Portero, is at the happy age of between twenty-eight and thirty. Or, possibly, she is as old as thirty-two. Her figure is slender and supple, with those bold expansions of the hips which, in dancing the fandango, make short work of the skirt. Add to these fascinating details the accurate information with which I have already supplied you on the subject of her exuberant bust, and you can picture her very well for yourself.

She has a fine erect head, clear and singularly expressive features, a warm complexion, a Grecian nose, with quivering nostrils, and a mouth adorned with pearly teeth, with a soft, black, downy growth on her upper lip. She is an Andalusian, overflowing with life and spirits, whose exuberance, however, is tempered by her graceful and truly refined demeanour. One can guess what a fire of passion smoulders within her.

My uncle was in perfection that evening. From time to time he discarded his philosophic calm in order to take a look at us and reply in Spanish to his fair friend's questions. He addressed her as "querida," in that indulgent tone which is peculiar to him, like a pasha who is signifying his approbation.

During the course of our conversation I discovered that things had gone on like this between them since the day after that famous scene at Villebon, whose lively incidents had doubtless conduced to this friendly reconciliation. How had my uncle managed to get round the ferocious native of Toulon? That I could never discover. However this may have been, after the play was over, we went off, all three of us, to the Cafe Anglais.

We had a capital supper, during which Madame Jean Bonaffe, feeling more at her ease under these intimate circumstances, gave free play to her fascinations. I could soon perceive that in her pleasure at forgetting her regrettable escapades of the past, her grief over her supposed widowhood, and also the short-lived and illegal marriage which she had contracted by mistake, she expected that my uncle would settle her at Paris. She appeared to speak of this happy prospect as of something upon which her mind was set, and it gave rise to a number of beautiful castles in the air.

Barbassou-Pasha, gallant and attentive as ever, listened to all these proposed arrangements for her felicity, in that good-natured, patronizing manner which he always maintains with women, and only departs from in the case of my aunt Eudoxia, who keeps him in check. Nodding his approval of everything she said, he went on eating and drinking, like a practical man who will not neglect the claims of a good supper, and he allowed the fair Andalusian to lavish all her attentions upon him.

About two o'clock in the morning, we took a brougham, drove back my aunt to the Rue de l'Arcade, where she occupies a splendidly furnished suite of rooms, and then returned home.

"What do you think of all that, my dear Louis? Hum!"

Our little circle has been augmented by a very pleasant and genial addition, Mr. Edward Wolsey, a nephew of the commodore's, who may very likely be engaged to Maud.

As I have become quite intimate with Commodore Montague's party, I generally join their group, without the smallest fear of raising a suspicion regarding these encounters. The attention which I pay to Kondje-Gul and to Suzannah have caused no little envy, for, as you know, Kondje-Gul pretends she does not dance. This peculiarity, together with her original fascinations with which a certain childish simplicity is mingled, give rise to the most extraordinary conjectures. What is the cause of all this reserve? men ask. Is it modesty, bashfulness, or pride? They know that she can dance splendidly, for she has been seen dancing occasionally at private parties with Maud and Suzannah. They think it must be due to some jealous *fiance*, her betrothal to whom is kept secret, and to whom she is devoted.

Lent having interrupted the course of public entertainments, our private parties which usually took place at Teral House, became the gainers by it. Maud and Suzannah felt more free and easy there, and Kondje-Gul experienced quite a childish

delight in holding what she called her "receptions." Our small circle was soon augmented by a dozen select friends, picked carefully from the ranks of their young ball-room acquaintances. There were one or two mothers among them whose presence did not interfere with the harmony of these charming gatherings, and the tone of elegant distinction which prevailed in no respect interfered with their exuberant gaiety.

This break in the giddy circle of fashionable dissipation, afforded quite a new happiness to Kondje-Gul and me. In the course of her initiation into the refinements of our life, her exotic charms had acquired some new and indescribable embellishments. We spent many a long evening alone together in that delightful privacy which affords the sweetest opportunities for communion between loving hearts, and we grew to feel like a modern Darby and Joan. I was quite proud of my handiwork, and contemplated with joy this pure and ideal being whose nature I had inspired, whose soul and whose heart I had moulded. The cultivation of this young and virgin mind, as I may be permitted to call it, so possessed by its Oriental beliefs, had produced a charming contrast of enthusiasm and calm reason which imparted a most original effect to her frank utterances of new ideas. I was often quite surprised to find in her mingled with her Asiatic superstitions, and transformed as it were by contact with a simpler faith, the substance of my own private sentiments and of my wildest aspirations. One might really think that she had borrowed her thoughts, nay, her very life, as it were, from me, and that her tender emotions had their source in my own heart.

Our happiness seemed so assured, and we had it so completely under our own control, that it would have appeared absurd for us to imagine it to be at the mercy of Fate. Still, in the midst of this tranquillity there sometimes arose in my mind an anxious thought. Light clouds floated across my clear azure sky, and often, as I sat by her side, I began to think, in spite of myself, about the future—about this marriage of which you yourself have reminded me, and from the obligations to which nothing could save me. However great the sacrifice might be, I could not even think of failing to carry out my uncle's wishes in this matter. My heart bound me to this adoptive father who had placed unlimited faith in my loyalty: my whole life was pledged to this chivalrous benefactor who had left all his fortune in my hands, nor could I permit the least suspicion of ingratitude on my part to pass over his mind.

But melancholy as was the recollection of this duty to which I had resigned myself, I must confess that, after all, this impression was but a fugitive one. I no longer attempted to struggle against the temptation to a compromise, by means of which I had determined to reconcile my passion for Kondje-Gul with my marital duties to Anna Campbell. The retiring nature of the latter would surely permit our union to be treated as one of those arrangements known as *mariages de convenance*, and my charming romantic connection with Kondje-Gul would always remain a secret. Moreover, my uncle, should he ever discover this after-match of my oriental life, was certainly not the man to be seriously scandalised at it, directly he assured himself that "the respectabilities" had not been violated.

By-the-bye, I should tell you that was a false alarm I sounded about my uncle! I calumniated him when I believed him to have committed anything so shocking as a double adultery.

We went again yesterday to the forest of Meudon, which we had almost given up visiting of late, my uncle having been engaged for the last fortnight upon "some important morning business," as he says. Well, we arrived at Villebon's restaurant, our usual destination. When we entered that celebrated room—empty this time—which had been the scene of the drama which you remember, the latter came back very naturally to our memory, and would have done so even without the superfluous aid of the grins with which our waiter greeted us. Equally naturally, and as becomes a dutiful nephew, who does not wish to appear indifferent to family matters, I, seeing my uncle cast a glance towards the window near which the incident that produced such momentous consequences occurred, took the opportunity of asking after my pseudo-aunt Christina, about whom I had not had any previous chance of questioning him.

"Christina!" exclaimed Barbassou-Pasha, "why, she's gone back!"

"Dear me! I thought she wanted to settle in Paris?"

His eye lightened up with a sly look.

"Oh, yes! She would have liked to do so very well," he replied. "In fact, we made the round of the upholsterers' shops,—and she fancied, up to the last moment, that it was all settled. But I had made up my mind, and I sent her back to Jean Bonaffe."

"The deuce you did!" I said, quite astonished at the news.

Then my uncle just closed one of his eyes, and looked at me out of the other, as he added—

"You see, I was not sorry to return that rascal the little trick he played me before!"

And, with that, Barbassou-Pasha began to whistle a hunting song, with all the calm complacency of an honest soul on satisfactory terms with his neighbour. I accompanied him whistling the bass, and we got on very well together that time.

I believe that after this explanation, you will at once renew the esteem which you used to accord to my uncle, and will join me in a sincere expression of regret for having suspected him for one moment in this matter:—in which, in reality, he had merely played the part of an avenging deity, punishing sinners with remorse by recalling to them the blisses of their lost Paradise. And I am ready to testify that he has spared no expense; for during the last three weeks he has had from me more than twenty thousand francs in pocket-money. I warrant you he has given his fair friend a jolly time of it, purposely holding the golden cup to her faithless lips, and letting them taste of all the pleasures—

The severe lesson of an abrupt return to her husband, Jean Bonaffe, after the awakening of such delightful anticipations, will certainly impress the guilty one, and engrave in her heart a keen remorse for her past misconduct.

CHAPTER XIII

We have been four months at Paris without anything to disturb the happy life which we have led, secure from all suspicions. Nothing can be more original or sweeter than this love concealed from all prying eyes, the exquisite pleasures of which you can imagine. Kondje, delighted with her triumphs, plays everywhere her part of enchantress.

My romance is, however, complicated by a circumstance which I must at once relate to you.

You will not have forgotten that my aunt had seen Kondje-Gul at Baroness de Villeneuve's party, and that she conceived a great liking for her. Their friendship having been cemented during several parties at the commodore's, where they met each other, my aunt very naturally invited Madame Murrah and her daughter to dinner one evening. She is fond of young people, as you know; and Suzannah, Maud, and Kondje-Gul formed such a charming trio, that she soon insisted on their coming to dine with her every Thursday. Indeed, Kondje has frequently met Anna Campbell there, for the latter has leave out from her convent twice a month. The consequence was, we became in time so completely involved in intimate relations together, that it would have been imprudent to make any break in them: moreover, Kondje-Gul was so very happy and so proud of this intimacy which allied her still more closely with me! All of them were charmed with her; even my uncle, who, delighted at the opportunity of conversing with her in Turkish, treated her with quite a display of gallantry.

Among the constant visitors at our house, I should have mentioned Count Daniel Kiusko, a fabulously rich young Slav, the owner of platinum mines in the Krapacks mountains, and in the forests of Bessarabia. This being his first visit to Paris, I found myself selected to act as his guide or bear-leader, and to introduce him to our gay world. It was a simple enough task, for that matter, since I had hardly anything to do but to present him in society.

He was tall, slenderly built, and a fine specimen of the young boyard, with that determined expression of countenance which suggests a habit of acting and being obeyed as the feudal lord. In less than a week, with the most lofty recklessness, he had thrown away half a million francs in the club at baccarat, and his other doings are all in the same vein. With such a start, you may be sure he has taken the world by storm, so that his friendship is sought after as a prize. A successful duel which he fought with a Brazilian made his reputation as a skilful swordsman.

His gratitude to me, and a sort of frank admiration of superior qualities, which he fancies he recognises in me, have won for me his friendship. I have quite become "his guide, philosopher, and friend." I find him a capital companion, and, like some modern Damon and Pythias, we hardly pass a day without seeing one another. At first he was rather surprised that I abstained from the promiscuous pleasures of the gay world; but he soon divined that I was restrained by the spell of a secret passion, and this placed me still higher in his estimation.

I gained credit with Kiusko by taking him into my confidence, and telling him that I had in truth a *liaison* with a

young widow, whose high position in society demanded extreme prudence on my part. With the tact of a thorough-bred gentleman, he never referred to the subject again. Being himself associated with us in our relations with the Montagues, through meeting them at my aunt's, he would never dream of my having any attachment in that quarter; indeed, he was now almost on an equal footing of friendship with me in our intercourse with the fair trio, and was spoken of as one of their "tame cats." Such was the position of things when the following event occurred.

It happened a few days ago. I was in my aunt's boudoir, talking about some matter, which I forget; she was knitting away at a little piece of ornamental work, with her usual business-like industry, and I was playing with her dog "Music," a young animal from Greece.

"By the bye, Andre," she said, "I have an important commission to discharge, concerning which I must consult you."

"All my wisdom is at your service, aunt."

"Let us talk seriously," she continued; "you have to undergo a regular cross-examination, and I command you to reply like an obedient nephew."

"Oh, you frighten me!"

"Don't interrupt me, please. In my person you see before you a family council."

"What, all at once, and without any preparation?—without even changing your dress?"

"You impertinent boy, do you mean to say this does not suit me?"

"On the contrary, I find it quite bewitching."

"Well, then?"

"All right, I ought not to have interrupted you."

"Very well! let us resume—let me see, what was I saying?"

"That in that handsome dark violet velvet dress you represent the grandmother of the family."

"Just so, you're quite right! Now, attention please! The trial has commenced, be on your guard."

"Right you are!"

"Well, what do you think of Mademoiselle Kondje-Gul Murrah?" she asked me point blank, looking me straight in the face.

This question was so unexpected that I felt myself blush like a girl of sixteen.

"Why," I answered, "I think her—most charming and beautiful."

"That's right! Pray don't alarm yourself, my dear young man!" continued my aunt with a smile.

"Oh, I'm not the least alarmed!"

"That's quite clear!—Well, you admit that you find her most charming and beautiful. Let us proceed. What is your present position with regard to her? Tell me the whole truth, and mind don't keep anything back."

I had found time to recover my self-possession.

"Take care," I said, laughing in my turn; "this question of yours may lead us much further than you imagine."

"That's all nonsense. Don't try to turn off my questions with jokes, and please leave my dog's ear alone! If you pull it about like that, you'll make it grow crooked. There, that'll do! Now, answer me seriously, and with all the respect which you ought to feel in speaking of a young lady like Kondje-Gul Murrah."

I was inspired with the brilliant idea of making game of her.

"Must I tell you the whole truth?" I replied. "Do you really require to know it?"

"I *demand* it," she said, "in its naked, unsophisticated reality."

"All right, aunt! you shall have it;" I said, in a confident tone. "I suppose you know that Mademoiselle Kondje-Gul is a Circassian. Well, she belongs to my harem; I bought her at Constantinople eight months ago."

My aunt split her sides with laughter.

"There now!" she exclaimed; "what ever is the use of expecting a word of sense from a lunatic like you?"

"You asked me for the truth, and I have told it to you!" I replied, laughing secretly at the trick I was playing her.

"Leave off talking rubbish! Can't you understand, you silly boy, that I am speaking to you about Kondje-Gul because I can see how the land lies? It is quite clear to me that between you two there is some sort of secret understanding; now what is it? I know nothing about it, but however innocent this mystery may be, I see too much danger about it not to caution you. Mademoiselle Murrah is not one of those drawing-room dolls with whom it is safe for a man to risk a little of his heart in the game of flirtation; no, the man who once falls in love with her will love her for ever, body and soul, he will be bewitched."

"Why, then, she must be Circe herself," I exclaimed: "it's a terrible look-out for me!"

"Oh, you need not laugh," she continued: "your lofty philosophical contempt would not serve you in the least. A beautiful sorceress like that girl is all the more dangerous because her own heart is liable to be kindled by the flames of her incantations. In her heart slumber passions which will devour her some day, both her and the man she loves. That is why I am reading you this lecture, with the object of warning you in time, before your youthful recklessness has carried you too far in this affair; especially as you are already betrothed to another."

Notwithstanding the semi-jocular manner which my aunt had preserved throughout this lecture, I could easily perceive that she was seriously alarmed on my behalf. I therefore abandoned my jesting tone, assuring her that neither my imagination nor my heart were in the smallest danger with Mademoiselle Kondje-Gul Murrah, and that "no change whatever would be made in our present relations." This jesuitical reply appeared to satisfy her.

"In that case," she continued, "I may set to work to get her married?"

"Get her married?" I exclaimed in astonishment.

"Certainly. Did I not tell you, before I began questioning you, that I had an important commission to discharge? My young cousin Kiusko adores her, he has begged me to see

Madame Murrah on his behalf, and I expect to call on her this very day, to set this important business in train."

Although I might have long ago foreseen the consequences of emancipating Kondje-Gul from her harem life, and the conflict which it would involve me in with our social customs, I must admit that this revelation of my aunt's intentions caused me no small anxiety. Kondje's remarkable beauty created too much sensation in the world for me to hope that rivals would not turn up in large numbers, against whom I should have to defend myself. Her personal independence, the wealth which her mother's establishment indicated, and her youth, all seemed to leave the field open to sanguine hopes, and to attempts to win her hand, to the open acknowledgment of which no obstacle appeared. Nevertheless, well prepared as I was for such attempts, and fully expecting to witness them, I was very much affected by the news that Kiusko was my rival. It was impossible for me to doubt that his determination to marry Kondje-Gul was the result of reflection as well as of love, and that it would be only strengthened by any obstacle. Of a calm and energetic nature, endowed with an iron will, and accustomed to see everything submit to his law, he had also preserved that freshness of the affections which would be intensified by the impulses of a first love.

All the same, and notwithstanding my friendship for him, I certainly could not think of explaining to him the strange situation in which he had in his ignorance placed himself. To proclaim Kondje-Gul to be my mistress would be to banish her from the society into which she had won her way: it would have wounded her spirit to the quick and determined her degradation, without reason or advantage either for Kiusko or for myself. Moreover, did I not owe a stricter fidelity to her than to this friend of yesterday?

I resolved accordingly to keep my counsel, and wait upon

events. I felt too confident of regulating them in my own interests to be afraid of the consequences. However, I was surprised by an incident which at first seemed insignificant. Having been informed of my aunt's projected visit to Kondje's mother, I went to her the same evening, thinking that she would at once tell me about it, but she said nothing. I thought, of course, that some obstacle had occurred which had deferred my aunt's negotiations.

The next day, without seeming to attach any importance to the matter, I questioned my aunt about it. She informed me that she had been to Madame Murrah's the day before.

"Did you commence your overtures on behalf of Kiusko's grand scheme?" I asked her.

"Yes," she answered.

"And—were they entertained?"

"Oh, you are going too fast! According to Mussulman usage, matters don't proceed at that rate. We did not get any further than the preliminaries. I explained our amorous friend's eager anxiety, and the next step is to consult Kondje-Gul."

"Meanwhile, does the mother appear favourable to your request?"

"It was not her duty to declare herself at the first interview," said my aunt. "She has, as you know, all the fatalistic composure of her race; still, when I described Daniel's fortune, I fancied she listened to me with some approval."

"Did she tell you what dowry she could give her daughter?"

"Dowry! are you mad? We talked in Turkish and discussed the matter in the Turkish way. I think I should have surprised

her exceedingly if I had given her the idea that I was asking, not only for Kondje-Gul herself, but for some pecuniary remuneration to the noble Kiusko for taking her. That would have been sufficient to upset all her ideas, for don't you know that in the East it is the husband, on the contrary, who always makes a present to the parents of the girl he wants to have? This arrangement, by the way, seems to me more chivalrous and more manly. Kiusko, for that matter, cares about as much for money as for a straw: he loves her, and that is enough for him."

I took good care not to disturb the illusive hopes which my aunt had already conceived. Being reassured by the manner in which Madame Murrah had played her part, it only remained for me to determine the time and the form of refusal best adapted to the circumstances.

While I was in the midst of these reflections, Count Kiusko came in, like any familiar friend, without being announced. He held out his hand to me with more than his usual cordiality. By his happy looks I judged that he had already had a word of encouragement from my aunt, and that he had come to learn in detail the result of her first attempt. Not wishing to disturb their interview, I pretended after a minute or two that I had some letters to write, and left them.

The following morning I was only just out of bed when Kiusko came up with his spurs on. We had decided the day before to ride together to the Bois. As he usually went to the rendezvous by himself, I guessed that to-day he wanted to appear to have been taken there by me, in order to cover his embarrassment, or perhaps his bashfulness when he met Kondje-Gul. Having made up my mind to avoid all confidences, I kept my valet in the room with me, dressing myself very deliberately, and without any compassion for Kiusko's impatience. This compelled us, directly we were mounted, to gallop to the Bois, a procedure not very favourable to confidential effusions.

We only joined the party at the Avenue of Acacias on their way back. I took care to watch Kiusko as he saluted Kondje-Gul. He blushed and stammered out a compliment addressed collectively to all the three girls. Kondje's countenance betrayed nothing more than the flush produced by her ride. We started off in two separate parties. From motives of discretion, I suppose, Kiusko remained behind with Suzannah and the commodore. Edward and I had gone in front with Kondje-Gul and Maud, who was quarrelling with her cousin upon the important question, as to whether we should gallop straight ahead or make a round between the trees. Kondje-Gul decided the matter by suddenly entering the cover.

"Who loves me, let him follow me!" she said, with a laugh.

I followed her, and in a few moments we found ourselves side by side.

"Oh, such a fine piece of news!" she said to me, as soon as Maud and Edward, who were behind us, were out of hearing.

"What is it?" I asked.

"Well, I must tell you that the day before yesterday your aunt came to see my mother while I was away, and there and then formally requested my hand in marriage for the noble Count Daniel Kiusko. My mother related this to me this morning, when I got up."

"And what did you answer her?"

"Oh, I laughed at first, and then I told mamma that she must inform you at once, so that you may decide upon the manner in which she shall repulse the enemy."

"That's simple enough," said I. "She has only to tell my aunt, when next she calls, that she has consulted you."

"Is it as simple as that?"

"Certainly," I said, with a feeling of annoyance at the idea that she knew of Daniel's love. "Is it not solely your will that has to be consulted?"

Kondje-Gul regarded me with astonishment.

"My will?" she said. "Good heavens! do you love me no longer?"

"Why should you imagine I love you no longer?" I answered.

"One might suppose that you wished to remind me of that horrible liberty which I am so much afraid of."

I then realised how stupid and abrupt I had been, and asked her forgiveness.

"You naughty fellow!" she said, pointing to the golden bracelet clasped round her arm.

We decided that I should go to her mother to concert with her and dictate to her the precise terms of a refusal which should cut short all Kiusko's hopes. We were just then emerging from the narrow avenue, and Maud and Edward were joining us again. Our ride came to an end without any other incident of note, except indeed that it appeared to me Daniel was watching Kondje and myself, as if he wanted to guess what had taken place during our *tete-a-tete*, which he had observed from a distance. I troubled myself no further about this, but made up my mind to take measures that very day to put an end to this stupid adventure.

About three o'clock I went to Teral House, and in an interview with Kondje-Gul's mother drew up the precise terms of her answer to my aunt, which consisted of a formula usually employed on similar occasions.

"Mademoiselle Kondje-Gul feels greatly flattered by the honour which Count Daniel Kiusko has intended to confer upon her, but is unable to accept it." To this we added, in order to convince him it was not one of those half-decisive answers which he might hope to overcome: "She desires to inform their friend confidentially that her heart is no longer free, and that she is engaged to one of her relations." This partly-confidential answer possessed the merits of a candid communication, after receiving which no honourable man could press her without giving offence. Moreover, it established a definite status, under which Kondje-Gul could shelter herself for the future from all importunate attempts on the part of my rival.

CHAPTER XIV

You are returning once more, my dear Louis, to your favourite occupation of knocking down skittles which you have set up yourself, and are trying to exercise your humorous spirit at my expense.

You tell me that my Oriental system of life crumbles away upon contact with the hard world, and with those sentiments which I venture to class among the antiquated prejudices of a worn-out civilisation.

You do not perceive, you subtle scoffer, that every one of your arguments can be turned against you to establish the superiority of the customs of the harem. Can't you see that all these mishaps, these troubles, and these outbursts of jealousy, which you have intentionally magnified, originate solely in Kondje-Gul's emancipation from the harem, and that none of them would have occurred if I had not departed from Turkish usages? Consider on the one hand the tranquillity of my amours with Zouhra, Nazli, and Hadidje, my easy life with them, as a poet and a sultan, secure from all annoying rivalries, and on the other hand look at these difficulties and contests arising all at once out of our social conventionalities.

I do not really know why I should waste any more time discussing the question with you.

Being now confident that after the declaration which Madame Murrah would next day make to my aunt, Kondje-Gul would be freed henceforth from the importunities of Count Kiusko, I soon recovered my peace of mind. I entertained no doubts as to the effect which such a decisive answer would produce upon Daniel. I knew that he was too deeply in love not to feel the blow severely.

I expected, accordingly, to hear that he was mourning in some secluded retreat over his lost hopes. For him to see Kondje-Gul again after such an unqualified refusal would only revive his sorrows and cause him more suffering. More than this, it would place her in an uncomfortable position since his declaration of love to her. But while I was convincing myself as to this necessity for him to break off his relations with her, great was my surprise at seeing him reappear among us the following day as calm as ever, and just as if no unpleasant incident had befallen him. Time went on, and still there was no change in this respect. One might even have said, to judge from his easy demeanour and from a certain increase of assurance in his manner, that he felt confident in the future success of his endeavours, and was only waiting for the happy moment when his aspirations would be realized.

I could not help being puzzled by this remarkable result of a decided rejection of his suit, but as I had so plainly avoided my rival's confidences in my embarrassment at the part I was playing, I could not now attempt to regain them. I began to suspect that Kondje-Gul's mother had rehearsed her part imperfectly, and at last made up my mind to question my aunt discreetly on this point.

"By the by, my dear aunt," I said to her one morning in a perfectly unconcerned tone of voice, "you have not told me anything more about Kiusko's intended marriage."

"Ah, there is no longer any question of it!" she answered me. "He presented himself too late: the fair Kondje-Gul's heart is occupied. She is even engaged to one of her own relations I hear."

"Then he seems to me to be bearing his disappointment very easily."

"Oh, don't be too sure about that! Daniel is not one of those whining lovers who publish their lamentations to the whole world. He loves her, as I could see by his sudden paleness when I announced to him the definite rejection of his offer; but he has an iron will, and you may be certain that if he is so calm, that only shows he still cherishes some hope. As for me, I won't believe in Kondje-Gul's marriage with her cousin, until I see them coming out of church together."

Now although it was of small consequence to me that Kiusko, in his robust faith, still preserved a remnant of hope, I must admit that I felt somewhat aggravated by his presumptuous pertinacity. As he had formally declared his love, Kondje-Gul could not henceforth feign to ignore it. There was an offensive kind of impertinence to her about that coolness of his, which affected to take no account of an engagement of which she had informed him as a justification for her refusal. However reserved he might be, and even if he never betrayed by a single word the secret feeling which he concealed so carefully during our intercourse as friends, it would be impossible for me not to feel the constraint of such a situation. So far as he was concerned, it did not seem to trouble him in the least. This demeanour, and this insolent confidence of his—such as might be expected in a petty feudal tyrant—irritated me inexpressibly; but an incident occurred, at first sight insignificant, which diverted the current of my suspicions into quite a different channel.

One morning, about ten o'clock, I was accompanying my

aunt upon one of her rounds of visiting the poor. As we happened to be passing Count Teral's house, I was very much surprised to see Daniel coming out of it. What had he been doing there? This was Kondje-Gul's lesson time, and certainly not the time of day for callers. This discovery put me into a state of agitation which it was extremely difficult for me to avoid showing.

I reflected, however, that it was quite possible Maud or Susannah had entrusted him with a message or with some book, which he had come to deliver. However that might be, I wanted to clear up the mystery. When half-way down the Champs Elysees, I pretended to have an order to give to a coachmaker, and leaving my aunt to return home alone, I went back to Teral House.

As I had anticipated, Kondje-Gul was shut up with her music-mistress. I sent up my name in the ordinary way, and was immediately introduced.

"What! is it you?" she said, pretending before her mistress to be surprised at such an early visit. "Have you come to play a duet with me?"

"No," I answered, "I was passing by this way, and I will only trouble you long enough to find out if you have formed any plans for to-day with your friends the Montagues."

"None," she replied, "beyond that they are expecting me at three o'clock."

"Then they did not send you any message this morning?"

"No. Has anything happened?" she added in Turkish.

"Nothing whatever," I replied, with a laugh. "My aunt brought me this way, so I thought I would come and say good morning to you."

"How kind and nice of you!" she said, with evident warmth.

She had not left her piano, and I remained standing, so as to show that I had only called on my way, to receive her orders. I shook hands with her, saying that I did not wish to interrupt her lessons any more, and took my departure.

It was evident that Kondje knew nothing about Daniel's visit. On my way out I spoke to Fanny, and gave her some instructions, telling her that I was going to send some flowers. This girl was quite devoted to me, and her discretion might be perfectly relied upon. However, as I did not wish her to think that I was questioning her about her mistress, I asked her in an indifferent manner if the count had not brought anything for me.

"I don't know, sir," she answered. "The count came an hour ago, but he told me to send in his name to Mademoiselle Kondje's mother, who was expecting him, I think, and who ordered me to show him into the small drawing-room, where she went to see him. When he left, he said nothing to me."

"Did he say nothing to Pierre?" I added.

"Pierre was not in, sir," replied Fanny. "The count only spoke to Madame Murrah."

"Ah, very well!" I said, carelessly.

These inquiries had led me to a curious discovery. What was the meaning of this private interview between Kondje's mother and Daniel? Determined to get to the bottom of this mystery, I went up without any more ado to Madame Murrah's private sitting-room. She did not appear surprised, from which I concluded that she knew I was in the house, and was prepared to see me. For my part I pretended to have come to settle some details connected with the house and the stables, for I was obliged to assist her in the management of all her domestic affairs. She listened to what I said with that deferential sort of smile which she invariably assumes with me. When she was quite absorbed in the calculations which I had submitted, I said to her all at once:

"By the way, what did Count Kiusko come here for so early in the day?"

I thought I noticed her face redden, but this was only a transient impression.

"The count?" she answered, in a most profoundly surprised tone. "I did not see him! Has he been here?"

"Why, Fanny showed him in here," I replied, "and you have spoken to him."

"Ah, yes! *this morning*," she exclaimed sharply, and with emphasis on these words. "Goodness me, what a poor head I have! I thought you said *yesterday evening*. I understand French so badly, you know. Yes, yes, he has been here. The poor young man is off his head. This is the second time he has been here to beg me for Kondje-Gul's hand. He is quite crazy! crazy!"

"Oh, then he has been before! But why did not you inform me?"

"It is true: I had forgotten to do so!" she replied.

I deemed it useless to appear to press her any more on the matter. Had Madame Murrah tried to keep me in ignorance of these visits of Count Kiusko's? Or was this merely a proof, or the contrary, of the slight importance which she attached to them? In any case, for me to let her see my distrust in her would only put her on her guard. So I broke off the subject, and resumed my household instructions, as if I had remarked nothing more important in this matutinal incident than the stupid pertinacity of a discomfited lover. A quarter of an hour afterwards I took my leave of her in quite a jaunty way.

Once out of the house, I considered the matter over calmly, and made my reflections upon it. Had I, by accident, stumbled upon a plot, or was my jealous mind alarmed without occasion by a foolish attempt which Kondje-Gul's mother could not avert? Accustomed as she was to a sort of passive submission, had she allowed herself to be cowed by a man who spoke in the tone of a master? Was it not possible that, in her embarrassment with the part she had to play, she had let out rather more than was prudent? Was anything more than this necessary in order to explain Daniel's conduct?

Without any kind of scruple Kiusko brought to the contest all the savage energy of a will constituted to bend everything before it. The choice of instruments was a matter of small importance to a man of his nature, the incompleteness of whose education had left him scarcely half-civilized. Accustomed to have all his own way, he made straight for his object, rushing like a bull at every obstacle. The suppleness of his Slavonic character displayed itself in this desperate game, in which, the happiness of his life was at stake. He loved Kondje-Gul, as I knew full well, with that blind love which admitted no compromise with reason. With the mother as his ally, he no doubt conjectured that the marriage would be brought about in accordance with Turkish custom without Kondje-Gul being consulted.

My first idea was to interfere violently and so frustrate this plot, but enlightened upon those manoeuvres, which afforded me an explanation of Daniel's incredible constancy after the repulse which he had sustained, I could see the folly of any provocation on my part, and the consequent danger of injuring Kondje-Gul and perhaps creating a scandal. Henceforth I hold the threads of these underhand intrigues: I am about to catch my rival in his own trap and mislead him as much as I please.

These reflections calmed me a little. After all, would it not be insane for me to lose my temper about a rivalry which, all said and done, was only one of the innumerable incidents which I had foreseen as consequences of Kondje-Gul's beauty? Such beauty would of course attract passionate admiration wherever she went. Good heavens! what would become of me if I took any more notice of Kiusko than of the rest of them? Besides, being informed now of all his movements, I was in a position to intervene whenever it became necessary to put an end to his hostile projects.

A great worry has come upon me, my friend.

I must tell you that there are some barracks in the Rue de Babylone; from which it follows that a great many officers lodge in the vicinity. Moreover, the garden of my house, although enclosed by a wall on the boulevard side, is not sufficiently screened to prevent daring eyes from peering into it from various neighbouring windows.

Now, as a few days of sunshine had favoured us with very mild weather, my houris did not fail to go and stroll about the lawns. Naturally enough they attracted the attention of some indiscreet persons whose curiosity had been quickened by the apparent mystery of this closed house, and by all the gossip in the neighbourhood about "the Turk." It also happens that the house adjoining mine is tenanted by the colonel, whence it results that from morn to eve, there is a constant coming and going of sergeant-majors, lieutenants and captains, who rival one another in casting fascinating

glances upon this corner of Mahomet's paradise.

I must do my houris the justice to say that they do not show themselves unveiled; still I will leave you to imagine the agitation which they cause among the whole regimental staff.

All this was certainly but an inconvenience which pure chance threw in my way, amid my methodical experiments with the new manners and customs of which I wish to show the superiority. It would not have been fitting for a sincere psychologist to convert a purely adventitious difficulty into a defeat; and the removal of my harem would have furnished a specious argument for some detractor of my doctrines who would not have failed to seize hold of this slight practical obstacle in order to raise a controversy. Then, too, I should have been violating human dignity and confessing the fragility of my system of social renovation if I had so lowered myself as to completely sequestrate the women after the fashion of some vile Asiatic satrap.

To be brief, I stood firm; and I conscientiously instructed Mohammed, who was already alarmed, not to interfere with the freedom of their diversions in the garden.

Being confident in the healthy effects of an application of the immortal principles, I had ceased to busy myself about this affair, when, as I arrived in the evening three days ago, I saw Mohammed hasten to me, looking scared. With signs of acute emotion, he begged of me to hear him privately, having an important communication to make.

I entered his room where I invited him to unbosom himself.

He then informed me—in a tone of genuine despair, I will admit—that the honour of the harem and also his own were terribly compromised. In point of fact, he had during the day surprised Zouhra at her window corresponding by signs with a young and superb nobleman who had come to one of the windows of the neighbouring house. This audacious lover, judging by his military uniform, bedizened with gold lace, must at the least be a *muchir* or general.

Had a thunderbolt fallen at Mohammed's feet it certainly would not have caused him greater consternation. The unfortunate fellow did not seem to doubt for one moment what punishment awaited him. But I reassured him, for as you may well suppose, with my system this useless practice is destined to disappear as being superfluous: the dignified position of eunuch not being compatible with our laws. However, under the circumstances, I did not think that I could dispense with opening a serious inquiry concerning this offence which, according to Mohammed, had been perpetrated repeatedly for some days past. Even letters, thrown over the walls, had been exchanged.

On the morrow then, I repaired to the house before the hour usually selected for this correspondence, and placing myself on the upper floor, I waited, screened by a curtain, thanks to which I could watch the manoeuvres of the accomplices, at my ease. Mohammed was moaning like a fallen man, deprived of his grandeur and dishonoured. I soon saw Zouhra appear, charmingly adorned and carrying a nosegay in her hand; but the other window, which had been indicated to me, remained unoccupied. After ten minutes or so she became restless and began to pace up and down her room in a way that conclusively proved her impatience.

Provided with a good opera-glass I carefully watched her goings-on.

Nearly half an hour elapsed. There was still nobody at the other window. Mohammed, who became more and more downcast, was beginning to fear that he would be unable to prove to me the full extent of my disgrace, when suddenly the swift approach of my houri to her window betokened something fresh. She lowered her nosegay by way of saluting, and my glasses were at once turned to the direction in which she was darting her glances.

On the third floor of the colonel's house I could see a splendid drum-major in full uniform, with large epaulets, his chest bedizened with broad gold braid and his hand resting upon his heart. As the room was not high enough to accommodate the lofty plume towering above his bearskin, my rival was leaning half out of the window, and his tricolour insignium seemed to pierce the sky.

I remained dazzled at the sight of him: he glistened like the sun!

With Zouhra it had been love at first sight. The pantomimic business gradually began on both sides; on the girl's part it was naive and still restrained; on the drum-major's, ardent and passionate, though now and then he struck a contemplative attitude. He showed her a letter and she showed him another one, which she held in readiness. The sight made a flush rise to Mohammed's brow.

In presence of such avowals doubt was no longer possible. The drum-major soon became emboldened and raised the tips of his fingers to his lips. His kisses journeyed through space; and then with his hands clasped he begged of Zouhra to return them.

I must confess that the wretched girl defended herself for a few minutes with bashful reserve. But she was so pressed and implored that at last I saw her weaken, and anxious and hesitating, she yielded.

I was betrayed!

Mohammed sank down, uttering a plaintive moan. For my own part I thought of my uncle's misfortune. Was it fate?

However, my uncle is not the only man who comes from Marseilles; I also come from that city, and although I am merely his nephew, I have at times enough of his hot disposition to feel as he felt after similar strokes of fate. Having been drawn into his irregular orbit, passing through the same phases as he passed through, I must expect that nothing will ever happen to me in the same way as it would happen to others, himself excepted. Thus the similarity of our adventures—the drum-major in my case taking the place of my uncle's Jean Bonaffe,—ought not to have surprised me; it should have been foreseen like a philosophical contingency previously inscribed in the book of destiny. And, indeed, to tell the truth, I should have considered the slightest departure from the precise law of fate illogical.

However, I was either in a bad disposition of mind or I had been too suddenly and speedily awakened from the presumptuous quietude into which I had sunk, for I will admit to you that on thinking over my case, I experienced at the moment a singular feeling of astonishment.

Horns are like teeth, a witty woman once said: they hurt while they are coming, but afterwards one manages to put up with them!

True as this remark of an experienced person may be, yet having my own ideas as to these vain appendages which I could not prevent from sprouting; and being, moreover, sufficiently provided with proofs which I had duly weighed, my first idea was to dart head first athwart this intrigue in which my dishonour was a certainty. Leaving Mohammed upon the divan where he had stranded, I hastened by way of the stairs to the guilty creature's room.

I softly opened the closed door, stepped gently over the carpet, and approached her from behind in time to catch her just as she had one hand on her heart and the other on her lips.

She gave a little shriek, while the drum-major, on seeing me appear so suddenly, made a gesture of despair. Then he drew back with such haste that his plume caught against the wall above the window, with the result that his bearskin was knocked off, and turning a sommersault fell into the courtyard.

Zouhra thereupon gave another shriek.

All this had occurred with the rapidity of a flash of lightning. My rival, closing his window, had disappeared like a jack-in-the-box.

We were alone.

"Ah! ha!" I then said to the unworthy creature, "so this is your conduct—"

She answered nothing; she still hoped, no doubt, that she would be able to deny the facts, with the brazen assurance of the woman who, although surprised in the act, puts on a grand air, and waxes wrathful as at an insult.

"Who was that man up there," I resumed, "with whom you were corresponding?"

"A man!" she finally answered with her strong Turkish accent which I will spare you. "I don't know what you mean—I don't know any men—I have never seen any!"

"But he was at that window—there."

"Well, what does that prove?" she retorted. "Does that concern me? Can I prevent people from coming to their windows?"

"No, but when they are there you might prevent yourself from making signs to them; and especially from returning the kisses they send to you."

"Signs, I? I made signs!" she exclaimed. "Ah! that is really too bad! Who do you take me for then?"

"Why, I surprised you, and I stayed your hand when you had your fingers raised to your lips."

"Well, can't I put my fingers to my lips now? What, am I not to have the right to make a gesture, without accounting for it, without being insulted? Did any one ever see a woman treated in such an odious fashion? Well, tie me up then!"

You are acquainted with women's tactics, my dear Louis: they are always the same in such cases. I put a stop to it all after letting her deny the facts.

"Come, come," I said to her. "This is not the time for you to play the part of a persecuted victim. For the last half hour I have been watching you from behind those curtains. I saw everything—with my opera-glass," I added, showing her the glass in proof of my assertion.

Struck by this victorious demonstration she stood there in consternation. For a moment I enjoyed the effect I had produced and then continued:

"I saw the letter which he showed you, and the one which you have in your pocket—I can still see a bit of it peeping out."

On hearing this she became very red; and with incredible swiftness drew forth the incriminating missive, which she tore into a hundred pieces.

"All right," said I. "It would seem then that you had written something very compromising to that soldier, whom you have never met and whom you don't know."

"It was a letter for the modiste," she replied with assumed indignation.

"Yes, and you no doubt wanted him to deliver it," I retorted in an ironical strain.

This last bitter dart went home and set her beside herself. She assumed a superb attitude.

"I shall not give you any explanation," she said. "Believe whatever you please. Do whatever you choose. As for myself, I know what I have to do now. Since I am spied upon and treated in this fashion I have had enough of leading such a life—I prefer to put an end to it at once!"

"And how do you purpose putting an end to it?" I resumed. "It will perhaps be necessary to consult me a little bit on that subject."

"But you are neither my husband nor my brother, my dear fellow," she exclaimed in the most airy way imaginable, "and I don't suppose that you are going to talk to me any more of those stupid Turkish rights. We are in Paris and I know that I am free!"

"Well, where will your freedom take you?"

"Oh! don't worry yourself about me—I should not have any trouble to secure a husband. Do you imagine, my dear fellow, that I should be embarrassed to find a *position*?"

This characteristic word showed me that she was far more completely initiated than I had suspected.

"And you expect," I retorted, "to obtain this *position* from that fine nobleman, eh?"

These disdainful words exasperated her; she lost all self-restraint and burnt her ships.

"That fine nobleman is a duke!" she exclaimed vehemently. "I will not allow you to insult him. And since you dare to threaten me, I will tell you that I love him and that he adores me, and that he offers to marry me and promises me every bliss—"

In spite of my misfortune I could not help laughing at this fiery indignant declaration to which Zouhra's Turkish accent imparted an irresistibly comic effect. My gaiety brought her anger to a climax.

Frenzied, decided upon everything, she darted to a chiffonier, drew out an illuminated card, upon which two doves were pecking one another, and threw it at me with a queenly air, exclaiming:

"There, my dear fellow you will see if I still have any need of you!"

I picked up the card and read what was written upon it:

LEDUC (D'ARPAJON),

Drum-Major of the 79th Regt. of the Line.

To the divine ZOUHRA—Everlasting Love!

It would be useless for me to describe to you the end of the scene.

When I had laughed enough, I allowed myself the delightful pleasure of undeceiving my faithless houri by explaining to her her unfortunate mistake as to the rank of her conqueror, whom she had mentally endowed with a fortune in keeping with the height of his plume.[A] I destroyed her dream of every bliss by reducing it to so much bliss as was procurable with a full pay of a franc and a half *per diem*.

[Footnote A: Zouhra with her imperfect knowledge of French had concluded that Leduc (D'Arpajon) meant "the Duke of Arpajon"—whereas, in reality, Leduc, a single word, was the drum-major's name; D'Arpajon implying that he came from, or belonged to, the little market town of Arpajon, not far from Paris.—*Trans.*]

As I made these crushing revelations you might have seen her gradually sinking and collapsing, with her pretty purple lips just parted, and her gazelle's eyes staring with frightened astonishment. She was the picture of consternation.

All at once she darted towards me and abruptly caught me in her arms.

"Ah! it is you that I love!—you that I love!" she exclaimed in a pathetic tone amid her transports.

I had some difficulty in releasing myself from her passionate embrace; still I eventually succeeded in doing so, but only to confront a fresh crisis of despair, whereupon I immediately confided Zouhra to the care of her maids.

Then, without any further explanations, which would have been superfluous, I withdrew.

Of course I am perfectly aware that you will try to derive from this mishap some argument intended to triumph over my discomfiture.

I would have you remark, however, that you have no right to seize upon a general fact—for infidelity is inherent in woman's nature—and draw deductions respecting my particular case. All that you can reasonably conclude is that the man who has four wives is bound to be deceived four times as often as the man who has but one wife.

That is certainly a weighty argument, I confess.

However all that may be, my misfortune having been made evident to me, and Zouhra being banished from my heart, it was necessary that I should come to a decision with regard to her.

The most simple course was to consult my uncle; his own experience in a similar mishap pointed him out as the best of advisers.

He listened to me, stroking his beard with the somewhat derisive phlegm of a practical man, who is not sorry to find that he has some companions in misfortune. It even seemed to me that I could detect a touch of malicious satisfaction, as if he still resented my conduct as an heir.

When I had finished he quietly remarked:

"What an old stupid you are! You should have let her get married without saying anything! In that way you would have saved us the expense of sending her back home again."

"Well, unfortunately it's too late now for that, uncle," I answered.

To be brief, as the Turkish law does not allow the desertion or dismissal of a cadine unless she be provided for, Zouhra is to be exiled to Rhodes. The pasha has established there for his own use, a kind of Botany Bay, which is a place both of retirement and rustication for his invalided wives who have lost their freshness with age. The place is an old abbey with spacious gardens planted with mimosas and orange trees, and was purchased by auction for some ten thousand francs. The island is delightful, and provisions are to be had there for nothing, according to what my uncle tells me. Judge for yourself: fowls cost twopence each, and everything else is to be had at correspondingly low prices. There are already eleven women there, and it does not cost more than nine thousand francs a year to keep them all on a proper footing, including the board and wages of their servants.

Find me among our own boasted institutions any one to be compared with that of my uncle—an institution established to provide for similar contingencies, and the arrangements of which are equally good.

CHAPTER XV

For the last three days that unworthy girl Zouhra has been on her way to Rhodes.

Well, what does that matter? I admit that I have only three wives left, that's all. And what of that? Is it fitting that you, my dearest friend, should try to make me feel ashamed of it?

While exercising your facetiousness, it seems to me that you especially level your irony at certain other worries necessarily occasioned by the position of Kondje-Gul and what you call the wooing of the "fierce Kiusko." Ye Gods! so I have a rival. Really, you make me laugh!

I fancy, however, that all this will inevitably end in a duel between us, which indeed, as time goes on, seems to me quite unavoidable.

One evening when I arrived rather late at Teral House by reason of one of those tedious dinners with which Anna Campbell's leaves-out were celebrated, I found Kondje-Gul quite downcast, and her eyes red with crying. I had left her a few hours before in the best of spirits, and delighted about a pretty little pony which I had given her in the morning, and which we had been trying. Surprised and alarmed at such a sudden grief as she evinced, and which had caused her to shed tears, I anxiously questioned her about it.

Directly I began speaking to her I saw that she wanted to conceal from me the cause of her affliction: but I pressed her.

"No, it's nothing," she said, "only a story which mamma told me."

But when she tried to smile, a sob broke out from her lips, and, bursting into tears, she threw her arm round my neck, nestling her head on my bosom.

"Good heavens! what's the matter, dear?" I exclaimed, quite alarmed. "Tell me all about it, I entreat you. What has happened? And why are you crying like this?"

She could not answer me. Her bosom heaved, and she seized my hand and covered it with kisses, as if in order to demonstrate her love for me in the midst of her distress.

I succeeded in calming her; and then, making her sit down by my side, with her hands in mine, I pressed her to confess her troubles to me. Her hesitation increased my alarm: she turned her eyes away from me, and I could see that she feared to reply to me. At last, quite frantic with anxiety, I resorted to my marital authority.

Then, with childlike submission, she related to me the following strange story, which filled me with astonishment.

After luncheon her mother had joined her in the drawing-room, when in the course of a general conversation she began to speak about their native country and their family, and about the pleasure it would be for them to revisit them after so long an absence. Kondje-Gul let her go on in this strain, thinking that she was just indulging in one of those dreams of a far-off future which the imagination is fond of cherishing, however impossible their realisation may be. But soon she was very much surprised by noticing that her mother was discussing this scheme as one which might be carried out at an early date. She then questioned her about it. At last, after a lot of fencing, Madame Murrah informed her that she had learnt a marriage was arranged between me and Anna Campbell, who had been betrothed to me for a long while past; also that this marriage would take place in six months' time, and that I should have to go away with my wife the day after the wedding.

The end of all these arrangements would be the abandonment of Kondje-Gul.

I was dismayed by this unexpected revelation. The plan of my marriage with Anna had remained a family secret, known only to my uncle, to herself, to my aunt, and to me. How had it got to Madame Murrah's ears? I was unable to conceal my uneasiness.

"But this marriage is true then?" continued my poor Kondje with an anxious look in my face.

"Nothing is true but our love!" I replied, distressed by her fears; "nothing is true but this, that I mean to love you always, and always to live with you as I do now."

"But this marriage?" she again repeated.

It was impossible for me to escape any longer from the necessity of making a confession which I had intended to have prepared her for later on.

"Listen, my darling," I said, taking her by the hands, "and above all things trust me as you listen to me! I love you, I love no one but you; you are my wife, my happiness, my life. Do you believe me?"

"Yes, dear, I believe you. But what about her?" she added in a tremble. "What about Anna Campbell? Are you going to marry her?"

"Come," I said, wishing to begin by soothing her fears; "if, as so often happens in your own country, I were obliged, if only in order to assure our own happiness, to make another marriage, would not you understand that this was only a sacrifice which I owed to my uncle if he required it of me—a family arrangement, in fact, which could not separate us from each other? What have you to fear so long as I only love you? Did you trouble yourself about Hadidje or Zouhra?"

"Oh, but they were not Christians! Anna Campbell would be your real wife; and your religion and laws would enjoin you to love her."

"No," I exclaimed, "neither my religion nor my laws could change my heart or undo my love for you. It is my duty to protect your life and make it a happy one; for are not you also my wife? Why should you alarm yourself about an obligation of mine which, if we lived in your country, would not disturb your confidence in me? Anna Campbell is not really in love with me: we are only like two friends, prepared to unite with each other in a conventional union, such as you may see many a couple around us enter upon—an association of fortunes, in which the only personal sentiments demanded are reciprocal esteem. My dear girl, what is there to be jealous of? Don't you know that you will always be everything to me?"

Poor Kondje-Gul listened to these somewhat strange projects without the least idea of opposing them. Still under the yoke of her native ideas, those Oriental prejudices in which she had been brought up were too deeply grafted in her mind to permit of her being rapidly converted by acquaintance with our sentiments and usages—very illogical as they often appeared to her mind—to a different view of woman's destiny. According to her laws and her religion, I was her master. She could never have entertained the possibility of her refusing to submit to my will; but I could see by the tears in her eyes that this very touching submission and resignation on her part was simply due to her devoted self-control, and that she suffered cruelly by it.

"Come, why do you keep on crying?" I continued, drawing her into my arms. "Do you doubt my love, dear?"

"Oh, no!" she replied quickly. "How could I mistrust you?"

"Well, then, away with those tears!"

"Yes," she said, giving me a kiss, "you are right, dear: I am very silly! What can you expect of me? I am still half a barbarian, and am rather bewildered with all I have learnt from you. There are still some things in my nature which I can't understand. Why it is that I feel more jealous of Anna Campbell than I was of Hadidje, of Nazli, or of Zouhra, I can't tell you; but I am afraid—she is a Christian, and perhaps you will love her better than me. I feel that the laws and customs of your country will recover their hold over you and will separate us. That odious law which you once told me of, which would enfranchise me, so you said, and make me my own mistress if I desired to leave you, often comes back to my mind like a bad dream. It seems to me that this imaginary liberty, which I don't want at any price, would become a reality if you get married."

I reassured her on this point. There is a much more persuasive eloquence in the heart than in the vain deductions of logic. During this extraordinary scene, in which my poor Kondje-Gul's mind was alarmed by the conflict going on between her own beliefs and what she knew of our society, I was quite sincere in my illusions concerning the moral compromise which, I fancied, was imposed upon me as an absolute duty. Singular as it may all appear to you, I had already been subjected too long to the influence of the harem not to have become gradually permeated by the Oriental ideas. The tie which bound me to Kondje-Gul had acquired a kind of sacred and legitimate character in my eyes.

However this may have been, her revelation disclosed an impending danger. It was clear to me that the news of the marriage arranged between Anna Campbell and myself could only have reached Madame Murrah through Kiusko. His relationship with my aunt had made him a member of our family, and he had been acquainted with our projects. I could easily understand that his jealous instincts had penetrated one side of the secret between Kondje and myself. He had at least guessed that she loved me, and that I was an obstacle to the attainment of his desires. He was following up his object. He wished to destroy Kondje-Gul's hopes in advance, by showing her that I was engaged to marry another.

With my present certitude of his mean devices, I began to wonder whether everything had been already let out through slips of the tongue made by Madame Murrah, in the course of those interviews which he had obtained with her either by chance or by appointment. For several days past I fancied I had remarked in him an increased reserve of manner. It was possible that, being convinced now of the futility of his hopes, his only object henceforth was to revenge himself on his rival by at least disturbing his feeling of security.

Yes! you are quite right: I love her! Why should you imagine I would wish to deny it, or dissemble it as a weakness? Did I ever tell you that the consequence of indulgence in the pleasures of harem loves would be to drown the heart, the soul, and the aspirations towards the ideal for the sole advantage of the senses? Where you seem to see the defeat of one vanquished, I find the triumph of my happiness and the enchantment of a dream which I am realizing during my waking hours. Compare with this secret and charming bond of union which attaches me to Kondje-Gul, the prosaic and vulgar character of those common intrigues which one cynically permits the whole world to observe, or of those illicit connections which the hypocritical remnant of virtue with us constrains us to conceal, like crimes, in the darkness. Deceptive frenzies they are, the enjoyment of which always involves of necessity the degradation of the woman and the contempt of the lover! You may preach and dogmatise as much as you like in your endeavours to uphold the superiority of our habits over those of the East, which you declare to be barbarous; you will never succeed in doing anything more than entangling yourself in your own paradox.

The fact is that in the refined epoch, so-called, in which we live, every description of non-legitimized union in love becomes a libertinage, and the woman who abandons herself to it becomes a profane idol. Whether she be a duchess, or a foolish maid, you may write verses over her fall, but you cannot forget it. The worm is in the fruit. My love for Kondje-Gul knows no such shame, and needs no guilty excuses. Proud of her slavish submission, she can love me without derogating in the least from her own self-respect. In Kondje's eyes, her tender embraces are legitimate, her glory is the conquest of my heart. I am her master, and she abandons herself to me without transgressing any duty. Being a daughter of Asia, she fulfils her destiny according to the moral usages and the beliefs of her native land: to these she remains faithful in loving me: her religion has no different rule, her virtue no different law.

That is why I love her, and why my heart is possessed by such a frank and open loyalty towards her. You speak to me about the future, and ask me what will happen when the time comes for my marriage to Anna Campbell? Well, the future

is still in the distance, my dear fellow; when it comes upon me we will see what I will do! Meanwhile I love and content myself with loving!

Will that satisfy you? Oh yes, I confess my errors, I abjure my pagan vanities, and my sultanic principles. I give up Mahomet! I have found my Damascus road. True love has manifested itself to me in all its glory, shining through the clouds; it has inspired me with its grace, and my false idols lie prostrate in the dust—Would you like me to make you a present of my harem? If this offer suits you, send me a line, and I will forward what remains of it to you with all despatch: you shall then give it my news, for it is six weeks now since I have seen my two sultanas. Only make haste—in eight days' time they are to return to Constantinople. The blessings of civilization are decidedly banes to these little animals. Liberty in Paris would soon ruin them. I have provided for them, and am sending them away.

I mention all this to show you in what happiness I bask. Reassured by my affection, and confident in the future, my Kondje-Gul has recovered that sweet serenity which makes our love such a delicious dream. As the fierce Kiusko is now unmasked, we laugh at his foolish plots as you may well imagine!

CHAPTER XVI

My aunt Gretchen van Cloth is in Paris!

Well, why do you assume your facetious tone on reading that? I know you and can guess your thoughts.

After all, Barbassou is a pasha, is it still necessary to remind you of that?

Well, the other day my uncle informed me that he would take me home to dine with him. I repaired to the boulevard at the appointed hour and we started in his brougham for Passy. On the way he told me what it was necessary I should know. We reached a rather nice looking house in the Rue Raynouard, from which you can see the boats floating down the Seine. There is a railing and a little garden in front. On hearing our footsteps, a young lady whom I at once recognised, from the recollections of my childhood, hurried to the door.

"Kiss your aunt," my uncle said to me: and I did as I was told.

We then entered a modest little drawing-room, the commonplace aspect of which, reminding one of furnished apartments, was improved by its general neatness and by a few bunches of flowers displayed in sundry odd vases. Three youngsters, the smallest of whom was between three and four years old, were eating bread and butter there. My uncle saluted each of them with a hurried kiss, and then they ran off to their nurse.

My aunt Gretchen is just reaching her thirty-fourth birthday. She confesses to her age. If she did not come from Amsterdam she ought to have been born there. She has blossomed like a flower among the tulips, and she looks like a Rubens, in that painter's more sober style, as in the portrait of the Friesland woman, with the prim pink and white flesh of the healthful natures of the North. You realise that good blood flows quietly and temperately beneath the pleasantly plump charms of this worthy Dutchwoman, who claims only her due, but is desirous of getting it. And she does get it. She has luxuriant light chestnut hair, and a very attractive face with the smiling, placid, and even somewhat simple expression of a good housewife, who is as expert in bringing up her children as in making pastry and pineapple jam. Being of a gay and amiable disposition, she greeted her husband with the ordinary, hearty affection of a woman who has never been a widow. After bringing him his foxskin cap she established him in a comfortable arm-chair, and then mixed his absinthe for him. I guessed that the captain was returning to old habits, with the dignified composure which he displays in everything.

They began to talk in Dutch, and as I looked at them without understanding it, my uncle said to me:

"Your aunt tells me that her kitchen range is too small to make any good *souffles*, and it worries her on your account."

"Oh! my aunt is too kind to disturb herself about such a trifling matter," I replied; "the pleasure I feel in seeing her again amply compensates me for this slight mishap."

"Well, instead of the *souffles* you shall have some *wafelen* and some *poffertjes*!" quickly rejoined my aunt with her kindly smile.

I remarked that she spoke French much better than formerly. However, probably on account of her voyages with the captain, who recruited his crews at Toulon, her Dutch accent has now become a Provencal one.

The dinner was delightful, substantial and plentiful, like the charms of my aunt, who was victorious along the whole line, and notably with the spicy sauce of a *gebakken schol*, which was excellently baked.

The conversation was simple and of a free and easy character, my uncle talking with all the freedom of a man who has a quiet conscience. He was as much at his ease in his Dutch household as any good citizen could be, and I perceived that my aunt knew absolutely nothing about him, unless it were the important position that he occupied in the spice trade. She gave him some news about the great doings of the Van Hutten firm of Rotterdam and Antwerp, in which he seemed to take a particular interest. It seems, too, that Peter van Schloss, junior, is married to a young lady of Dordrecht, who presented him with twins after six months of matrimony, a circumstance which my uncle found very natural. Old Joshua Schlittermans, having been utterly ruined by the failure of Gannton Brothers of New York, has now taken to drink.

When the coffee was served (Dirkie had brought it from Amsterdam, purchasing it on the Damplaatz, at the corner of Kalver Straat), my aunt filled a long porcelain pipe which my uncle took from her hands and lighted, puffing out clouds of smoke, with the serene gravity of some worthy burgomaster at home. We drank some schiedam and two sorts of dry curacoa. While my aunt sat knitting at the table she questioned me as to my occupations, asking me if I were working in my uncle's establishment; and upon my replying affirmatively to her, she gave me some very good advice, telling me to be very industrious so that I might take my uncle's place later on.

At half-past ten we rose from table and went into the drawing-room. Dirkie got everything ready for a game of dominoes, and they began to play in the Dutch fashion. My uncle kept the markers, and noted the points made: he himself speedily scored between three and four hundred, and then, feeling satisfied with his success, he said:

"Well, give us a little music!"

My aunt did not require any pressing, but went to the piano in a very good-humoured manner. She opened the top so that the instrument might give out a louder sound, then passed behind and arranged everything; and suddenly I heard the splendid introduction of Haydn's seventh symphony in *F major* bursting forth, while my aunt turned the handle with rare skill and gracefulness. (I recognised the superb instrument mentioned in the fourth legacy of the famous will.)

I must admit that if my aunt played the minuet rather quickly, she executed the *andante* in a very delicate style, and the *scherzo* and the *finale* were both dashed off in a spirited way. At the last chord, I applauded with sincere enthusiasm.

"She plays very well, doesn't she?" my uncle quietly asked me, in a modest tone. "You, who are a connoisseur—"

"Oh! she plays perfectly," I rejoined, without stinting my praise.

"And besides she puts expression into it," he resumed. "One

can see that she feels what she plays."

My aunt kissed him for this compliment, which he paid her with the gravest assurance.

"Ah! you are still a flatterer!" she said to him.

As may readily be guessed, some of Strauss's waltzes and two or three polkas followed the classical symphonies, together with the overtures of "Don Giovanni" and "Fra Diavolo." It was really a perfect concert till midnight. But by that time my aunt's plump arm being somewhat tired it was necessary to bring the entertainment to a close.

Now, my dear fellow, I am not one of those who give way to the stupid prejudices of our foolish traditions; still less am I one of those who seek to evade frivolous objections, or fight shy of plain and open discussion. I have myself officially abandoned polygamy, that is true—but you are meditating another attack upon my uncle—I see it and I feel it—and from the depths of your troglodytic intellect you intend to drag out some commonplace hackneyed argument accompanied by frivolous sarcasms, and directed, not at the point in question, but all round it. As you are even incapable of understanding your own so-called virtue in its true and primitive sense, you will no doubt repeat your usual stupid remarks, denouncing my uncle's conduct as scandalous.

Let us go straight to the moral point, without haggling over words. My uncle, who has the advantage of being a Turk, distributes himself between his two wives, like a worthy husband faithful to his duty. Do you presume to blame him? In that case what have you to say to our friends A. B. C. D. E. F. (I spare you the rest of the alphabet, and it is under-stood that the reader and present company are excepted), our friends, I say, who deceive their wives for the sake of hussies who have several protectors, as they are well aware? It is not

a question here of fighting on behalf of the holy shrine of monogamy. With how many faithful, irreproachable husbands are you acquainted? Those hussies are mistresses, you will say to me! I know it: that is to say, they are females who belong to everybody. The question is settled: my uncle is a virtuous man by the side of our friends. As he is incapable of such vulgar and promiscuous intrigues he has a supplementary household, that is all! Like the prudent traveller who is acquainted with the length of the journey he judiciously prepares relays.

Compare that family gathering at my aunt Van Cloth's with those unhealthy stolen pleasures of debauched husbands who feel ashamed and tremble with the fear of being surprised. My uncle is a patriarch and takes no part in the licentiousness of our times. So much for this subject.

I have just received a most unforeseen blow, my dear Louis, and even while I write have scarcely recovered from the alarm of a horrible machination from which we were only saved by a miracle.

I told you about my poor Kondje-Gul's passing grief on account of her mother's foolish ideas. Reassured as to the future by my vows and promises, she was too amenable to my influence to refuse to submit to a trial which I was forced by duty to prepare her for. Proud at the thought that she was sacrificing her jealousy for me, sacrificing herself for my happiness, her tears having been dried up by my kisses, I found her the day after this cruel blow to her heart as expansive and confiding as if no cloud had darkened our sky.

But a very few days after I was quite surprised to observe a sort of melancholy resignation about her. I attributed this trouble to some of the childish worries which her mother's temper occasionally gave her. However, after several days had passed like this, I came to the conclusion that the cause of her sadness must be something more than a transitory one, and that she was harassed by some new grief which even my presence was not sufficient to dissipate. By her replies to me, which seemed to be pervaded by more than usual tenderness, I judged that—in her fear of alarming me, no doubt,—she wished to conceal from me the real cause of her anxiety.

One evening at one of our little parties at the Montagues, which had begun as a concert, but was converted by us, in our gay and sociable mood, into a dance, Maud had trotted me off to make up a quadrille. Kondje-Gul, who, as you know, never dances, had withdrawn into the boudoir adjoining the drawing-room, where she was looking through the albums. I suspected nothing, and was engaged in a frivolous conversation with Maud, when from where I stood, through the glass partition which separated the two rooms, I noticed Kiusko come and sit down by her side. It was natural enough that, seeing her alone, he considered himself bound not to leave her so, for that might have looked like a want of politeness on his part. It seemed to me, moreover, from their faces, that their conversation was upon indifferent topics, and was being conducted in that tone of ordinary friendliness which was usual between them.

He was turning over the pages of an album as he talked to her. I had no reason to pay much attention to this *tete-a-tete*, and was not even intending to follow it, but once, near the end of the quadrille, my eyes being again turned by chance in Kondje-Gul's direction, I saw her rise up all of a sudden, as if something that Daniel had said had excited her suddenly. I thought I saw her blush, raising her head proudly and answering him in an offended tone.

The dance being now over, I left Maud, and, agitated by an anxious kind of feeling, walked up to the boudoir. They were standing up, and Kiusko's back being turned to the door, he did not see me enter. Kondje-Gul saw me and said:

"Andre, come and give me your arm!"

At this unusually bold request, Daniel could not repress a gesture of astonishment, and cast a bewildered glance at me. I advanced, and she seized my arm with a convulsive movement, and addressed herself to my rival:

"This is the second time, sir, that you have declared your love to me. Let me tell you why I decline it: I am the slave of Monsieur Andre de Peyrade, and I love him!"

If a thunderbolt had fallen at Daniel's feet, it could not have startled him more than this. He turned so pale that I thought he was going to faint. He gazed at both of us with a desperate and ferocious look, as if some terrible thought was revolving in his mind. His features were contracted into such a savage expression that I instinctively placed myself between him and Kondje-Gul. But, all at once, frightened no doubt at his own passion, he gave one glance of despair and rage, and fled from the room. Kondje-Gul was all of a tremble.

"What has happened, then?" I asked her.

"I will tell you all about it," she answered, in a voice still quivering with emotion. "I am going home with my mother. Come after us as soon as we are off."

CHAPTER XVII

Half an hour later I joined Kondje-Gul again at her house. She had sent Fanny out of the room, and was waiting for me. When she saw me, she threw her arm round my neck, and the long pent-up tears seemed to start from her eyes like a fountain.

"Good heavens!" I exclaimed, "what is it, then?"

And taking her on my knees like a child, I held her in my arms; but she soon recovered her energy.

"Listen, dear," she said in a firm voice, "you must forgive me for what I have just done: you must forgive me for having concealed my thoughts and my troubles from you, even at the risk of distressing you."

"I forgive you, everything," I answered immediately, "go on, tell me quickly."

"Well, then! For a whole week I have been deceiving you," she continued, "by telling you that I had no troubles, and that I did not know the cause of that sadness which I could not conceal from you. I was afraid of making you angry with my mother, by confessing to you that it was she who was tormenting me."

"Your mother!" I exclaimed: "and what had she to say to you, then?"

"You shall hear all," she said, with animation, "for I must justify myself for having kept a secret from you. I daresay you remember," she continued, "that a fortnight ago she spoke to me about your marriage, telling me that you were going to leave me."

"Yes, yes, I understand," I said. "What then?"

"My mother had made me promise to keep this revelation a secret, because it was necessary, so she said, that Count Kiusko should not suspect that we loved each other. She said that he had expressly attributed my refusal to become his wife to some hope which I doubtless entertained of marrying you."

"Well, go on; tell me what has occurred since."

"You know the state of trouble you found me in that night. I could not hold back my tears, and you commanded me to tell you all. At last you reassured me with so much warmth of feeling, that after that I did not believe anyone but you. Quite happy at the thought of sacrificing myself to your will, and to your peace of mind, I left off thinking about my alarms, and regretted them as an insult to our love; I repeated to my mother all your kind promises, and thought that I had set her mind at rest. Imagine my astonishment at hearing her, a few days afterwards, return to the subject: she had seen the count again, who had declared that your uncle would disinherit you if you did not carry out his wishes."

"And did you believe all that?"

"No," she replied promptly, "for you had not told me so! But then my mother, seeing that I would only believe you, changed her tactics: she spoke about Count Kiusko, his wealth, and his love for me."

"She did that, did she?"

"Oh, forgive her!" she continued; "she gets anxious both on my account and her own. She is alarmed about the future, and fancies she sees me deserted by you! Well, it was simply a cruel struggle for me, in which my heart could not betray you. I suffered through it, and that's all! But three days ago, I don't know what can have passed during your aunt's party, my mother, on our way home, said to me in a decided manner that she had resolved 'to live no longer among the infidels,' and intended 'to return to the land of the Faithful, in order to expiate the great wrong she had committed by living here.'"

"I was dismayed at this resolution of hers. As she based it upon our faith, I could not oppose her, for that would have been a sacrilege, but I could at least invoke her affection for me, and entreat her not to leave. Then, while I was on my knees before her, and was kissing her and crying, she startled me by saying: 'You shall not leave me; for, when I go, I shall take you away with me'!"

"Why, she must be crazy!" I exclaimed.

"Well, dear," added Kondje-Gul, "you can easily understand what a thunderbolt this was to me! I felt it so painfully that I nearly swooned away. My mother was alarmed and called for Fanny. The next day, I attempted to prevail upon her to change her mind, declaring that it would kill me to be separated from you. I thought I had mollified her, for she kissed me and said that all she cared about was my happiness. But this evening, while we were in the carriage on our way to Suzannah's, she spoke again to me about Count Kiusko. I have a presentiment that the greatest enemy to our

love and happiness is that man; and that he it is who has been influencing my mother, hoping, no doubt, that when separated from you I should no longer be able to resist her wishes.

"Well, you know the rest, I had gone into the boudoir while you were dancing, when the count came and sat down by my side.—'Is it true that you are going away?' he said to me, after a minute or so. 'Who could make you believe such a thing?' I replied coldly. 'Why, something your mother told me which seemed to imply it.' I remained silent—he did not venture to follow up the subject, and said nothing more for a few minutes. I kept my eyes on a book which I was looking through, for I felt that his eyes were fixed upon me. 'Perhaps you will regret Andre a little,' he continued, 'but what can you do? He is not free,—and besides, do you suppose he would have loved you?'"

"At this question, the cruel irony of which wounded me to the quick, I was possessed by some mad impulse, I raised my head and replied to him in such a scornful tone that he rose up in confusion. Just then you came in. I wished to overwhelm him with my contempt so as to destroy all further hopes he might cherish. You know what I said—"

"And quite right, too! For it was necessary to put a stop to his nonsense. I will attend to it."

"But what if my mother wants to separate us?"

"Your mother, indeed!" I exclaimed; "your mother who sold you, abandoned you to the life of a slave, do you think she can come and claim the rights which she has thrown away?"

"Can you defend me against her, then?"

"Yes, dear, I will defend you," I exclaimed in a passion, "and now set your mind at ease. There is a miserable plot at the bottom of all this, which I intend demolishing. When I leave you I am going to Count Kiusko, and I assure you that he sha'n't trouble you any more: after that I shall see your mother."

"Good heavens!" said Kondje-Gul, "are you going to fight him?"

"No, no," I answered with a laugh, in order to remove her fears; "but you must understand that it is necessary for me to have an explanation with him."

In the morning I returned home and arranged all my affairs ready for any eventuality; then when all was in order I went after two of my friends, and asked them to hold themselves ready to act as my seconds in an affair which I might be compelled by grave circumstances to settle that very day. Having obtained their promise to do so, I proceeded to Kiusko's in the Rue de l'Elysee.

When I arrived at his house, I saw from the windows being open that he was up. A footman, who knew me, was standing under the peristyle. He told me that he did not think his master would see anyone then. I gave him my card and instructed him to send it up at once to the count. In a minute or two after he returned and asked me to come up to his master's private room: he showed me into a little smoking-room adjoining the bedroom, to which the count's intimate friends only are admitted. I had hardly entered it when Daniel appeared; he was dressed in a Moldavian costume which he uses as a dressing-gown.

"Hullo, here's our dear friend Andre!" he said when he saw me, in such an indifferent tone that I could detect in it the intentional affectation of a calmness to which his pale countenance gave the lie.

Still he did not hold out his hand to me, nor did I proffer mine; he sat down, indicating to me an arm-chair on the other side of the fire-place.

"What good fortune has brought you here so early this morning?" he continued, taking a few puffs at his cigar.

"Why, I should have thought you expected to see me," I replied, looking him straight in the face.

He returned my look with a smile.

"I expected you, without expecting you, as they say."

By the peculiar tone in which he uttered these words, I could see that he was determined to make me take the initiative in the matter upon which I had come.

"Very well!" I said, wishing to show him that I guessed his mind. "I will explain myself."

"I am all attention, my dear fellow," he answered.

"I have come to speak to you," I continued drily, "about Mademoiselle Kondje-Gul Murrah, and about what passed yesterday between her and you."

"Ah, yes! I understand: you are referring to the somewhat severe lecture which I drew upon myself, and to the confidential communication she made me."

"Precisely so," I added; "you could not sum up the two points better than you have done: a lecture, and a confidence. Now as one outcome of the second point is that I am responsible for all Mademoiselle Murrah's acts, I have come to place myself at your command respecting the lecture she thought fit to give you."

"What nonsense, my dear fellow!" he exclaimed, puffing a cloud of smoke into the air. "After all I only had what I deserved, for I can only blame my own presumption. Besides the very anger of such a charming young lady is a favour to the man who incurs it, so that my only regret is that I offended her. I should therefore really laugh at myself to think that I could hold you responsible for this little incident: nay, I will go so far as to say that, strictly speaking, I should owe you an apology for what you might be justified in complaining of as an act of disloyalty between friends, but for the fact that I can plead as my excuse the complete ignorance in which you left me of certain mysterious relations. You must know very well that a simple word from you, my relative, my *friend*, would have made me stop short on the brink of the precipice."

I appreciated the reproachful irony concealed in this last sentence; but I had gone too far to trouble myself about remorses of conscience regarding him.

"So then," I replied, "you have nothing to say, no satisfaction to demand of me in respect to this lecture?"

"None whatever, my dear fellow!" he answered, in the same easy tone which he had preserved all along. "And I may add that there could be nothing more ridiculous than a quarrel between two friends like you and me upon such a matter!"

"Let's think no more about it then!" I continued, imitating his composure. "Since you take it so good-naturedly, I sha'n't press it. But, having settled this first point, it remains now for us to discuss what you have termed the *confidence*."

At this he could not repress a slight gesture. His dark eye flashed up, but for a moment only: he was soon quite calm again.

"Ah, yes!" he said carelessly; "now we've come to the second point."

"This is the point of importance for me," I added; "and I am going to ask you, on my side, what you propose to do after this revelation?"

"I must compliment you, my dear fellow, for upon my word it's a most wonderful romance. Do you really mean to say that this beautiful young lady whom we have all been admiring from a distance, fascinated by her charms, and who like a young queen has been starring it in the most aristocratic drawing-rooms of your society, exciting enthusiastic praise wherever she goes,—that she is your slave?—You must admit that no mortal man could help envying you!"

"Do your compliments," I continued, "imply an engagement, on your part, to abandon importunities, which you now recognise to be useless?"

"Oh, indeed!" he exclaimed, with a laugh; "so you're going to ask me now to make *my* confession?"

Exasperated by this imperturbable composure of his, which I could not break down, I again looked him straight in the face, and asked—

"Do you mean to say you refuse to understand me?"

"No, my good sir!" he answered, resuming his peculiar smile, "I understand you perfectly well; you want to pick a quarrel with me, or to force me to demand satisfaction from you for a matter to which I do not attach as much importance as you do. Between ourselves, a duel would be an act of folly."

"Do you understand, at any rate," I retorted, "that I forbid your ever presenting yourself before Mademoiselle Kondje-Gul Murrah again?"

"Fie! my dear fellow! What do you take me for? After such an astonishing confession on her part, I should prove myself deficient in the most ordinary discretion, if I did not henceforth spare her my presence; so you may set your mind at ease on that point."

"Do you also imply by this evasive answer that you will abandon certain plots with her mother, which I might describe in terms that would not please you?"

"*Corbleu!* I should be too heavily handicapped in such a game, you must admit. Nor do I think that the good lady would be of much service to me, from what I know of her. Moreover," he added, "you have made me your confidences, as a friend, and, late though they arrive, I shall feel bound by them henceforth, if only on the ground of the mutual consideration, which, in grave circumstances, relations owe to each other."

The idea, then, occurred to me of provoking him in another way; but I clearly realised that, as he was playing such a perfidious part, it would be dangerous for me to commit this imprudence.

"Come, my dear Daniel," I said, as I rose from my chair, "at any rate, I can see that you have a very good-natured disposition."

"Of course I have," he replied; "and yet there are people who accuse me of evil designs."

The most formidable perils are those which you feel darkly conscious of, without being able to discern either the enemy

or the snare. This interview with Kiusko left almost an impression of terror on my mind. Knowing him to be as brave as I did, I felt convinced that his insensibility to my insults could only be due to the calculated calm of an implacable will, which was pursuing its object, whether of love, of vengeance, or of hatred, with all the energy of desperation.

Notwithstanding the humiliations he had undergone, I made sure that he had by no means given up the game. He meant to have Kondje-Gul, even if he had to capture her forcibly, and to carry her off as his prey. When I considered his sinister calm, which seemed to be abiding its opportunity, I wondered whether we were not already threatened by some secret machinations on his part.

Still I was not the man to be overcome by childish panics; so I soon got over this transitory feeling of alarm. I knew that after all we were so unequally matched, that I need not seriously fear his success. However determined Kiusko might be not to abandon the cowardly *role* he had assumed, I felt sure that an open affront at the club would compel him to fight.

Feeling reassured by this consideration, I decided to be guided in my action by the result of the interview which I was going to have with Kondje-Gul's mother. It was necessary for me to commence by putting a stop to the foolish proceedings of this woman, who was perhaps acting unintentionally as Kiusko's accomplice in schemes the object of which she could not foresee. It was eleven o'clock, an hour at which I knew I should find her alone, while Kondje-Gul was taking her lessons: I went accordingly to Teral House.

When I arrived a carriage was coming in and drawing up under the portico. I saw Madame Murrah get out of it. She could not avoid showing some annoyance on observing me.

Rather surprised at her taking such an early drive, I asked her to go into the drawing-room. She went there before me, and, seeing me take an arm-chair, she sat down on the divan in her usual indolent manner, and waited to hear what I had to say.

The scene which I am now going to relate to you, my dear Louis, was certainly, according to our ideas, a remarkable one. I tell it you just as it happened; but you must not forget that, for the Circassian woman, there was nothing in it which was out of conformity with her principles and the ideas of her race.

"I have come to talk with you," I said, "upon a serious subject, the importance of which perhaps you do not comprehend; for, without intending it, you are causing Kondje-Gul a great deal of trouble."

"How am I causing my daughter trouble?" she answered, as if she had been trying to understand.

"By continually telling her that I am going to leave her in order to get married,—by telling her that you wish to go away, and have even decided to take her with you. She is of course alarmed by all these imaginary anxieties."

"If it is so decreed by Allah!" she said quietly, "who shall prevent it?"

I had been expecting denials and subterfuges. This fatalistic utterance, without answering my reproaches, took me quite aback and made me tremble.

"But," I replied in a severe tone, "Allah could not command you to bring unhappiness to your daughter."

"As you are going to be married—"

"What matters my marriage?" I answered. "It cannot in any way affect Kondje-Gul's happiness! She knows that I love her, and that she will always retain the first place in my affections."

Madame Murrah shook her head for a minute in an undecided manner. The argument which I had employed was a most simple one.

At last she said: "Your wife will be an infidel; and, according to your laws, she will be entitled to demand my daughter's dismissal."

Dumb-founded at hearing her raise such objections, when I had fancied that I only needed to express my commands, I gazed at her in complete astonishment.

"But my wife will never know Kondje-Gul!" I exclaimed. "She will live in her own home, and Kondje-Gul will live here, so that nothing will be changed so far as we are concerned."

Upon this reasoning of mine, which I thought would seem decisive to her, the Circassian reflected for a moment as if embarrassed as to how she should answer me. But suddenly, just when I thought she was convinced, she said:

"All that you have said would be very true, if we were in Turkey; but you know better than I do that in your country, your religion does not permit you to have more than one wife."

"But," I exclaimed, more astounded than ever at her language, "do you suppose, then, that Kondje-Gul could ever doubt my honour or my fidelity?"

"My daughter is a child, and believes everything," she

continued. "But, for my own part, I have consulted a lawyer, and have been informed that according to your law she has become as free as a Frenchwoman, and has lost all her rights as *cadine* which she would have enjoyed in our country. Moreover I am informed that you can abandon her without her being able to claim any compensation from you."

I was struck dumb by this bold language and the expression with which it was accompanied. This was no longer the apathetic Oriental woman whose obedience I thought I commanded like a master. I had before me another woman whose expression was thoughtful and decided—I understood it all.

"While informing you that your daughter is free," I said, changing my own tone of voice, "this lawyer no doubt informed you also, that you could marry her to Count Kiusko?"

"Oh, I knew that before!" she replied, smiling.

"So you have been deceiving me these two months past, by leaving me to believe that you had answered him with a refusal?"

"It was certainly necessary to prevent you from telling him what he now knows.—The silly girl told him everything yesterday."

"How do you know that?"

I saw her face redden.

"I know it. That's enough!" she replied defiantly.

Feeling certain that Kondje-Gul had not told her anything of the incident of the day before, I divined that she had just left

Kiusko's, where she had been, no doubt, during our interview.

"May I ask you, then, what you propose to do, now that Count Kiusko knows everything?" I continued, controlling my anger.

"I shall do what my daughter's happiness impels me to do. You cannot marry her without being obliged to give up your uncle's fortune. If Count Kiusko should persist in wishing to make her his wife, knowing all the circumstances that he now does, you can understand that I, as her mother, could not but approve of a marriage which would assure her such a rich future."

At this I could no longer restrain myself, but exclaimed:

"Oh, indeed! Do you imagine I shall let you dispose of her like that, without defending her?"

"No, of course, I know all this.—And that's the very point upon which I consulted a counsel; but, according to what he has advised me, I should like to ask what authority you can claim over my daughter? What rights can you set up against mine?"

"Well, I should like to remind you also that I can ruin your comfortable expectations by killing Count Kiusko," I said, quite beside myself with rage.

"If so it is written!" she rejoined in a calm voice.

Exasperated by her fatalistic imperturbability, I felt moved by some furious and violent impulse. I got up from my chair to calm myself. I could see that for two months past I had been duped by this woman, who had been pursuing with avidity a vision of unexpected fortune, and that nothing could now divert her from this pursuit. I felt myself caught in their abominable toils.

Sitting motionless on her divan, with her hands folded over her knees, she regarded me in silence.

"Well!" I said, coming close to her again, "I can see that your maternal solicitude is all a question of money. For what sum will you sell me your daughter a second time, and go back to live by yourself in the East?"

She hesitated a moment, and then she said:

"I will tell you in a week's time."

By her deceitful looks I judged that she still placed some hope in Kiusko, and that she probably wished to wait until she could make sure about it, one way or the other—but from motives of discretion I held my tongue, and took leave of her.

CHAPTER XVIII

Events had succeeded each other with such strange rapidity since the day before, that I felt like one walking in a dream. First, Kondje-Gul's revelations of her mother's duplicity, then my discussion with Daniel, and now finally this cynical dialogue with the Circassian, in the course of which she had just confessed her schemes quite openly; all these things had given such a succession of rude shocks to my spirit, which had been reposing until then in the tranquil assurance of undisturbed happiness, that I had hardly found time to estimate the extent of my misfortune. Overwhelmed with distress when I perceived the possibility of losing Kondje-Gul, I almost thought I should go mad. I made a desperate struggle against the despair which was taking possession of my mind. It was necessary for me to carry on the contest in order to defend my very soul and life, yet I felt my soul slipping out of control. Like a mystic fascinated by his vision, I might have allowed myself to be deluded by a vain mirage of security, for I had never imagined that my rights could be disputed. I had been living in the peaceful but foolish confidence that I could obtain redress, when necessary, by the sword, for my rival's presumption.

And now I had woke up in consternation at finding myself caught in this stupid trap which I had permitted them to set in my path. Kondje-Gul's mother had become Kiusko's accomplice. How was I to defeat this conspiracy between two minds animated by consuming passions, resolute and pitiless, who were determined not to be deterred by any scruples or any sense of honour? I could now see my weakness; I was paralysed and defenceless against this wretched woman who, in order to constrain her daughter and dispose of her future, had only to claim her legal authority over her. She could take her from me, and carry her away. Once back in Turkey, supported by the horrible laws of Islam, all she need do was to sell her to Kiusko and thus give her up to him.

My mind was struck by a sudden idea. Was it not the height of folly on my part to give way to childish alarms, and to defer action until after Kiusko and the Circassian had matured their plans? Was it not possible for me to escape, carrying Kondje-Gul off with me, and placing her out of reach of their pursuit?

As soon as this idea had taken possession of my mind, it fixed itself there, and soon developed into a resolution. I felt surprised that it had not occurred to me earlier, and decided to put it into execution that very day. I knew that Kondje-Gul would follow me, for we had often cherished the idea of taking a journey together alone, and I had promised her we would carry it out some day. In order to assure our successful escape, I resolved to give her no notice beforehand, lest she should let it out to her mother.

It was necessary, however, to provide for the consequences of this disappearance, and the gossip which would inevitably result in connection with it. Well, after a good deal of hesitation, I confided the whole matter to my uncle.

"You old stupid!" said he to me, "why, I have known all about your little love-knot for the last six months!"

"What! do you mean to say you knew that Kondje-Gul?—"

"Lord bless you! Don't you suppose that I heard enough from Mohammed to make me keep my eyes open?"

After I had come to a complete understanding with my uncle, I made my own arrangements. I was expected to dinner at Kondje's that day. I found her quite sad; and on the pretext of giving her some distraction, I ordered the carriage at about half-past eight, as if for a drive to the Bois. We started off.

As soon as we were alone, she said to me:

"Good gracious, Andre! whatever has been passing between you and my mother? I am worried to death. She has been talking again to me about my departure with her, and Fanny believes that she is making her preparations for it already.— She is going to carry me away."

"All right, never mind her!" I answered with a laugh; "you're out of danger already."

"How so?"

"I'm taking you away! You won't go back to the house, for we are off to Fontainebleau, where we shall both of us remain in concealment, while watching events."

Need I describe to you her joy? In the Champs Elysees we got out, as if in order to walk, and I sent back the carriage. An hour after this, a cab set us down at the railway station!

We spent a delightful week in the forest, playing truant. Fanny, who is a reliable girl, has joined us here. We really had a narrow escape; for it seems that Madame Murrah had, the very day we made our flight, got everything planned for leaving the day after. When she found in the morning that Kondje-Gul was gone, she nearly had a fit. Kiusko came to the house, being sent for at once; all of which pretty clearly indicates an understanding between them. The Circassian of course rushed after me to the Rue de Varennes, noisily demanding her daughter. So my aunt got to know all about it! My uncle, whom I had taken into my confidence, put them at once completely off the scent, by replying that I had started for Spain.

We are safe! Everything has been accomplished, as if by enchantment. For fifteen days past my Kondje-Gul has been settled in a charming cottage at Ermont, in the middle of the forest, hidden away like a daisy in a field of standing corn. She has disappeared from view, leaving no more traces behind her than a bird in its flight through the air; and I am back in Paris, as if I had just returned from a journey. I have sent word to Madame Murrah that her daughter, having resolved to become a Christian, has taken refuge in a remote convent. You may picture to yourself her rage; but, as she is henceforth powerless, I fear her no more. Being a foreigner, and in her precarious position, she cannot venture to charge me with abduction, and, as you may imagine, I am not likely to let her take us by surprise. In order to get rid of her, I have offered to give her an annuity to live in Turkey, but she has declined it.

There can be no doubt that Kiusko guides her, and that they have by no means given up their game, but are ready to resort to any violence. You may be sure I keep a sharp eye on them, and am prepared for them. The contest, however, is too unequal for me to alarm myself very much. My uncle, who never troubles himself much with legal scruples, telegraphed to a couple of his old sailors, Onesime and Rupert, to come up from Toulon: they were born on our Ferouzat estate, and are, moreover, his "god-children." They are ridiculously like him, except that one of them is two inches taller than the captain. Their godfather has installed them at Ermont, and I don't mind betting that, with a couple of strapping fellows like them about the place, any attempt at carrying off Kondje-Gul in my absence would meet with a few trifling obstacles!

As to myself, I defy them to get on my scent.

Being accustomed to taking morning rides, I could find my way to our happy cottage home by various routes, starting from opposite sides of the city. Once on the road, it was impossible to follow me, even at a distance; for I should soon recognize any one on horseback who appeared too inquisitive about my journey. Moreover, if these tactics failed, the pace at which Star goes would easily baffle any pertinacious pursuit. I often stay for two or three days at this delicious retreat. My uncle delights in coming there from time to time to take his madeira.

In short, after the little adventures we have lately gone through, we are now leading a very pleasant existence.

You can see what a simple matter it is.

My famous system, you will tell me, has come to grief. Here I am, all forlorn, among the ruins of my harem, running my head against impossibilities opposed to our laws, morals, and conventionalities, with my last sultana leaning on my arm; here I am, like some little St. John,[B] reduced to shady expedients in order to get a minute's interview with my mistress, imprisoned in her tower. I am trembling between our caresses, you will say, lest a commissary of police should come to cut the golden thread upon which my remaining blisses hang, and force me by legal authority to give back Kondje-Gul to her cruel mother.

[Footnote B: Referring to a familiar French nursery-legend similar to that of Santa Claus.—*Trans.*]

Well, my dear friend, I will answer you very briefly, I am in love! Yes, I am in love! These words are a reply, I think, to everything; although I must own that fear of the commissary, which certainly does threaten my felicity, has considerably humbled my Oriental pride—I am in love! I have burnt my essay for the Academy.

Well, then, I have abjured my polygamy. What more can I say to you?

To-day I must confide to you a most valuable discovery I have made; for I beg you to believe that love is not, as so many foolish people imagine, an extinguisher to the fire of the human intellect. On the contrary, it stimulates the perceptions; and an enthusiastic lover, who is familiar with the elements of science, can extend therein his field of observations quite as easily as persons whose hearts are whole.

As an example of this, then, I have just been realising the beauty of a charming phenomenon of nature—a most ordinary one, and yet one which so far has remained, I think, completely unobserved. I refer to the spring!

As a great artist, you of course know, as well as any one in the world, that this is the season which leads from the winter to the summer; but what I feel sure you don't know is the full charm of this transitory period, in which the whole forest awakens, in which the bushes sprout, and the young birds twitter in their nests!

According to Vauvenargues, "The first days of spring possess less charm than the growing virtue of a young man."

Well, it would ill befit me to depreciate the value of such an axiom, coming from the pen of such a great philosopher; still, and without wishing to disdain his politeness in so far as it is really flattering to myself at this particular moment of

my career, I do not hesitate to raise my voice after his, and assert, without any pretence of modesty, that this charm is at least as great in the case of Flora's lover as in mine, and that it is only fair to accord to each his just portion. If my budding virtue possesses ineffable charms, no less powerful are those of the lilacs and the roses. It is really, I assure you, a wonderful spectacle. You ought to have witnessed it! Some day I will tell you all about it, as I have just been doing to my uncle, who finds it all very curious, although he professes only to understand me "very approximately."

Getting up at sunrise, Kondje and I take a run through the coppices, her little feet all wet with the dew. We feel free, merry, and careless, dismissing the commissary to oblivion, and trusting to each other's love, the full charms of which this solitary companionship has revealed to us. I do not risk more than two excursions to Paris each week, one to my aunt Eudoxia's, and one to my aunt Van Cloth's. Having made these angel's visits, and performed various family duties, I vanish, by day or by night as the case may be, eluding the vigilance of the spies who have no doubt been set at my heels by the unscrupulous mother, or by *that rascal Kiusko*, as we now call him. These adventures augment my rapturous felicity; and if time and destiny have shorn me of the privilege of my sultanship, which you say rendered me so proud and vain, I retain at all events the glory of being happy.

I am in love, my dear fellow; and therefore I dream and forget. But there is another still darker speck on my serene sky. Anna Campbell is just approaching her eighteenth birthday, and I cannot think of this without a good deal of melancholy. Although my uncle is delighted to take occasional walks here, at the end of which he finds a capital glass of madeira waiting for him, he, as you are aware, is not a person of romantic temperament, and has already noted with his scrutinising eye the ravages caused by a double passion, which bodes no good for his daughter's married life.

The other night, on my return from my aunt Van Cloth's, he questioned me very seriously on the subject. As to my disappointing his hopes, he knows that the idea of such a thing would not even occur to me. That is a matter of honour between us.

I spoke of a further delay before preparing my poor Kondje-Gul for the blow. He seemed touched at this token of the sincerity of my entirely filial devotion to him.

The commissary has at last come; we have been discovered!

Yesterday afternoon we were sitting in the garden, under the shade of a little clump of trees. My uncle, in a big arm-chair, was smoking and listening, while I read to him the newspapers, which had just been brought to us. Suddenly Kondje-Gul, who was standing a few steps off from us, arranging the plants for her window, uttered a suppressed cry, and I saw her run up to me all at once, pale and trembling.

"What's the matter, dear?" I said to her.

"Look there! look there!" she answered, in a terrified voice, pointing towards the house, "my mother!"

At the same moment, on the door-step of the cottage, through which she had passed, and found it empty, appeared the Circassian.

She was accompanied by a man.

"This is my daughter, sir," she said to him.

I sprang forward to throw myself in front of Kondje-Gul.

"Come, don't agitate yourself, my dear fellow!" said my uncle. "Do me the favour of keeping quiet!"

Then, rising up as he would to receive guests, he walked a few steps towards Madame Murrah, who had advanced towards us, and addressing himself to the man, said to him:

"Will you inform me, sir, to what I am indebted for the honour of this visit from you?"

"I am a Commissary of Police, sir, and am deputed by the court to assist this lady, who has come to demand the restitution of her daughter, illegally harboured by you at your house."

"Very well, sir," continued my uncle; "I am delighted to see you! But be so kind, if you please, as to walk into the house, where we can consider your demand more comfortably than in this garden."

"Take care," said the Circassian to the commissary: "they want to contrive her escape!"

"Nothing of the sort, my dear madam," replied my uncle: "this gentleman will tell you that we could not venture to do such a thing in his presence. Your daughter will remain with us to answer any questions which may be put to her. I am taking her arm, and if you will kindly follow us, I shall have the honour of showing you the way."

Onesime and Rupert might be distinguished in the dim perspective, waiting apparently for a signal from the captain to remove both the commissary and the unwelcome lady visitor.

Our hearts were beating fast: Kondje-Gul could hardly restrain her feelings. We went in, and my uncle, as calm as ever, offered chairs to Madame Murrah and to the emissary of justice. Then he addressed him again, saying:

"May I inquire, sir, whether you are provided with a formal warrant authorizing you to employ force to take this young lady away, according to her mother's wish?"

"I have the judge's order!" exclaimed Madame Murrah with vehemence.

"Excuse me, excuse me," continued my uncle, "but let us avoid all confusion! Be so kind, if you please, madam, as to permit the commissary to answer my question. We are anxious to observe the respect which we owe to his office."

I felt done for. How could we resist the law? My poor Kondje cast despairing looks at me.

"Madame Murrah being a foreigner, sir," answered the officer of the law, "as you appear to understand, my only instructions are to accompany her, and, in the event of opposition being made to her rights, to draw up a report in order to enable her to bring an action against you in a court of justice."

"Ah!" continued my uncle. "Well, then, sir! you may proceed, if you please, to take down our replies. In the first place, then, the young lady formally declines to return to her mother."

"That's false!" said the Circassian. "She is my daughter, and belongs only to me! She will obey me, for she knows that I shall curse her if—"

"Let us be quite calm, if you please, and have no useless words!" replied my uncle. "It is your daughter's turn to reply.—Ask her, sir."

The commissary then addressed himself to Kondje-Gul, repeating the question. I saw her turn pale and hesitate, terror-stricken by her mother's looks.

"Do you want to leave me, then?" I said to her passionately.

"Oh, no!" she exclaimed. Then turning towards the commissary, she added in a firm voice: "I do not wish to go with my mother, sir."

At this the Circassian rose up in a fury.

Kondje-Gul fell on her knees before her, supplicating her with tears, in piteous tones.

In my alarm I rushed forward.

"Get her out of the room; take her away!" my uncle said to me sharply.

My poor Kondje-Gul resisted, so I took her up in my arms and carried her out. At the door I found Fanny, who had come up, and I left my darling in her care.

Madame Murrah darted forward to follow her daughter, but my uncle had seized her by the wrist, and forcing her down again, said to her in Turkish:

"We have not finished; and if you stir, beware!"

"Sir," exclaimed the Circassian, addressing the officer of the law, "you see how violently they are treating me, and how they are threatening me!"

All this had taken place so quickly that the commissary hardly had time to intervene with a gesture. Onesime and Rupert were strolling about outside the window.

"Excuse me for having sent this child out, sir," continued my uncle; "but you are, I believe, sufficiently acquainted already with her decision. Moreover, she is there to reply afresh to you, if you desire to question her alone, secure from all influence and pressure. It remains for me to speak now upon a subject which she ought not to hear mentioned. After her refusal to follow her mother, which she has just given so clearly, be so good as to add on your report that I also refuse very emphatically to give her up to her."

"You have no right to rob me of my daughter," exclaimed the Circassian, who was nearly delirious with rage.

"That is just the point we are about to discuss," replied my uncle. "Firstly, then, allow me to introduce myself to you, sir," he continued, quite calmly; "and to explain my position and rights in this matter. My name is *The Late* Barbassou, ex-General and Pasha in the service of His Majesty the Sultan—ranks which entitle me to the privileges of a Turkish subject."

The commissary smiled and nodded to him, thus indicating that the name of Barbassou-Pasha was already known to him.

"As a consequence of these rights, sir," continued my uncle, "my private transactions cannot come before the French courts; so that this affair must be settled entirely between Madame Murrah and myself. I should even add, while expressing to you my regrets for the inconvenience which it is causing you, that it is I who have brought about this very necessary interview. I presented myself twice at Madame Murrah's house in Paris, with the object of bringing this stupid business to a conclusion. For reasons, no doubt, which you are already in a position to estimate, she refused to see me. I arranged, therefore, that she should be informed yesterday that her daughter was concealed in this house; and

I came here at once myself, in order to have the pleasure of meeting the lady. There you have the whole story."

"I refused to see you," said Kondje-Gul's mother, "simply because I do not know you! And I ask the judge to order the restitution of my daughter, which the Ambassador of our Sultan supports me in demanding. I have his order to this effect."

Here the commissary intervened, and, addressing my uncle, whose imperturbable composure quite astounded me, said gravely:

"Would you oblige me, sir, by stating your motive for refusing to give up this young lady to her mother? According to our laws, as you are aware, this is a circumstance which, notwithstanding the purely voluntary character of my mandate, I am bound to enter in my report."

"Certainly, sir," replied my uncle, "your request is a very proper one, and I will at once reply to it, as I would have done in the presence of the consul of His Excellency the Turkish Ambassador, were it not that Madame Murrah has strong motives for avoiding such an explanation before him, between good Mussulmans like herself and me."

"I understand you," continued the commissary, suppressing another smile at this declaration of Barbassou-Pasha.

"Sir," added my uncle, "I have the advantage of being a Mahometan; and according to the special customs of my country, with which you are acquainted, this lady sold me her daughter by a straightforward and honourable contract, sanctioned by our usages, recognized and supported by our laws: these laws formally enjoin me to protect her, and to maintain her always in a position corresponding with my own rank and fortune, while they forbid me ever to abandon her. Under the same contract this lady duly received her 'gift' or legitimate remuneration, which had been estimated, fixed, and agreed to by her. Therefore, as you will perceive, sir," he added, "no discussion in this case would ever be listened to by an Ottoman tribunal, and Madame Murrah's suit would be ignominiously dismissed."

"We are in France," said Madame Murrah, "and my daughter has become free!"

"To conclude, sir," continued my uncle, without taking any notice of this objection, "this lady and I are both subjects of His Majesty the Sultan. Ours is simply a private dispute between fellow-Turks, coming entirely under the jurisdiction of our national tribunals, and is one in which your French courts, as you will understand, have no authority to interfere."

"You are not my daughter's husband!" exclaimed the Circassian; "she does not belong to you any longer, for you have given her to your nephew, a Giaour, an infidel!"

"Quite true, madam!" replied my uncle. "But," he continued, "these are details in a private dispute, with which this gentleman is not concerned. And I fancy he has by this time obtained sufficient information."

"Certainly, sir," said the officer of the law, rising from his seat. "I have taken down your replies, and my mission is accomplished."

Barbassou-Pasha, upon this conclusion, saluted him in his most dignified manner and conducted him out with every polite attention.

The Circassian, exasperated beyond measure, had not moved: rage was depicted on her whole countenance, and she looked like one determined to fight it out to the bitter end.

"I must insist upon speaking to my daughter," she said passionately, "and then we shall see!"

Just as he caught these words, my uncle came in, leading my poor Kondje-Gul by the hand.

"Come, you silly old fool," he said to Madame Murrah, changing his tone quite suddenly, "you can see now that there is nothing left to you but to submit. Swallow all your stupid threats! You will make a good thing out of it all the same—for I give your daughter in marriage to my nephew!"

I thought I must have misunderstood him.

"Uncle!" I exclaimed, "what did you say?"

"Why, you rascal, I see that I must give her to you, since you love each other so consumedly!"

Kondje-Gul could not repress a scream of joy. We both threw ourselves into my uncle's arms at the same time.

"Yes," he said, "what a jolly couple they look! But it was your aunt Eudoxia who led me at last to play this card! Here I am nicely balked of all my fine schemes!"

"Oh!" exclaimed Kondje-Gul, "we will love each other so much!"

"Well, well! There, they're quite smothering me! May the good God bless you! go along. But now we shall have to come to an understanding with this excellent mother; for according to these infernal French laws, which complicate everything, her consent is necessary for your marriage."

"I certainly shall not give it," said Madame Murrah furiously.

"All right! We will see about that," he continued. "That is a matter to be arranged between us, and for that purpose I shall go to your house to-morrow. Only, I give you warning, no noise, please, no silly attempts to carry off your daughter, otherwise we shall wait until she is of age in two years' time, and then you will have nothing."

Don't be surprised, Louis, if for the rest of this page I scrawl like a monkey. At the recollection of this scene, my eyes are quite obscured by a veil of mist. By Jove, so much the worse! for now it's all breaking into real tears.

Dear me, what a brick of an uncle he is to me!

Notwithstanding Barbassou-Pasha's Turkish tactics, and in spite of the happiness which for the moment quite over-whelmed us, my poor Kondje-Gul began to tremble again with fear after the departure of her mother, whom we knew to be capable of any mad act. We decided that, in order to avoid a very real danger, we would take her that very day to the convent of the Ladies of X.; this we did. Before she becomes my wife she is going to become a Christian, in pursuance of the wish which, as you know, she has expressed a long time since, of embracing my faith. This visit, which will account to the world for her disappearance, will be explained quite naturally by this *finale* of our marriage; and if people ever discover anything about this queer story of our amours, well—I shall have married my own slave, that's all.

Eh? What? You incorrigible carper! Is it not, after all, a charming romance?

A fortnight has passed since the intervention of the commissary. Kiusko has gone: he disappeared one morning.

My aunt Eudoxia, who has taken us under her special care, goes to see Kondje-Gul every day at the convent. She is charming in her kindness to us, but still we have our anxieties. The negotiation of the maternal consent is an arduous task, for the Circassian makes absurd pretensions; my uncle, however, undertakes to bring her down.

What will you say next, I wonder? That I am reduced to buying my own wife? I flatter myself that I shall find happiness in that bargain! How many others are there, who have done the same, that could say as much as that?

CHAPTER XIX

Here's a fine business! It is my uncle who has got into trouble this time! My aunt Eudoxia has found out everything, and I have just spent two days in helping my aunt Van Cloth to pack up and get back to Holland with my long string of cousins, the fat Dirkie, the cooking moulds, and the barrel-organ following by goods' train.

It was a veritable thunderclap!

I have told you all about this Dutch household and its patriarchal felicity, its sweetmeat and sausage pastries, and its inimitable tarts—less appetizing, however, than my aunt's fine eyes. I have told you about their quiet family evenings with my uncle's pipe and schiedam, in which domino-parties of three were varied by the delightful treat of a symphony from one of the great masters, executed in a masterly style by a pretty little plump hand covered with pink dimples.

Once or twice a week, as became a favourite and affectionate nephew, I came into the midst of this idyll of the land of tulips; and always quitted it full of sweetmeats and good advice.

However, the day before yesterday, Ernest, the second of my cousins, who is five years old, suddenly caught a violent fever; he grew scarlet in the face, and his stomach swelled up like a balloon.

My poor aunt, having exhausted all her arsenal of aperients and astringents against what she reckoned to be an indigestion due to preserved plums, quite lost her head. In the afternoon the child grew worse. Where in Paris could she find a Dutch doctor? She could only place confidence in a Dutchman. At the end of her wits with fear, she thought she would go after my uncle or me; so, without thinking any more about it, as she knew our address, she takes a cab and gets driven to the Rue de Varennes, believing in her simplicity that this was where our shops and offices were.

She arrives and asks for my uncle. Being seven o'clock, the hall-porter tells her that the captain will soon be in, shows her to the staircase, and rings the bell; one of the men-servants asks her for her name, and then opens the folding doors, announcing—

"Madame Barbassou!"

It is my aunt Eudoxia who receives her.

My aunt Van Cloth, who is distracted with anxiety, thinks that she sees before her some lady of my family, and in order to excuse herself for disturbing her, begins by saying that she has come to see Captain Barbassou, *her husband*.

Imagine the stupefaction of my aunt Eudoxia! But being too astute to betray herself, she lets the other speak, questions her and learns the whole story. Then, like the good soul that she is, and feeling sorry for poor Ernest and his swollen stomach, she rings and orders the carriage to be ready, so that she may go as soon as possible to her own doctor; upon which my aunt Van Cloth, who is of an effusive nature, embraces her most affectionately, calling her her dearest friend.

Just then my uncle arrives.

I was not present; but my aunt Eudoxia, who continues to laugh over it, has related to me all the details of the affair. At the sight of this remarkable fusion of "the two branches of his hymens," as she termed it, the Pasha was positively dumbfounded. All the more so as my aunt Van Cloth, who understood no more about this extraordinary position of affairs than she did of Hebrew, threw herself into his arms, and exclaimed:

"Ah! Anatole! here you are, dear!—Our Ernest is in danger!"

The bravest man will quail occasionally; and at this unfortunate and unavoidable attack, which tore asunder the whole veil of mystery, the splendid composure with which Nature has armed my uncle Barbassou really deserted him for a moment. But, like a man who is superior to misfortunes of this sort, when he found himself caught he did not on this occasion, more than on any other, waste any time over spilt cream.

"Quick! we must go and fetch the child!" he said.

And taking advantage of the fact that my aunt Van Cloth was hanging to him, he carried her off without any more ado, and went out by the door, without leaving her time to kiss the Countess of Monteclaro, as she certainly would have done out of politeness. From the ante-room he dragged her down to the carriage, where he packed her in.

I was coming down from my own chambers just as he returned from this summary execution. Although about the last thing I expected to come in for was the climax of a tragic occurrence, I could see easily enough that my uncle had experienced some little shock; but the announcement of dinner and the ordinary tone of my aunt's reception creating a diversion, I did not feel certain until we were seated at table that there was some storm in the air which was only restrained from bursting by the presence of the servants. The Pasha, sitting in silence with his head bent down into his plate, seemed to be absorbed by some abstruse considerations, which caused him that evening to forget to grumble at the cook. My aunt, on the contrary, sparkling with humour, and in her most charming and gracious mood, suggested by her smiles a certain lightness of heart: he eyed her suspiciously from time to time, like a man with an uncomfortable conscience.

When the meal was over we returned to the drawing-room, and coffee being served, remained there alone. The Countess of Monteclaro, still as gracious as ever, made some sly thrusts at him, the significance of which escaped me somewhat. The captain evidently was keeping very quiet. Finally, after half an hour, as I was about to leave, and he showed symptoms of an intention to slip off, she said to him, in her most insinuating manner—

"I will detain you for a minute, my dear; I must have a little conversation with you about a matter on which I want to take your advice."

I kissed the hand which she held out to me, and which indicated that my presence was not wanted.

"Well, good night, old good-for-nothing!" she added, as she accompanied me as far as the door of the adjoining room.

What passed after I left, none will ever know. My aunt, with her exquisite tact, has only related to me the original and amusing side of the matter, laughing at her unfortunate discovery in the lofty manner of a noble lady who is smoothing over a family trouble. Apart from her very genuine affection for my uncle, she entertains also a certain esteem for him, which she could never depart from before his nephew.

As for myself, I remained still in ignorance of everything until nine o'clock, when the Pasha joined me again at the club, where he had particularly asked me to wait for him.

At the first glance I guessed that there had been a row. Without saying a word, he led me into a little detached room: there he fell into an arm-chair, and shook his head in silence, as he looked at me.

"Good gracious! what's the matter, uncle?" I asked.

"Pfuiii!" he replied, staring with his full eyes, and prolonging this kind of whistling exclamation, like a man who is breathing more freely after a narrow escape.

His gestures were so eloquent, his sigh so expressive and so reinvigorating, that I waited until he had given complete vent to it. When I saw him quite exhausted by it, I continued, feeling really anxious—

"Come! what is it?"

"Oh, I've just had such a nasty turn!" he answered at last, "Pfuiii!"

I respected this new effort at relief, which, moreover set him right this time.

"You've had some words with my aunt, I suppose?" I added, at a venture, recollecting the cloud which seemed to hang over us at dinner.

"A regular earthquake!" he drawled out, in that appalling Marseilles accent which he falls into whenever he is overcome by any strong emotion. "Your aunt Eudoxia has discovered the whole bag of tricks! The story of the Passy house, your aunt Gretchen, the children, Dirkie, and the whole blessed shop!"

"But, perhaps she has only suspicions—the consequence of some gossip she has heard?"

"Suspicions?" he exclaimed; "why, they have met each other!"

"Nonsense, that's impossible!—Are you really sure of this?"

"*Te!* Sure indeed? I should think so! I return home to dinner, come into the drawing-room, and I actually find them both there, talking together. They were kissing each other!"

"The deuce!" I exclaimed, quite alarmed this time.

"Well, that was a stunner, wasn't it, my dear boy?"

"It was indeed! Whatever did you do?"

"I separated them, carrying Gretchen back at once to her carriage."

"Then now I understand the chill which seemed to be over us all dinner-time. So, after I went out, you had a heavy downfall?"

"Pfuiii!" my uncle began again.

This last sigh seemed to lose itself in such a vista of painful souvenirs, that the whole of Theramene's narrative would certainly have taken less time to tell. I proceeded as quickly as I could, foreseeing that my intervention would be necessary.

"Had I not better run over to my aunt Gretchen's?" I asked him.

"Yes, I certainly think you had. I promised that, except in case of Ernest's illness proving serious, they should all leave Paris to-morrow! You may still have time to arrange that this evening," he added, looking at the clock.

"All right, I'm off!" I replied, rising up.

As I was about to go out, he called me back.

"Ah! above all," he continued sharply, "don't forget to tell Eudoxia to-morrow that it is you who have undertaken this business, and that as for me, I have not stirred from here!"

"That's quite understood, uncle," I answered, laughing to myself at the blue funk he was in.

Needless to add, I did not lose any time. In a quarter of an hour I was at Passy. It so happened that a favourable crisis had come over Ernest and relieved him, and he gave no further cause for anxiety. My aunt Gretchen, who had gone through all this business as a blind man might pass under an arch, without knowing anything about it, did not evince the least surprise on hearing that my uncle "having received a telegram which had obliged him to leave Paris that evening, had commissioned me in his absence to send her off immediately to Amsterdam." She entrusted me with no end of compliments for the Countess of Monteclaro, whose acquaintance she was charmed to have made.

The next morning she was rolling away in the express, delighted to have made such an agreeable and enjoyable visit.

A week has now passed since this affair, and beyond that my

uncle is still quite humiliated by a malicious sort of gaiety affected by my aunt, who often calls him "The Pasha," instead of "The Captain," which is the title she always gave him formerly, everything has resumed the harmonious tranquillity of the best regulated household. Attentions, politenesses, gallantries, &c., are quite the order of the day. Only he is ruining me with all the presents he lavishes upon her; and I have been forced to make serious complaints on the subject to my aunt, who has laughed insanely at them, maintaining that it is "the sinner's ransom." Still, some kind of restrictions are necessary in families, and I have warned her that, if it continues, I shall stop "the late Barbassou's" credit, seeing that he is dead.

"You see what a simple matter it is, as my uncle says," I added.

But she only laughed again, louder than ever. We have got on no further.

Louis, go and hang yourself! I was married yesterday, and you were not there!

The ceremony was very fine. It was at the church of Sainte Clotilde; all the Faubourg St. Germain was there, delighted at Kondje-Gul's conversion, and with her beauty, her charming manners, and the romance connected with our marriage. Everyone was there who has made any name in the world of art, not to speak of that of finance. There was Baron Rothschild, who had a long conversation with my uncle. Three special correspondents for London newspapers were present, and all our own Paris reporters. High Mass, full choral; Faure sang his *Pie Jesus*, Madame Carvalho and Adelina Patti the *Credo*.

At the entrance, the crowd nearly crushed us. Barbassou-Pasha, Count of Monteclaro, gave his arm to the bride. Poor

Kondje, what agitation, what emotion, what delight she evinced! I escorted Madame Murrah in a splendid costume, tamed but very dignified still, and playing her part with noble airs, like a fatalist. "It was written!" She started off the same day to Rhodes, where my uncle is finding a position for her—as head manager of his Botany Bay.

The Countess of Monteclaro was there, and Anna Campbell was smiling all over as she acted, in company with Maud and Susannah Montague, as bridesmaid to her friend Kondje-Gul.

It took them all exactly an hour to pass in procession through the vestry. We had to sign the register there, and my uncle headed it with his self-assumed title of "*The late* Barbassou," to which he clings.

Then came the deluge of congratulations, my beautiful Christian wife blushing in her emotion, with her garland of orange-flowers. (Well, yes! And why not? It's the custom, you know.)

At two o'clock, back to the house, a family love-feast, and preparations for the flight of the young couple to Ferouzat. Peace and joy in all hearts. My uncle, at last admitted to absolution, quivering with pleasure at hearing my aunt Eudoxia calling him no longer "Pasha," but "Captain," as of old.

Everywhere Love and Spring!

Come now, Louis, quite seriously, are you, who have made the experiment, quite sure that one heart suffices for one veritable love? I am anxious to know.

When evening arrived, the Count and Countess of Monteclaro accompanied us to the railway station. They will join us at the end of the month.

I leave you to imagine for yourself all the kisses and salutations, promises and grandparents' advice.

While my aunt was exhorting Kondje-Gul, my uncle favoured me with a few words on his part.

"You see," he said to me quietly, standing by the side of our carriage, "there is one thing which it is indispensable for you not to forget, and that is never on any account to have *two wives*—in the same town!"

Louis, I think my uncle is a little wanting in principle.

Choose from Thousands of 1stWorldLibrary Classics By

A. M. Barnard
Ada Leverson
Adolphus William Ward
Aesop
Agatha Christie
Alexander Aaronsohn
Alexander Kielland
Alexandre Dumas
Alfred Gatty
Alfred Ollivant
Alice Duer Miller
Alice Turner Curtis
Alice Dunbar
Allen Chapman
Alleyne Ireland
Ambrose Bierce
Amelia E. Barr
Amory H. Bradford
Andrew Lang
Andrew McFarland Davis
Andy Adams
Angela Brazil
Anna Alice Chapin
Anna Sewell
Annie Besant
Annie Hamilton Donnell
Annie Payson Call
Annie Roe Carr
Annonaymous
Anton Chekhov
Archibald Lee Fletcher
Arnold Bennett
Arthur C. Benson
Arthur Conan Doyle
Arthur M. Winfield
Arthur Ransome
Arthur Schnitzler
Arthur Train
Atticus
B.H. Baden-Powell
B. M. Bower
B. C. Chatterjee
Baroness Emmuska Orczy
Baroness Orczy
Basil King
Bayard Taylor
Ben Macomber
Bertha Muzzy Bower
Bjornstjerne Bjornson

Booth Tarkington
Boyd Cable
Bram Stoker
C. Collodi
C. E. Orr
C. M. Ingleby
Carolyn Wells
Catherine Parr Traill
Charles A. Eastman
Charles Amory Beach
Charles Dickens
Charles Dudley Warner
Charles Farrar Browne
Charles Ives
Charles Kingsley
Charles Klein
Charles Hanson Towne
Charles Lathrop Pack
Charles Romyn Dake
Charles Whibley
Charles Willing Beale
Charlotte M. Braeme
Charlotte M. Yonge
Charlotte Perkins Stetson
Clair W. Hayes
Clarence Day Jr.
Clarence E. Mulford
Clemence Housman
Confucius
Coningsby Dawson
Cornelis DeWitt Wilcox
Cyril Burleigh
D. H. Lawrence
Daniel Defoe
David Garnett
Dinah Craik
Don Carlos Janes
Donald Keyhoe
Dorothy Kilner
Dougan Clark
Douglas Fairbanks
E. Nesbit
E. P. Roe
E. Phillips Oppenheim
E. S. Brooks
Earl Barnes
Edgar Rice Burroughs
Edith Van Dyne
Edith Wharton

Edward Everett Hale
Edward J. O'Biren
Edward S. Ellis
Edwin L. Arnold
Eleanor Atkins
Eleanor Hallowell Abbott
Eliot Gregory
Elizabeth Gaskell
Elizabeth McCracken
Elizabeth Von Arnim
Ellem Key
Emerson Hough
Emilie F. Carlen
Emily Bronte
Emily Dickinson
Enid Bagnold
Enilor Macartney Lane
Erasmus W. Jones
Ernie Howard Pie
Ethel May Dell
Ethel Turner
Ethel Watts Mumford
Eugene Sue
Eugenie Foa
Eugene Wood
Eustace Hale Ball
Evelyn Everett-green
Everard Cotes
F. H. Cheley
F. J. Cross
F. Marion Crawford
Fannie E. Newberry
Federick Austin Ogg
Ferdinand Ossendowski
Fergus Hume
Florence A. Kilpatrick
Fremont B. Deering
Francis Bacon
Francis Darwin
Frances Hodgson Burnett
Frances Parkinson Keyes
Frank Gee Patchin
Frank Harris
Frank Jewett Mather
Frank L. Packard
Frank V. Webster
Frederic Stewart Isham
Frederick Trevor Hill
Frederick Winslow Taylor

Friedrich Kerst
Friedrich Nietzsche
Fyodor Dostoyevsky
G.A. Henty
G.K. Chesterton
Gabrielle E. Jackson
Garrett P. Serviss
Gaston Leroux
George A. Warren
George Ade
Geroge Bernard Shaw
George Cary Eggleston
George Durston
George Ebers
George Eliot
George Gissing
George MacDonald
George Meredith
George Orwell
George Sylvester Viereck
George Tucker
George W. Cable
George Wharton James
Gertrude Atherton
Gordon Casserly
Grace E. King
Grace Gallatin
Grace Greenwood
Grant Allen
Guillermo A. Sherwell
Gulielma Zollinger
Gustav Flaubert
H. A. Cody
H. B. Irving
H.C. Bailey
H. G. Wells
H. H. Munro
H. Irving Hancock
H. R. Naylor
H. Rider Haggard
H. W. C. Davis
Haldeman Julius
Hall Caine
Hamilton Wright Mabie
Hans Christian Andersen
Harold Avery
Harold McGrath
Harriet Beecher Stowe
Harry Castlemon
Harry Coghill
Harry Houidini

Hayden Carruth
Helent Hunt Jackson
Helen Nicolay
Hendrik Conscience
Hendy David Thoreau
Henri Barbusse
Henrik Ibsen
Henry Adams
Henry Ford
Henry Frost
Henry James
Henry Jones Ford
Henry Seton Merriman
Henry W Longfellow
Herbert A. Giles
Herbert Carter
Herbert N. Casson
Herman Hesse
Hildegard G. Frey
Homer
Honore De Balzac
Horace B. Day
Horace Walpole
Horatio Alger Jr.
Howard Pyle
Howard R. Garis
Hugh Lofting
Hugh Walpole
Humphry Ward
Ian Maclaren
Inez Haynes Gillmore
Irving Bacheller
Isabel Cecilia Williams
Isabel Hornibrook
Israel Abrahams
Ivan Turgenev
J.G.Austin
J. Henri Fabre
J. M. Barrie
J. M. Walsh
J. Macdonald Oxley
J. R. Miller
J. S. Fletcher
J. S. Knowles
J. Storer Clouston
J. W. Duffield
Jack London
Jacob Abbott
James Allen
James Andrews
James Baldwin

James Branch Cabell
James DeMille
James Joyce
James Lane Allen
James Lane Allen
James Oliver Curwood
James Oppenheim
James Otis
James R. Driscoll
Jane Abbott
Jane Austen
Jane L. Stewart
Janet Aldridge
Jens Peter Jacobsen
Jerome K. Jerome
Jessie Graham Flower
John Buchan
John Burroughs
John Cournos
John F. Kennedy
John Gay
John Glasworthy
John Habberton
John Joy Bell
John Kendrick Bangs
John Milton
John Philip Sousa
John Taintor Foote
Jonas Lauritz Idemil Lie
Jonathan Swift
Joseph A. Altsheler
Joseph Carey
Joseph Conrad
Joseph E. Badger Jr
Joseph Hergesheimer
Joseph Jacobs
Jules Vernes
Julian Hawthrone
Julie A Lippmann
Justin Huntly McCarthy
Kakuzo Okakura
Karle Wilson Baker
Kate Chopin
Kenneth Grahame
Kenneth McGaffey
Kate Langley Bosher
Kate Langley Bosher
Katherine Cecil Thurston
Katherine Stokes
L. A. Abbot
L. T. Meade

L. Frank Baum
Latta Griswold
Laura Dent Crane
Laura Lee Hope
Laurence Housman
Lawrence Beasley
Leo Tolstoy
Leonid Andreyev
Lewis Carroll
Lewis Sperry Chafer
Lilian Bell
Lloyd Osbourne
Louis Hughes
Louis Joseph Vance
Louis Tracy
Louisa May Alcott
Lucy Fitch Perkins
Lucy Maud Montgomery
Luther Benson
Lydia Miller Middleton
Lyndon Orr
M. Corvus
M. H. Adams
Margaret E. Sangster
Margret Howth
Margaret Vandercook
Margaret W. Hungerford
Margret Penrose
Maria Edgeworth
Maria Thompson Daviess
Mariano Azuela
Marion Polk Angellotti
Mark Overton
Mark Twain
Mary Austin
Mary Catherine Crowley
Mary Cole
Mary Hastings Bradley
Mary Roberts Rinehart
Mary Rowlandson
M. Wollstonecraft Shelley
Maud Lindsay
Max Beerbohm
Myra Kelly
Nathaniel Hawthrone
Nicolo Machiavelli
O. F. Walton
Oscar Wilde

Owen Johnson
P.G. Wodehouse
Paul and Mabel Thorne
Paul G. Tomlinson
Paul Severing
Percy Brebner
Percy Keese Fitzhugh
Peter B. Kyne
Plato
Quincy Allen
R. Derby Holmes
R. L. Stevenson
R. S. Ball
Rabindranath Tagore
Rahul Alvares
Ralph Bonehill
Ralph Henry Barbour
Ralph Victor
Ralph Waldo Emmerson
Rene Descartes
Ray Cummings
Rex Beach
Rex E. Beach
Richard Harding Davis
Richard Jefferies
Richard Le Gallienne
Robert Barr
Robert Frost
Robert Gordon Anderson
Robert L. Drake
Robert Lansing
Robert Lynd
Robert Michael Ballantyne
Robert W. Chambers
Rosa Nouchette Carey
Rudyard Kipling
Saint Augustine
Samuel B. Allison
Samuel Hopkins Adams
Sarah Bernhardt
Sarah C. Hallowell
Selma Lagerlof
Sherwood Anderson
Sigmund Freud
Standish O'Grady
Stanley Weyman
Stella Benson
Stella M. Francis

Stephen Crane
Stewart Edward White
Stijn Streuvels
Swami Abhedananda
Swami Parmananda
T. S. Ackland
T. S. Arthur
The Princess Der Ling
Thomas A. Janvier
Thomas A Kempis
Thomas Anderton
Thomas Bailey Aldrich
Thomas Bulfinch
Thomas De Quincey
Thomas Dixon
Thomas H. Huxley
Thomas Hardy
Thomas More
Thornton W. Burgess
U. S. Grant
Upton Sinclair
Valentine Williams
Various Authors
Vaughan Kester
Victor Appleton
Victor G. Durham
Victoria Cross
Virginia Woolf
Wadsworth Camp
Walter Camp
Walter Scott
Washington Irving
Wilbur Lawton
Wilkie Collins
Willa Cather
Willard F. Baker
William Dean Howells
William le Queux
W. Makepeace Thackeray
William W. Walter
William Shakespeare
Winston Churchill
Yei Theodora Ozaki
Yogi Ramacharaka
Young E. Allison
Zane Grey